Linguistics and the Bible

McMaster Divinity College Press
McMaster New Testament Studies Series, Volume 9

Christian Mission: Old Testament Foundations and New Testament Developments (2010)

Empire in the New Testament (2011)

The Church, Then and Now (2012)

Rejection: God's Refugees in Biblical and Contemporary Perspective (2015)

Rediscovering Worship: Past, Present, and Future (2015)

The Bible and Social Justice: Old Testament and New Testament Foundations for the Church's Urgent Call (2015)

The Letter to the Romans: Exegesis and Application (2018)

Is the Gospel Good News? (2019)

Linguistics and the Bible

Retrospects and Prospects

edited by
STANLEY E. PORTER,
CHRISTOPHER D. LAND,
and
FRANCIS G. H. PANG

☙PICKWICK *Publications* • Eugene, Oregon

LINGUISTICS AND THE BIBLE
Retrospects and Prospects

McMaster New Testament Studies Series, Volume 9
McMaster Divinity College Press

Copyright © 2019 Wipf and Stock Publishers. All rights reserved. Except for brief quotations in critical publications or reviews, no part of this book may be reproduced in any manner without prior written permission from the publisher. Write: Permissions, Wipf and Stock Publishers, 199 W. 8th Ave., Suite 3, Eugene, OR 97401.

Pickwick Publications
An Imprint of Wipf and Stock Publishers
199 W. 8th Ave., Suite 3
Eugene, OR 97401

McMaster Divinity College Press
1280 Main St. W.
Hamilton, ON, Canada
L8S 4K1

www.wipfandstock.com

PAPERBACK ISBN: 978-1-5326-5910-2
HARDCOVER ISBN: 978-1-5326-5911-9
EBOOK ISBN: 978-1-5326-5912-6

Cataloguing-in-Publication data:

Names: Porter, Stanley E., 1956–, editor. | Land, Christopher D., editor. | Pang, Francis G. H., editor.

Title: Linguistics and the Bible : retrospects and prospects / edited by Stanley E. Porter, Christopher D. Land, and Francis G. H. Pang.

Description: Eugene, OR: Pickwick Publications, 2019. | McMaster New Testament Studies Series 9. | Includes bibliographical references and indexes.

Identifiers: ISBN 978-1-5326-5910-2 (paperback). | ISBN 978-1-5326-5911-9 (hardcover). | ISBN 978-1-5326-5912-6 (ebook).

Subjects: LCSH: Bible.—New Testament—Language, style. | Greek language, Biblical—Grammar.

Classification: BS537 L39 2019 (paperback). | BS537 (ebook).

Manufactured in the U.S.A.   07/11/19

Contents

Preface / vii
Contributors / ix
Abbreviations / xi

Introduction: A Retrospect and Some Prospects / 1
—*Stanley E. Porter, Christopher D. Land, and Francis G. H. Pang*

PART 1: LINGUISTICS

1   Linguistics and Biblical Studies: An Ongoing Journey / 9
    —*Randall K. J. Tan*

2   The Past, Present, and Future of the Opentext.Org
    Annotated Greek Corpus / 28
    —*Christopher D. Land and Francis G. H. Pang*

3   Clause Structuring and Transitivity: Advantages
    of OpenText.org and Its Prospects / 63
    —*Chris S. Stevens*

4   The Future of New Testament Lexicography: Remodeling
    Relational Semantics and Componential Analysis through
    Distributional Corpus Analysis / 87
    —*Ryder A. Wishart*

5   The Limits of Linguistics: Subjectivity, Metaphysics,
    and the Interpretive Enterprise / 112
    —*David J. Fuller*

Part 2: Translation and Exegesis

6   Key Terms, the Lexicon, and How Languages
    Accommodate Translation / 145
    —Scott Berthiaume

7   The Human One? A Controversial
    CEB Translation Choice / 166
    —Cynthia Long Westfall

8   What is the Relationship between Exegesis
    and Our Views of Greek, or Vice Versa? / 185
    —Stanley E. Porter

9   The Benefits of Being an "Outsider": Mark 4:12
    as an Epexegetic Ἵνα Clause / 210
    —Mark Proctor

10 What the Church Should Do to the Sexually Immoral Man:
    Examining the Ideational Meaning of 1 Corinthians 5 / 233
    —Esther G. Cen

    Index of Modern Authors / 251
    Index of Ancient Sources / 255

Preface

THE 2016 H. H. Bingham Colloquium in the New Testament at McMaster Divinity College in Hamilton, Ontario, Canada, held on June 17, was entitled "Linguistics and the Bible: Retrospects and Prospects." This Colloquium was the twentieth in a continuing series held here at MDC, and the first entirely devoted to questions of linguistics in relation to the Bible. Due to the growth of interest in linguistic matters at MDC, we believe that it is important to showcase and promote further such work through our annual Bingham Colloquium. This conference also expanded our usual format for the conference by providing a number of parallel sessions besides our list of plenary speakers. We also organized the conference according to the three major elements of our Centre for Biblical Linguistics, Translation, and Exegesis (CBLTE). This original outline is partly reflected in the organization of this volume. We were able to invite three scholarly guests to participate in the conference as plenary speakers, one a biblical linguist, another a translator, and the third a biblical exegete. They provided a range of helpful perspectives on our admittedly expansive topic. We also invited some of our own graduate students to propose papers for presentation in the parallel sessions, and these were then refereed for inclusion in this volume.

We have organized the papers around two broad topics that encompass the main areas of the conference: Linguistics, and Translation and Exegesis. The papers in the Linguistics section are themselves diverse, but with an admitted focus upon the work that the CBLTE is doing with OpenText.org. The section on Translation and Exegesis has representation from both of those topics within it. The vision of the conference to explore the three major emphases of our Centre was fulfilled, even if the number of papers within each topic is not equal. Even though we do not explicitly emphasize linguistics

Preface

within the graduate programs of MDC, we have attracted a number of students in that area due to the interests of our faculty—even if they are not exclusively interested in such areas, as the papers included here attest—and so it is appropriate that we feature that area. Nevertheless, these papers provide some new and different perspectives on all three of the topics represented.

The Bingham Colloquium is named after Dr. Herbert Henry Bingham, who was a noted Baptist leader in Ontario, Canada. His leadership abilities were recognized by Baptists across Canada and around the world. His qualities included his genuine friendship, dedicated leadership, unswerving Christian faith, tireless devotion to duty, insightful service as a preacher and pastor, and visionary direction for congregation and denomination alike. These qualities endeared him both to his own church members and to believers in other denominations. The Colloquium has been endowed by his daughter as an act of appreciation for her father. We are pleased to be able to continue this tradition.

The first volumes of the Bingham Colloquium were published by Eerdmans Publishing, but since 2010 all of the volumes in this series have been published by McMaster Divinity College Press, in conjunction with Wipf & Stock Publishers of Eugene, Oregon, in the McMaster New Testament Series. We appreciate this active and continuing publishing relationship.

I finally would like to thank the individual contributors for their efforts in the preparation and presentation of papers that make a significant contribution to linguistics, translation, and exegesis of the Bible. We were pleased to welcome several outside scholars to present their scholarship as part of the Colloquium, and we look forward to welcoming them back at some time in the future. I am particularly gratified that several of our students have had their work accepted for publication in this volume. I would especially like to thank my New Testament colleagues, Christopher Land and Francis Pang, for organizing the conference out of which this volume emerges, and for working together with me to edit this volume for publication. We would like to thank the staff and student helpers and volunteers at McMaster Divinity College, all of whom were integral in creating a pleasant environment and a supportive atmosphere for the colloquium.

—Stanley E. Porter

Contributors

SCOTT BERTHIAUME is Dean of Academic Affairs at Dallas International University, Dallas, TX

ESTHER G. CEN is a PhD candidate in New Testament at McMaster Divinity College, Hamilton, ON, Canada

DAVID J. FULLER is Managing Editor of McMaster Divinity College Press, as well as a recent PhD graduate in Old Testament at McMaster Divinity College, Hamilton, ON, Canada

CHRISTOPHER D. LAND is Assistant Professor of New Testament and Linguistics at McMaster Divinity College, Hamilton, ON, Canada

FRANCIS G. H. PANG is Assistant Professor of New Testament at McMaster Divinity College, Hamilton, ON, Canada

STANLEY E. PORTER is President, Dean, and Professor of New Testament, as well as holder of the Roy A. Hope Chair in Christian Worldview, at McMaster Divinity College, Hamilton, ON, Canada

MARK PROCTOR is Assistant Professor of New Testament at Lee University, Cleveland, TN

CHRIS S. STEVENS is Associate Pastor at Redeemer Traverse City Church in Traverse City, MI, as well as a PhD candidate in New Testament at McMaster Divinity College, Hamilton, ON, Canada

Contributors

RANDALL K. J. TAN is Vice President of Biblical Research at Global Bible Initiative

CYNTHIA LONG WESTFALL is Associate Professor of New Testament at McMaster Divinity College, Hamilton, ON, Canada

RYDER A. WISHART is a PhD student in New Testament at McMaster Divinity College, Hamilton, ON, Canada

Abbreviations

AB	Anchor Bible
BAGL	*Biblical and Ancient Greek Linguistics*
BBR	*Bulletin for Biblical Research*
BDAG	Bauer, Walter, et al. *Greek-English Lexicon of the New Testament and Other Early Christian Literature*. 3rd ed. Chicago: University of Chicago Press, 2000.
BDF	Blass, Friedrich, and Albert Debrunner. *A Greek Grammar of the New Testament and Other Early Christian Literature*. Translated and revised by Robert W. Funk. Chicago: University of Chicago Press, 1961.
BibInt	Biblical Interpretation Series
BLG	Biblical Languages: Greek
CurBR	*Currents in Biblical Research*
CBQ	*Catholic Biblical Quarterly*
CTL	Cambridge Textbooks in Linguistics
ExpTim	*Expository Times*
FN	*Filología Neotestamentaria*
JBL	*Journal of Biblical Literature*
JETS	*Journal of the Evangelical Theological Society*
JGRChJ	*Journal of Greco-Roman Christianity and Judaism*
JSNTSup	Journal for the Study of the New Testament Supplement Series

Abbreviations

JSS	*Journal of Semitic Studies*
LBS	Linguistic Biblical Studies
LSJ	Liddell, Henry George, et al. *A Greek-English Lexicon*. 9th ed. Oxford: Clarendon, 1996.
MJTM	*McMaster Journal of Theology and Ministry*
MNTS	McMaster New Testament Studies
MSJ	*The Master's Seminary Journal*
Neot	*Neotestamentica*
NIBCNT	New International Biblical Commentary on the New Testament
NICNT	New International Commentary on the New Testament
NIGTC	New International Greek Testament Commentary
NTM	New Testament Monographs
PNTC	Pillar New Testament Commentary
ResQ	*Restoration Quarterly*
SBG	Studies in Biblical Greek
SBT	Studies in Biblical Theology
SNTG	Studies in New Testament Greek
SSN	Studia Semitica Neerlandica
TDNT	Kittel, Gerhard, and Gerhard Friedrich, eds. *Theological Dictionary of the New Testament*. Translated by Geoffrey W. Bromiley. 10 vols. Grand Rapids: Eerdmans, 1964–1976.
TENTS	Texts and Editions for New Testament Study
TUGAL	Texte und Untersuchungen zur Geschichte der altchristlichen Literatur
TynBul	*Tyndale Bulletin*
WBC	Word Biblical Commentary
WTJ	*Westminster Theological Journal*
ZNW	*Zeitschrift für die neutestamentliche Wissenschaft und die Kunde der älteren Kirche*

Introduction

A Retrospect and Some Prospects

STANLEY E. PORTER, CHRISTOPHER D. LAND,
AND FRANCIS G. H. PANG

Human beings have been thinking about language for a long time, at least as far back as Plato and Aristotle in the western intellectual tradition, and language continues to be an object of detailed study within the diverse and ever-changing field of linguistics. Similarly, people have been describing, translating, and interpreting the biblical languages and biblical texts for a very long time, more recently with help from linguistically-informed biblical scholars who apply various linguistic approaches to the text of the Bible and its languages.

The Centre for Biblical Linguistics, Translation, and Exegesis operates at McMaster Divinity College in Hamilton, Ontario, Canada, in order to support the linguistic exploration of ancient languages and texts, in particular the Greek of the New Testament. By various means, the Centre supports individuals and projects who are applying linguistic methods to the Bible for the purposes of linguistic analysis, translation, and exegesis. It also hosts events, with the goal of fostering collegial, collaborative dialogue regarding the biblical languages, their translation, and the ways that linguistic methods can contribute to the interpretation of biblical texts.

On June 17, 2016, the Centre hosted the annual Bingham Colloquium at McMaster Divinity College in Hamilton, Ontario. This event, which was preceded the previous afternoon by more informal discussion about the activities of the Centre and the possibilities for linguistics in biblical studies, allowed for faculty and students from McMaster Divinity College to

1

interact with one another and with other interested scholars from other institutions. It included some plenary papers, some parallel papers, and a great many casual conversations during coffee breaks and mealtimes. It allowed new relationships to form and led to productive reflection on some of the ways in which linguistics has already entered into the discourse of biblical studies and some of the ways in which it might play a greater role in the future. This volume includes a number of the papers presented at that conference. We were unfortunately not able to publish them all, nor can we publish the stimulating conversations that were held between papers. It is our hope that the CBLTE will continue to host the Bingham Colloquium periodically, so that these unpublished conversations can not only continue but also include more voices. The prospects surrounding linguistics and biblical studies are promising, but the past has shown that the road to progress is slow and that more workers are needed. It has also shown that progress happens more quickly through collaborative exploration. At the Centre, we do not seek to advocate only one way of describing the biblical languages, but to encourage the generation of new descriptions that can move our understanding of Hebrew, Aramaic, and Greek out of the past and present and into the future.

This volume is divided into two major sections: Linguistics, and Translation and Exegesis. The first major section of this volume contains essays that discuss the application of linguistics in biblical studies from a variety of different perspectives. Randall Tan opens this section with an essay detailing the views he has developed over the course of his career about the ways modern linguistics should be integrated into the wider enterprise of biblical studies. His essay focuses on four main topics: (1) the reason why biblical studies needs the insights of modern linguistics, (2) the most productive aspects of modern linguistics that biblical scholars can utilize, (3) the kinds of corpora, tools, and communities needed to facilitate the incorporation of modern linguistics into biblical studies, and (4) the kinds of free use requirements necessary to facilitate this work. Many of the points made in Tan's essay are then exemplified in the next essay, where Christopher Land and Francis Pang narrate the story of OpenText.org, a freely accessible, web-based initiative to develop annotated Greek texts and tools for linguistic analysis. In their essay, they chronicle the developments of the collaborative OpenText.org project, beginning with the initial efforts of Stanley E. Porter, Matthew Brook O'Donnell, and Jeffrey T. Reed over fifteen years ago and continuing up until the present. They then discuss recent developments and future plans for the project, plans that are even now being brought to fruition. Following this essay, Chris Stevens also addresses the OpenText.org project, but with a focus on its usability in linguistic analysis of the New Testament. In Stevens's essay, he evaluates the current abilities and future applications of OpenText.org for biblical studies by applying a method that analyzes the clause structuring and transitivity patterns in Phil 2. Stevens employs the search capabilities of OpenText.org as they have been integrated into Logos Bible Software to collect data for his analysis, but finds that many improvements are required to yield accurate results.

Another area in which linguistics can make a contribution to biblical studies is the use of quantitative approaches to lexicography, which are now facilitated by computational tools that can manage large amounts of data—much larger than the relatively small corpus of the New Testament. The fourth essay of this volume, written by Ryder Wishart, addresses this topic from the perspective of neostructuralist lexical semantics. Wishart makes the argument that New Testament approaches to lexicography should be quantitative in orientation, following a framework of distributional corpus analysis within which both componential analysis and relational semantics can be remodeled in a way that upholds the motivating values of qualitative structuralist semantics. In the final essay of this section, David Fuller engages the relationship between linguistics and hermeneutics, a relationship he sees as an underexplored area in biblical studies because linguistics has traditionally been oriented towards the goals of historical criticism. Fuller relates the hermeneutical critiques raised against the traditional subject/object distinction to the current state of linguistics in biblical studies, engaging in dialogue along the way with Gadamer, Heidegger, and Ricoeur. Fuller's thesis is that, if linguistic analysis is to make advances in biblical studies, the hermeneutical critiques from continental philosophy need to be heeded.

The second major section of this volume, also comprising five essays, addresses the two other components of the colloquium: Translation and Exegesis. In the first essay of this section, Scott Berthiaume investigates the notion of key terms in translation, where key terms are defined according to the topical foci that a speech community uses to signify cultural themes or messages. He bases his work on several years of observation as a Bible translator of the Northern Pame language, an Otomanguean language located in the eastern part of San Luis Potosí, Mexico. His essay is concerned primarily with the question of how and why some terms used in translation gain traction in the wider use of the target language while others do not, finding that terms already used in a wider language context have the advantage of being well known, but are more susceptible to semantic shift or loss of meaning, and that prescribing terms, while having the advantage of being more precise, may or may not be successful because their incorporation is ultimately dependent upon the community's use of them over many years. In the second essay of this section, Cynthia Long Westfall also addresses matters of Bible translation, namely the decision made by the editors of the Common English Bible (CEB) to render the idiom ὁ υἱὸς τοῦ ἀνθρώπου as either "The Human One" or "the human being" (rather than the traditional "son of man"). To assess this decision, around which lies some controversy, Westfall evaluates several interpretive variables, including the semantics of the idiom in the New Testament in relation to its corresponding idioms in Hebrew and Aramaic in the Old Testament, the semantic distinctions between the CEB's translation and the formal equivalent phrase "The Son of Man," and the CEB's translation in light of its own goals for translation and modern translation theory.

The final essays of the volume are oriented to matters of exegesis. In the third essay of this section, Stanley Porter explores the contents of a number of recent or well-known books on exegesis to assess the role they give to the Greek language in the exegetical process. Based on his evaluation, Porter then examines the contrast between traditional grammar, which is found in most of the exegesis books, and modern linguistic approaches to the Greek language, in particular Cognitive-Functional Linguistics and Systemic Functional Linguistics. In the next essay, Mark Proctor challenges the common interpretation of Mark 4:12 that takes the ἵνα clause as expressing purpose, arguing instead that the ἵνα clause should be understood as epexegetical—that is, elaborating on the unfortunate situation of "those outside" (ἐκείνοις τοῖς ἔξω) God's kingdom. This entails that Jesus's parabolic instruction should be understood as a pedagogical concession where he explains to "outsiders" the nature of God's rule. In support, Proctor provides a detailed account of the ἵνα-clause functionality throughout the Gospel of Mark to show that its use in Mark 4:12 would have been comfortably understood by Mark's original readers as epexegetical. In the final essay, Esther Cen makes use of discourse analysis modeled through a Systemic Functional Linguistic perspective to address the subject matter of 1 Cor 5—that is, what the discourse is about. Cen concludes that the focus of this part of Paul's letter is not on the immoral man, but rather on what the church has failed to do, how the church should view this issue, and what the church should do in moving forward.

The range of essays found within this volume attests to the progress that has been made in linguistically-informed study of the Bible, in particular the Greek of the New Testament. However, if these essays show anything, they also show that there is much further opportunity for creative engagement between the study of Greek and the implementation of various linguistic models such as is attested and promised here.

Part 1

Linguistics

1

Linguistics and Biblical Studies
An Ongoing Journey

RANDALL K. J. TAN

INTRODUCTION

AROUND FIFTEEN YEARS AGO, early in my doctoral studies, I encountered an article called "Studying Ancient Languages from a Modern Linguistic Perspective," written by Stanley Porter.[1] After reading that article and Porter's other writings, I became deeply troubled that much of New Testament studies continued to rely on traditional grammar and premodern linguistic work. I became convinced that the scientific study of language is critical if we want to better understand the language and texts of the New Testament. This realization started me on a journey that would radically change the direction of my PhD studies, a journey I have continued on for my entire scholarly career.

Over the course of my career I have developed a number of views on how modern linguistics should factor into the wider enterprise of biblical studies. In this essay, I will focus on four areas in particular. First, I will briefly examine why the wider field of biblical studies needs the insights of modern linguistics. Second, I will make some modest suggestions about which aspects of modern linguistics give "the most bang for their buck." Third, I will provide some recommendations concerning what kinds of corpora, tools, and communities are needed to facilitate smoother incorporation of

---

1. Porter, "Studying Ancient Languages," 147–72.

modern linguistics into biblical studies. Finally, I will discuss what kinds of freedom for reuse are required to facilitate this type of work.

EXPLAINING THE NEED FOR MODERN LINGUISTICS

The first topic of discussion is the need for applying modern linguistics to the wider field of biblical studies. For a well-rounded consideration it is necessary both to count the costs and to demonstrate the benefits of modern linguistics. On the cost side of the ledger, modern linguistics uses vocabulary and concepts quite different from those found in traditional Greek grammars, and these are foreign to many biblical scholars.[2] To make matters worse, because advocates of integrating modern linguistics into biblical studies draw from different theories, the use of the same terms are often used in multiple and often contrasting ways.[3] To use a well-known example, once someone learns a term like "verbal aspect," they are immediately confronted by prolonged and complicated debates about how aspect is to be understood. And it can be difficult to find objective criteria to determine who is right. Confronted with this steep learning curve and uncertainty, many scholars are tempted to retreat to their comfort zone, the traditional grammars they were trained to use.

Despite the difficulties, these scholars should be prompted in the other direction. Traditional biblical scholars recognize that the so-called "traditional grammar" that continues to take pride of place in some circles did not pass down from the time of the apostles to the present fully formed and unchanged.[4] They understand some of the weaknesses in traditional

---

2. This situation results in part because the field of linguistics is vast and diverse. Phonetics, phonology, morphology, syntax, semantics, and pragmatics form a six-part core that moves up from the level of sound to meaning (Aronoff and Rees-Miller, "Preface," xv). There are also various fields of inquiry that look at the areas scholars use linguistics to explore. A partial list includes historical linguistics, psycholinguistics, sociolinguistics, neurolinguistics, computational linguistics, and all areas falling under applied linguistics. Applied linguistics is itself a broad field. While it started with a focus on language pedagogy, learning, and acquisition, it has expanded to include anything that fits Brumfit's widely cited definition of applied linguistics as "the theoretical and empirical investigation of real-world problems in which language is a central issue" (Simpson, "Introduction," 2).

3. Robin Lakoff observes that different sub-disciplines and competing theory in linguistics often use mutually unintelligible language ("Nine Ways of Looking at Apologies," 200).

4. Michael Frede traces the origins of traditional grammar in *Essays in Ancient Philosophy*, 337–60. Hadumod Bussmann describes traditional grammar as "A type of

lexicons and grammars. They may even acknowledge that the great grammarians and scholars of the nineteenth century would not ignore a century of advances in theory and tools. However, many scholars still neglect the insights of modern linguistics because they are not yet confident that they can be relied on.[5] Part of the challenge is that biblical studies is still in the early phases of understanding biblical languages through these newer paradigms, and it is simply hard to be certain about drawing conclusions using either traditional or newer paradigms.

Fortunately, scholars generally understand the inevitability of at least some uncertainty in scholarship. The task thus becomes making a convincing case for the strengths of using modern linguistic theory in biblical studies, but also proactively admitting the unresolved ambiguities and uncertainties that remain. Scholars also generally understand the importance of evidence. Often, however, traditional scholars do not understand what new kinds of evidence need to be considered, why the insights of modern linguistics improve understanding of language, or how these insights can be shown to be true. Traditional grammars often observed the same phenomena that some scholars are now looking at through the lens of modern linguistics. Thus, those advocating for the use of modern linguistic models need to explore where the evidence used in traditional grammars and commentaries was more or less accurately judged according to modern linguistic criteria. To do this well, the similarities and distinctions between modern and classical paradigms need to be thoroughly mapped, respecting the wisdom of many who have gone before while still scrutinizing the work of past generations.[6]

---

grammar first developed in Europe in the eighteenth century, based on Aristotelian logic and ancient Greek and Latin grammars, often as an aid to learning these languages and interpreting classical texts" (*Language and Linguistics*, 1032).

5. As Porter points out, this is partly attributable to the fact that "many of the standard critical tools for studying the biblical languages predate the development of modern linguistics" (*Linguistic Analysis*, 84). Perhaps the dominance of different versions of Chomskyan generative grammars in theoretical linguistics in the United States during much of the second half of the twentieth century was a significant factor. As Kanavillil Rajagopalan notes, Chomsky's exclusive focus on language structure, elevation of native speakers, and neglect of the communicative function of language led to widespread disassociation of applied linguistics from contemporary theoretical linguistics ("Philosophy of Applied Linguistics," 402–4) Applied linguists turned to other competing theories (Harris, "Linguistics in Applied Linguistics," 106–9). For works that apply some form of modern linguistics to Hellenistic Greek, see Palmer, "Comprehensive Bibliography."

6. Porter aptly notes, "The promise of linguistics is not necessarily that new insights are to be gained (although many new ones have already been realized), nor that it will

Admittedly, such a task has several daunting challenges before it, but the fact that all biblical scholars share a reliance on the biblical texts ensures some common ground in the efforts for progress. While no native speaker of Hellenistic Greek is alive today, we still have the texts that native speakers have written. These are the only real evidence available for researching the texts and language of the New Testament.[7] Porter makes this point clear in the following quotation:

> The study of the New Testament is essentially a language-based discipline. That is, the primary body of data for examination is a text, or, better yet, a collection of many texts written in the Hellenistic variety of the Greek language of the first century CE. Whatever else may be involved in the study of the New Testament ... to remain a study of the New Testament it must always remain textually based, since the only direct access that we have into the world of the New Testament is through the text of the Greek New Testament.[8]

Since the study of the New Testament is essentially a language-based discipline, it is necessary to highlight next how modern linguistics contributes to a fundamentally empirical approach.[9] This is particularly true in

---

overthrow all traditional opinions (although a number of unfounded traditional opinions have been called into question). The promise of linguistics is that it can provide a proper interpretive foundation for a text-based discipline—which, after all, is what biblical studies is supposed to be" (*Linguistic Analysis*, 92). In discussing the preservation of standard nomenclature and the use of modern linguistic categories and terms only when essential in his *Fundamentals of New Testament Greek* textbook for beginning students, Porter notes that there are many good reasons to adopt modern linguistic terminology throughout, but that there are many even better reasons not to do so (see also Porter, "Usage-Based Approach to Teaching New Testament Greek," 127–28). I would argue that the situation is analogous when dealing with scholars in biblical studies in general. This is because, while biblical scholars are learned and accomplished in their own specialties, they face the same obstacles as beginning students when newly confronted with modern linguistics. Removing unnecessary access barriers is thus a good idea.

7. Linguists generally work with living languages, which have native speakers. They can ask these speakers to make judgments about the language and do experiments using these speakers as subjects. Linguists also work with text corpora. On elicitation of native speaker judgments, see Munro, "Field Linguistics," 130–49. On experiments, see Ahlsén, "Neurolinguistics," 460–71. On corpora, see Stubbs, "Language Corpora," 106–32; O'Keeffe and McCarthy, *Corpus Linguistics*.

8. Porter, "Discourse Analysis and New Testament Studies," 14.

9. An empirical approach naturally entails that any linguistic analysis would be descriptive rather than prescriptive. No New Testament interpreter can claim a position of unique privilege and insight based on native speaker knowledge and intuition. Even if

modern computer-assisted corpus-based linguistics, where any theorizing is dependent on the facts and patterns that are empirically discovered in the text. For example, each judgment found in traditional grammars and lexicons can be examined, querying the corpus to see if a given judgment matches the available data. Thus, I will now turn attention to what I believe to be the fundamental benefits of using modern linguistics as an empirical science—namely, that it is based on systematic observation of the data, where the data and analyses are made publicly available, and where the data and analyses are open to testing and are potentially replicable or falsifiable.

THE MOST BANG FOR THE BUCK

Since learning new linguistic theories and their associated esoteric language demands a heavy investment, it is important to communicate to the larger biblical studies guild the aspects of modern linguistics that give "the most bang for the buck." The most important benefit of modern linguistics is perhaps its ability to help us systematically and comprehensively describe what the texts and language say—no more, no less. Considering the complexity of language and texts, three things stand out to me. First, language is multi-faceted and requires a multi-angled, multi-disciplinary approach. For example, language can at least be viewed as a social fact, as a psychological state, as a set of structures, or as a collection of outputs.[10] Because language has both formal and functional dimensions, functional linguistic theories like Halliday's Systemic Functional Grammar are likely to provide more satisfactory and holistic descriptions than formal theories of grammar, like the various versions of Chomskyan generative grammar.[11] Nev-

---

native speakers were available (and they are not), their judgments should be checked by empirical means.

10. Bauer, *Linguistics Student's Handbook*, 3.

11. Much of the work in various versions of Chomskyan generative grammar has operated at seemingly implausibly high levels of abstraction and complexity because of its assumption of the universal innate knowledge of grammar. Key ideas of various versions have also been modified or fully abandoned over the last half century (e.g., transformations, government and binding, principles and parameters) (see Swan, "Grammar," 559). As a result, in surveying the literature on corpus linguistics and applied linguistics for mentions of Chomsky and Chomskyan generative grammar, I have found that the general picture is that its dominance in theoretical linguistics in the United States has not translated into much impact (or has even had negative impact) on various areas of study of real-world language and real-world language issues. A notable exception is head-driven phrase structure grammar, which originated from the tradition of generative grammars and yet is an advanced practical formalism useful for describing and processing natural

ertheless, no theory comprehensively describes every aspect of language and so different theories potentially contribute valuable insights from different perspectives.[12] If individual scholars practice principled eclecticism and communities of researchers collaborate in multi-perspectival research, then vastness and diversity can be an asset rather than a weakness.[13] It is important then for scholars to not work in isolation; instead, there needs to be an effort to seek out dialogue, invite multi-disciplinary research collaboration, and build long-term, sustainable communities with colleagues who come from diverse disciplines and perspectives.

Second, in principle, different levels of language can be analyzed separately. However, because the primary body of data we analyze is corpus instances that belong to an ancient text of which there are no native speakers, we often need to be more careful not to make claims about meaning that are too sweeping or distinctions that are too narrow beyond what the available evidence clearly supports. Neatly dividing up the respective contributions of syntax and semantics in particular can be problematic.[14] Consequently, caution and humble restraint need to be taken concerning the degree of comprehensiveness and certainty claimed in individual studies. Then, researchers also will be better situated to help colleagues exercise more caution and restraint in their claims.

---

language. For example, the Global Bible Initiative found head-driven phrase structure grammar to be useful for building its own Greek and Hebrew syntax treebanks. The openly licensed complete syntactic treebank for the Nestle 1904 and SBLGNT editions of the Greek New Testament, as well as the documentation for these treebanks, may be accessed through biblicalhumanities.org's dashboard (online: http://biblicalhumanities.github.io/dashboard/).

12. As Simpson notes, "no one description, model or view of language will suffice for all intentions: one's understanding of language will depend to an extent on one's particular concern of the time" ("Introduction," 6).

13. Schiffrin et al. make a similar point in relation to discourse analysis ("Introduction," 5). Porter's recommendations on how to employ a model of multidisciplinary exegesis in *Linguistics Analysis*, 93–112 merit further consideration as one way forward. Any implementation of eclecticism should always be principled and take into account the relative compatibility and respective applicable domains of each theory, method, or tool employed.

14. Some, including linguists in the Systemic Functional Linguistics tradition, even reject the traditional distinction between lexis (i.e., lexical semantics treated in a lexicon) and grammar (i.e., morphological patterns discussed in grammar books). Instead, they see the lexico-grammar of language as a continuum of paradigmatic systems, with grammar at one end and lexis at the other. See, e.g., Hasan, "Grammarian's Dream," 184–211; and Hasselgård, *Corpus Perspectives*.

Third, out of context, linguistic forms are under-specified. They are bustling with a range of potential meanings. However, in context, they become much more specific, with bundles of meaning selected by lexical and grammatical combination patterns.[15] The whole linguistic utterance in context thus means both more and less than the sum of its parts. Half a century ago, James Barr famously debunked several kinds of linguistic mistakes that result from failure to adequately recognize how function and context narrow down meaning potential and specify meaning in actual usage in text.[16] Similar problems persist in contemporary biblical studies.[17] This is why better empirical methods and tools need to be developed that can clearly demonstrate why interpreters should not try to make a word, phrase, or clause mean every possible meaning it might have in isolation. More systematic attention needs to be paid to the phraseology, the syntax, the rest of the surrounding co-text, and any other contextual information to disambiguate meaning as clearly and accurately as the evidence will allow.

A COMMON INFRASTRUCTURE FOR STUDYING TEXTS AND LANGUAGE

In order to better understand the language and texts of the New Testament, there needs to be an infrastructure that supports (a) systematic observation of the data, (b) complete and intelligible accounting for all data and analysis, (c) testing of research hypotheses, and (d) reuse of prior work to create new work. Once established, this infrastructure will make linguistic research much easier to explain to the wider guild of New Testament

---

15. Corpus linguistic work is turning up increasing evidence of the importance of multi-word units, and may support John Sinclair's claim that lexis is more important than grammar in meaning creation. See Greaves and Warren, "Multi-Word Units," 212–26; Granger and Meunier, *Phraseology*; Herbst et al., *Phraseological View of Language*.

16. Barr, *Semantics of Biblical Language*. These include "illegitimate totality transfer," "illegitimate identity transfer," and confusing lexical items with the concepts they may be used to represent. Such mistakes are easy to commit if informed views of linguistics are not fully assimilated.

17. While some might disagree, I think that the πίστις Χριστοῦ debate is a clear example of this kind of linguistic mistake. In my opinion, consideration of the linguistic purposes of nominalizing a process into an entity and Paul's clear spelling out of the process with Christ as the object of believing (esp. Gal 2:16) in itself obviates the need for any debate. Paul did not intend to be ambiguous. If this simple observation is insufficient to convince many, fortunately others have also provided more thorough sound linguistic arguments to show where the weight of the linguistic evidence properly lies. See esp. Porter and Pitts, "πίστις," 33–53; Cirafesi, "ἔχειν πίστιν," 5–37.

studies and also easier to involve other scholars in doing new work together in collaboration.

Biblical scholars are helped by the fact that biblical studies revolves around a relatively small, specialized corpus of the biblical texts as the primary source data.[18] So, the logical first target is to build an open corpus of these texts. The OpenText.org project, started by Stanley Porter, Jeffrey Reed, and Matthew Brook O'Donnell, was a pioneering project in this arena. It was a web-based initiative to collaborate with and serve the scholarly community by developing annotated Greek texts and tools for their analysis.[19] It built an infrastructure to make systematic observation of the syntax of the Greek New Testament. It offered a complete and intelligible accounting of the Greek text at the clause and word group levels. I had the privilege of playing a part in its early development, which planted a seed of open scholarship that continues to flourish in me. My appreciation for the need to use cutting-edge technology was likewise sparked by watching the technological marvels that my then-close-collaborator on the OpenText.org project, Matthew Brook O'Donnell, came up with. It is a great joy to me to know that Christopher Land and Francis Pang are now spearheading OpenText.org 2.0. The OpenText.org project's contributions as a trailblazer should not be overlooked. I expect OpenText.org 2.0 to further expand its contributions.

To support the work of groups like OpenText.org 2.0, Jonathan Robie and I co-founded a group called biblicalhumanities.org, based on the idea of facilitation and enabling. We have started to bring together a community of computer scientists, biblical scholars, and digital humanists who are already working on creating open digital resources for biblical studies. These are people and groups doing similar things to OpenText.org 2.0 in different areas of biblical studies. Our aim is to facilitate collaboration and the building of an enabling infrastructure to use those resources more fully and effectively.

We think the first step is to build a machine-readable annotated corpus of the Greek New Testament that empowers flexible expansion and is freely licensed. By freely licensed, I mean there is no need to ask permission

---

18. Advantages of a smaller, specialized corpus include time and cost savings on setting up the base corpus and greater feasibility of adding multiple levels of linguistics annotations comprehensively. As Almut Koester notes, smaller, specialized corpora better enable one to interpret the language and text in context and to balance quantitative and qualitative analysis ("Building Small Specialized Corpora," 67).

19. See http://opentext.org/about/overview.html.

to reuse, remix, build on, or otherwise work with the corpus in any way without any restrictions, except to give credit where credit is due.[20] As a starting point, the corpus could consist of a base Greek New Testament text, textual variants, morphology, syntax treebanks, and a lexicon. Because users can reuse, remix, and build freely, we expect to generate a virtuous circle where more use of the material made available will lead to their improvement and augmentation as well as the creation of new resources as additional modules. Most of these basic ingredients are already available and can be viewed on biblicalhumanities.org's dashboard.[21] For Greek syntax alone, besides OpenText.org's annotations, there are multiple versions of the Global Bible Initiative's Greek syntax trees and PROIEL's dependency trees. Through the efforts of scholars working in the Classics, especially various groups working within the Perseus orbit, there is no shortage of digital Greek texts from the Hellenistic and other periods that can eventually be incorporated as well—that is to say if the volume of work can be handled. On biblicalhumanities.org's dashboard, various references and links are provided to resources, such as OpenGreekandLatin's machine-corrected versions of Swete's Septuagint, Migne's Patrologia Graeca, Cramer's Catenae, and LACE's conversions of a massive number of other Greek texts from scanned images into machine encoded texts.[22]

A second vital step is still largely missing. So, we are talking with our existing and potential partners, including OpenText.org 2.0, about building open source user-friendly software tools and interfaces. The idea is that open data still needs well-designed open source software to enable any individual or team of scholars to add to, delete, replace, or reorganize any of the existing modules of annotation data. The tools should allow for maximum flexibility for users to define what they want to annotate, their

20. The guidelines of biblicalhumanities.org, of which I am one of the co-founders, on free licenses is as follows: "For content that is not code, we like Creative Commons Licenses. For code, we like MIT, Apache, and GPL[;] see http://choosealicense.com. We encourage licenses that require attribution, we dislike licenses that require asking permission—that just doesn't scale" (http://biblicalhumanities.githuo.io/guidelines/). Suber highlights the point that the three influential public statements on open access, the Budapest Open Access Initiative (February 2002), the Bethesda Statement on Open Access Publishing (June 2003), and the Berlin Declaration on Open Access to Knowledge in the Sciences and Humanities (October 2003) essentially define open access as going beyond removing price barriers to removing permission barriers, except for the obligation to attribute the work to the author (*Open Access*, 7–8).

21. See http://biblicalhumanities.github.io/dashboard/.

22. See http://biblicalhumanities.github.io/dashboard/.

17

own framework, and labels. For users without the ability to take the open source code and modify it, the tools would be designed to be as extensible as possible to meet most foreseeable basic needs. For users able to build on the open source code, we likewise expect to start a virtuous circle where more use of the tools will lead to their improvement and augmentation, as well as the creation of new user-friendly software tools and interfaces. By setting up this infrastructure, we will be able to study the texts and language of the Greek New Testament on firmer empirical grounding, whatever the method or perspective.

A simultaneously needed third step is to cultivate a worldwide community of scholars who use this annotated corpus not only to conduct and publish their own research, but also to collaborate with one another to improve and build on the corpus.[23] As participants and resources increase, the corpus for New Testament studies can be extended to include other Hellenistic texts, and other levels and kinds of linguistic annotation can be added as modules. The growing community will also serve as a natural source of both collaboration and peer review for any research based on the corpus. Open scholarship with open data on open-source software augments both the ability to collaborate and to conduct thorough peer review because both the data and analyses are fully furnished. Together the community can help its members to validate their theories by testing and evaluating (a) whether proposed theories come up with compatible and convincing answers to many or all questions, (b) whether they apply to related sorts of data (i.e., range of coverage), and (c) how tightly they account for the linguistic details. The strength and diversity of support (or lack thereof) from members of the community would validate or cast doubt on research hypotheses.[24]

WHY IS A "TRIPLE OPEN" APPROACH OPTIMAL?

Even if one were to agree mostly with the approach I have suggested so far, one may still have reservations about allowing reuse of their research.

---

23. The Global Education and Research Technology section at the Society of Biblical Literature (SBL) Annual Meetings, which Nicolai Winther-Nielsen and I co-founded, serves in part to gather and build this global community of biblical scholars. On this program unit, see https://www.sblsite.org/meetings/Congresses_ProgramUnits.aspx?MeetingId=29.

24. I have adopted the four criteria James Paul Gee proposed to evaluate validity for discourse analysis, keeping the first three intact, but interpreting the community's level of support as based on their conclusions about how well the first three criteria are met (*Introduction to Discourse Analysis*, 113–14).

Some may need more convincing that the optimal approach is to practice corpus-based linguistic study within the framework of open scholarship with open data on open source software (which I have nicknamed a "triple open" approach). In what follows I will unpack the thought process that led me to this conclusion.

Writing is a technology.[25] It was a tremendous technological achievement that enabled humans to keep records and communicate over distance and time.[26] Gutenberg's mechanical movable type printing press vastly extended the reach of writing and introduced the era of mass communication. Run-of-the-mill use of digital technology to serve up digitized books and articles further extends the reach of writing and print. These are the technologies that empower scholarship and spread knowledge today. However, they appear ill-equipped to continue to support the information explosion all fields are experiencing.

What are the typical challenges of doing research? The challenges that come to my mind first are data gathering (for both primary and secondary sources), developing and documenting of methods, and making sure my results are replicable or falsifiable. When publication is taken into consideration, I think about spatial limitations (e.g., the word or page limit), temporal limitations (e.g., the length of the publication process and shelf life of the publication), and format limitations (e.g., the type of data and visualizations that can be fitted into standard print formats).

Because most data sources are still in print form or digital formats that imitate print, data gathering still involves a lot of legwork: a trip to the library or bookstore, ordering books through interlibrary loan or even purchasing them, locating and accessing individual digital documents, etc. Because the sources are scattered, integrating the information gained from them is time consuming. Even with digital documents, one often has to read and search them separately and toggle between documents to extract what is needed.

Moreover, the same kinds of limitations that one faces when publishing research are faced by the authors of the research one is consuming. Spatial, temporal, and format limitations usually mean that not all the relevant data or analyses can be published. Even in the rare occasions when they are made fully available, they are usually presented in print-dictated forms that

---

25. See Burton et al., *Linguistics for Dummies*, 295–306.

26. The description of this problem at http://osinitiative.org/about-osi/ is quite helpful.

are not very reusable, e.g., not stored in relational databases or annotated with machine-readable markup languages. Furthermore, copyright restrictions typically limit the extent to which the data and analyses can be reused in further research. To make matters worse, space limitations often hinder authors from fully documenting and explaining their thought process and methods with clarity.

Last, access to scholarship, even if one could overcome this communication gap, is hindered by the "Closed Access" model where ownership resides largely outside the academy in the hands of commercial companies. Scholarly research is quarantined behind access barriers (whether print or digital in nature) and held for what sometimes feels like a king's ransom. Access barriers in turn help perpetuate the situation where information is scattered, fragmented, and difficult to effectively gather and integrate. Unless a researcher is privileged enough to have easy access to a well-heeled research library or is independently wealthy, enormous financial and intellectual expense is demanded even to attempt to understand other people's research, let alone successfully decipher them.[27] With so many accessibility problems, much research does not achieve any kind of wide circulation, much less enjoy sufficient attention to warrant replication or falsification. The overall result is ever-worsening knowledge fragmentation and an ever-widening access gap.[28]

Scholars in the wider academic world have begun to address similar kinds of problems with a worsening access gap and knowledge fragmentation. The fields of technology and the sciences have led the way.[29] These efforts are already starting to address most obstacles and concerns effectively and to tilt the global political, legal, and cultural environment in favor of freedom of access. On the one hand, they provide abundant inspiration, impetus, and models for biblical studies to press ahead. On the other hand,

---

27. In fact, even the wealthiest libraries in the world can no longer keep up with the cost and suffer serious access gaps, notably including Harvard and Yale (Suber, *Open Access*, 30). See also Swan, "Overview of Scholarly Communication," 9.

28. Suber identifies the need for "a system of research dissemination that scales with the growth of research volume." For example, if a hypothetical library can afford 100 percent of the research literature it covers today and its library budget and the price of that literature increases at the same rate (so we are taking price inflation out of the equation), then if the literature grows by just five percent a year, in twenty years that library would only be able to afford to cover 37.7 percent of that expanding research (*Open Access*, 41–42).

29. Pomerantz and Peek disambiguate the many meanings of "open" and sort through various open movements in "Fifty Shades of Open."

they are demonstrating that the concerns and objections to open scholarship, which mainly center on economic issues and permissive reuse rights, are not insuperable, and that, in any case, the benefits outweigh the costs.[30] Given that my main concern is to show how open access, open data, and open scholarship augment one another, I will focus primarily on reasons why biblical scholars should join the larger global scholarly world in solving knowledge fragmentation and access barrier problems.[31]

A necessary, though not sufficient, ingredient to resolve accessibility problems is open access (OA). As Suber points out,

> OA benefits literally everyone, for the same reasons that research itself benefits literally everyone. OA performs this service by facilitating research and making the results more widely available and useful. It benefits researchers as readers by helping them find and retrieve the information they need, and it benefits researchers as authors by helping them reach readers who can apply, cite, and build on their work. OA benefits nonresearchers by accelerating research and all the goods that depend on research, such as new medicines, useful technologies, solved problems, informed decisions, improved policies, and beautiful understanding.[32]

---

30. Eve, in *Open Access and the Humanities*, offers a balanced, critical investigation of the potential benefits, the problems to overcome, and the controversies surrounding open access in the context of the humanities. In the sciences and many other fields, open access has focused on journal publication because it is low-hanging fruit and most research is disseminated in that form. For the humanities, because a higher proportion of research is disseminated in monograph form, at least some monographs should come into consideration for open access as well. Eve devotes a full chapter to the promise and challenges involved with open access for monographs in the humanities (112–36).

31. In essence, for most articles and monographs, the benefits of open access far outweigh any potential financial gain for the authors. This is because copyright mainly protects the economic interests of publishers rather than authors, unless the work is sufficiently popular to generate substantial royalties for the authors. Scholars who support open scholarship do not have to publish all of their work under open licenses. For example, they are free to leverage their more financially viable works to subsidize their less popular, basic research. For those concerned about what would happen to publishers, alternative models are already being tested in the larger scholarly world that may continue to fund publishers to play their roles in a more sustainable way. See, e.g., Suber, *Open Access*, 125–61; Eve, *Open Access and the Humanities*, 43–85, 125–36. Open licenses like the Creative Commons licenses provide the same protections against libel and false attribution as traditional commercial licenses. Eve fully addresses and allays concerns about scholarly integrity and undesirable use (*Open Access and the Humanities*, 102–11).

32. Suber, *Open Access*, ix. Suber provides a partial list of good scholarly reasons to exceed fair use: quoting long excerpts; distributing full-text copies to students or colleagues; burning copies on CDs for parts of the world with poor or unaffordable internet

Beyond open access, open data is also vitally important for the integrity of biblical studies as an empirical scientific discipline. This is because data is as much a product of scholarship as publications.[33] First of all, scholars can look at the data others used to reach a conclusion and analyze it for themselves. Moreover, if the data is relevant for further research, either along the same lines or along different lines, the data can be reused and built on without having to go through the process of collecting the data. Further, with the "triple open" approach advocated here, the data is tied directly to the common infrastructure and open corpus of the Greek New Testament—either built directly on the annotations provided by others or from one's own revisions to those annotations or one's own additional contributions. The common infrastructure and corpus thus becomes a common hub that provides convenient, comprehensive access to research data for all. One recurrent frustration in reading biblical research is that all the raw data and datasets that underlie findings are rarely fully and readily available. Most often, it is simply too time consuming to re-gather the data and reanalyze it simply to see if I agree or not with others' conclusions. In fact, I think it is unnecessarily inefficient and wasteful not to make it a lot easier to fully digest, interact, and build on previous research. How could I as a scholar possibly possess the time and resources to work in more than a small subspecialty if I continually run up against a wall of artificial scarcity? I would rather spend my time sifting through thousands of more pages of material, thinking, and producing new work than metaphorically walking miles with a bucket to get some drinking water from the nearest river or well. By contrast, the common infrastructure and open corpus would metaphorically supply tap water directly to the researcher's home.

Open source software is likewise indispensable. Without the freedom to run, study, modify, and redistribute the software that provides enhanced access to the research and its underlying data, scholarship will continue to be hamstrung. It is definitely not trivial or inexpensive to develop new

---

access; distributing modified versions with enhancements like semantic annotation; migrating texts to new formats or media; creating archive copies for long-term preservation; incorporating works in a database or mashup; producing audio recordings of texts; translating texts into other languages; indexing, text-mining, or other kinds of text processing (ibid., 73–74). Eve elaborates further on many of these good scholarly reasons from the perspective of humanities scholars (*Open Access and the Humanities*, 96–101).

33. Pomerantz and Peek note that "data is as much a product of scholarship as publications, and there is an increasing sentiment among scholars that it should therefore be made public" ("Fifty Shades of Open").

software and user interfaces from scratch just to be able to work better with any research and its underlying data.[34] When all these ingredients are in place, then scholarship can be opened. Open scholarship combines open access texts, open data, and open-source software to provide openness at every stage of a research project and enables replication, confirmation, revision, falsification, and further building on it.[35]

In line with all three steps spelled out above, biblicalhumanities.org is working to grow a community, but not to own it or control it. We seek to help create the environment needed to enable open scholarship in biblical studies with open data on open source software. We also attempt to get everyone to collaborate by recommending that everyone follow at least three dictums with all of the data, scholarship, and software they contribute to this enabling infrastructure: (a) make it freely accessible, (b) make it interoperable, and (c) make it intelligible.[36] With Greek, a way to conceive of the whole enterprise is to think of biblicalhumanities.org as working to put together a freely reusable, ever growing digital Greek New Testament corpus with accompanying modules for textual variants, morphological analysis, syntactic analysis, lexical analysis, and any other levels of linguistic analysis. The benefits do not end with freely reusable resources. Scholars are free to mix and match, revise, and build on them, whichever way they need.[37] Instead of all rights reserved by the author, users are granted almost

---

34. For those unfamiliar with programming, Eve provides a simple explanation of why it is extremely hard to understand how a program works or to change how it behaves without the original source code (*Open Access and the Humanities*, 92–93).

35. Perceptive readers may have noticed that I have used "open scholarship" in two different ways. Where "open scholarship" co-occurs with "open data" and "open source software," the component of making the result of one's research open access is foregrounded. Where "open scholarship" occurs on its own, as here, it refers to the overall process and product that combines open access, open data, and open source software, without foregrounding any one component. For my purposes, open science and open scholarship are near synonyms, with the term open scholarship potentially being broader in geographical and intellectual focus, if the word "science" in "open science" is construed too narrowly. The Open Scholarship Initiative changed its name from the Open Science Initiative apparently to explicitly expand its geographical and intellectual focus. See http://osinitiative.org/about-osi/.

36. By interoperable, we are referring to the ability to communicate, exchange data, and use that data meaningfully and accurately in terms of the technology used. By intelligible, we are referring to ensuring this similar ability by using comprehensible human language in communicating with other human researchers.

37. OpenContent.org offers a helpful definition of the range of freedoms users enjoy: "1. Retain the right to make, own, and control copies of the content (e.g., download,

the same rights as the author, except for some rights the author chooses to reserve in a "some rights reserved" approach.[38]

With this kind of an infrastructure in place to empower and showcase linguistically-informed scholarship, it will be much easier to clearly and fully explain and demonstrate work to the larger field of biblical studies. Various access barriers (e.g., the ones that result from the limitations of print, from the closed access model of scholarly publication, and communication problems that stem from unintelligible use of language) would be removed and misunderstandings and misconceptions would be less likely to occur. Less miscommunication and more effective communication will in turn lead to more time and effort being spent on engaging in substantive discussions and resolving real issues of serious disagreement. The lowering of barriers and the improved communication will likewise create a more conducive environment for collaborative scholarship, where a larger number of colleagues would be more likely to be both more willing and able to do new work together.

CONCLUSION

Empirical science is social and accumulative in the sense that researchers are meant to build on and improve each other's work.[39] Open scholarship with open data on open source software works exceptionally well to remove various access barriers and to empower (a) systematic observation of the data, (b) complete and intelligible accounting for all data and analyses, (c)

---

duplicate, store, and manage) 2. Reuse the right to use the content in a wide range of ways (e.g., in a class, in a study group, on a website, in a video) 3. Revise the right to adapt, adjust, modify, or alter the content itself (e.g., translate the content into another language) 4. Remix the right to combine the original or revised content with other material to create something new (e.g., incorporate the content into a mashup) 5. Redistribute the right to share copies of the original content, your revisions, or your remixes with others (e.g., give a copy of the content to a friend)" (http://opencontent.org/definition/).

38. The only right that should always be reserved is attribution, i.e., to give credit where credit is due. Reserving some other rights may be appropriate and helpful in particular circumstances. See especially https://creativecommons.org/choose/ for other choices and the considerations that lead to them. The "ShareAlike" option, which would ensure that any derivatives would be available to the community under the same terms as the original, is perhaps the most valuable and worthy of consideration. It would serve a similar function to GNU's General Public License (GPLv3) copyleft feature (see https://www.gnu.org/licenses/quick-guide-gplv3.html). For more details particularly relevant to the humanities, see Collins et al., "Guide to Creative Commons."

39. Gee, *Introduction to Discourse Analysis*, 114.

viable testing, potential replication, or falsification of any research, and (d) remixing and building upon the shoulders of any research. It effectively addresses the problems of knowledge fragmentation and access barriers while furthering mass dissemination of knowledge and empowering the building on and advance of biblical studies in ways that were previously unfeasible and mostly unimaginable for previous generations in biblical studies. The world has changed for the better. The question is whether biblical studies is ready to take full advantage of these positive changes at this time.

On a more personal note, once the basic open data, open scholarship, and open source software are in place, I will finally be able to begin to do the kinds of research I could only dream about when I was a PhD student. For example, I dreamt about compiling, for both Greek and Hebrew, corpus-based reference grammars, producing corpus-based lexicons, writing comprehensive discourse commentaries for every biblical book, and building biblical theologies for the whole Bible firmly on the foundation of thorough corpus-based linguistic analysis for the entire relevant corpus. I was naïve enough to not realize it at the time, but my dreams would require far more than the efforts of a single scholar in a single lifetime, however ambitious and resourceful. While I do hope that one day I will be able to enter the "Promised Land" and get a taste of the coming glory, my dream is now that future generations of scholars can be the ones to fully realize these kinds of dreams and beyond by having the necessary enabling infrastructure built for them by the current generation.

Can all of this be done? I believe so. The larger global scholarly community is already moving in the direction of open scholarship. The humanities and biblical studies might lag behind, but they will most likely follow suit. This constitutes a conducive, general environment and will also furnish abundant models of success for biblical studies to emulate. Linguistics and corpus linguistics in particular supply abundant theoretical and methodological models that could potentially produce valid, fruitful insights and perspectives into the biblical texts. Multi-disciplinary collaboration and global sharing of research and data is increasingly seen as a desired norm, even if it is not yet the actual norm in most fields of research. For biblical studies in particular, many of the components needed to build an enabling infrastructure, such as that envisioned by biblicalhumanities.org, have already been contributed to the biblical studies community on open licenses by various enterprising individuals and groups. Although not a prophet, I think it is safe to predict that it is not a question of whether, but of when. My hope is that the time is much nearer at hand than when I first started on my personal journey to apply modern linguistics to the study of the Greek New Testament more than fifteen years ago.

BIBLIOGRAPHY

Aronoff, Mark, and Janie Rees-Miller, eds. *The Handbook of Linguistics*. Oxford: Blackwell, 2002.
Barr, James. *The Semantics of Biblical Language*. Oxford: Oxford University Press, 1961.
Bauer, Laurie. *The Linguistics Student's Handbook*. Edinburgh: Edinburgh University Press, 2007.
Burton, Strang, et al. *Linguistics for Dummies*. Ontario: Wiley, 2012.
Bussmann, Hadumod. *Routledge Dictionary of Language and Linguistics*. Edited and translated by Gregory P. Trauth and Kerstin Kazzazi. London: Routledge, 1996.
Cirafesi, Wally. "ἔχειν πίστιν in Hellenistic Greek and Its Contribution to the πίστις Χριστοῦ Debate." *BAGL* 1 (2012) 5–37.
Collins, Ellen, et al. "Guide to Creative Commons for Humanities and Social Science Monograph Authors." Edited by James Baker et al. http://oapen-uk.jiscebooks.org/ccguide/.
Creative Commons Corporation. "Creative Commons." https://creativecommons.org/.
Davies, Alan, and Catherine Elder, eds. *The Handbook of Applied Linguistics*. Oxford: Blackwell, 2004.
Eve, Martin Paul. *Open Access and the Humanities: Contexts, Controversies and the Future*. Cambridge: Cambridge University Press, 2014.
Frede, Michael. *Essays in Ancient Philosophy*. Minneapolis: University of Minnesota Press, 1987.
Free Software Foundation. "GNU Operating System." https://www.gnu.org/.
Gee, James Paul. *An Introduction to Discourse Analysis: Theory and Method*. 2nd ed. London: Routledge, 2005.
Granger, Sylviane, and Fanny Meunier, eds. *Phraseology: An Interdisciplinary Perspective*. Amsterdam: John Benjamins, 2008.
Harris, Tony. "Linguistics in Applied Linguistics: A Historical Overview." *Journal of English Studies* 3 (2001–2) 99–114.
Hasan, Ruqaiya. "The Grammarian's Dream: Lexis as Most Delicate Grammar." In *New Developments in Systemic Linguistics*. Volume 1. *Theory and Description*, edited by M. A. K. Halliday and Robin P. Fawcett, 184–211. London: Pinter, 1987.
Hasselgård, Hilde, et al., eds., *Corpus Perspectives on Patterns of Lexis*. Amsterdam: John Benjamins, 2013.
Herbst, Thomas, et al., eds., *The Phraseological View of Language: A Tribute to John Sinclair*. Berlin: de Gruyter, 2013.
National Science Communication Institute. "The Open Scholarship Initiative." http://osinitiative.org/.
O'Donnell, Matthew Brook, et al. "The OpenText.org Project." http://opentext.org/about/overview.html.
O'Keeffe, Anne, and Michael McCarthy, eds. *The Routledge Handbook of Corpus Linguistics*. Routledge Handbooks in Applied Linguistics. London: Routledge, 2010.
OpenContent.org. http://opencontent.org/.

Palmer, Micheal. "A Comprehensive Bibliography of Hellenistic Greek Linguistics." http://greek-language.com/Palmer-bibliography.html.

Pomerantz, Jeffrey, and Robin Peek. "Fifty Shades of Open." *First Monday* 21 (May 2016). http://journals.uic.edu/ojs/index.php/fm/article/view/6360.

Porter, Stanley E. *Linguistic Analysis of the Greek New Testament: Studies in Tools, Methods, and Practice*. Grand Rapids Baker Academic, 2015.

———. "Studying Ancient Languages from a Modern Linguistic Perspective: Essential Terms and Terminology." *FN* 2 (1989) 147–72.

———. "The Usage-Based Approach to Teaching New Testament Greek." *BAGL* 3 (2014) 120–40.

Porter, Stanley E., and Andrew W. Pitts. "πίστις with a Preposition and Genitive Modifier: Lexical, Semantic, and Syntactic Considerations in the πίστις Χριστοῦ Discussion." In *The Faith of Jesus Christ: Exegetical, Biblical, and Theological Studies*, edited by Michael F. Bird and Preston M. Sprinkle, 33–53. Milton Keynes: Paternoster, 2009.

Porter, Stanley E., and D. A. Carson, eds. *Discourse Analysis and Other Topics in Biblical Greek*. JSNTSup 113. Sheffield: Sheffield Academic, 1995.

Robie, Jonathan, et al. "biblicalhumanities.org." http://biblicalhumanities.github.io/.

Schiffrin, Deborah, et al., eds. *The Handbook of Discourse Analysis*. Oxford: Blackwell, 2001.

Simpson, James. "Introduction: Applied Linguistics in the Contemporary World." In *The Routledge Handbook of Applied Linguistics*, edited by James Simpson, 1–8. Routledge Handbooks in Applied Linguistics. London: Routledge, 2011.

Suber, Peter. *Open Access*. The MIT Press Essential Knowledge Series. Cambridge, MA: MIT Press, 2012.

Swan, Alma. "Overview of Scholarly Communication." In *Open Access: Key Strategic, Technical and Economic Aspects*, edited by Neil Jacobs, 4–11 Oxford: Chandos, 2006. http://eprints.soton.ac.uk/252427/1/asj1.pdf.

Winther-Nielsen, Nicolai, and Randall Tan. "The Global Education and Research Technology Section." https://www.sblsite.org/meetings/Congresses_ProgramUnits.aspx?MeetingId=29.

2

The Past, Present, and Future of the OpenText.org Annotated Greek Corpus

Christopher D. Land and Francis G. H. Pang

INTRODUCTION

WHEN LOOKING BACKWARDS AND forwards in time, it is difficult not to reflect upon the significance of technology and the ways that technology has been—and will no doubt continue to be—a significant factor in the history of humanity and its various endeavours. This includes academic endeavours, of course, including even the humanities. In this essay, we will trace the history of one specific research endeavour, before making a few remarks about its promising future. The effort in question is the OpenText.org project, which was initiated almost twenty years ago by Stanley Porter, Matthew Brook O'Donnell, and Jeffrey T. Reed.[1] We are excited to take up this project both because of its goals and because of its methods.

In many respects, OpenText.org was ahead of its time, both technologically and linguistically (within New Testament studies, at least), and so its development has not exactly proven to be a steady forward march. It is a visionary project, however, and its future prospects are rich and varied. By pooling together their diverse skills and resources more than fifteen years

---

1. This article originally appeared as "The Past, Present, and Future of the OpenText.org Annotated Greek Corpus," in *The Language and Literature of the New Testament: Essays in Honor of Stanley E. Porter's 60th Birthday*, edited by Lois K. Fuller Dow et al., 69–105 (BibInt 150. Leiden: Brill, 2017). It has been used with the permission of the publisher of the volume.

ago, O'Donnell, Porter, and Reed displayed the kind of collaborative and innovative spirit that has become characteristic of the digital humanities. Eschewing the isolation that so frequently characterizes scholars in the humanities, they set out to accomplish something that none of them could have accomplished independently.[2] Today, the OpenText.org project retains this same spirit, and the vision of its founding partners remains as relevant as ever.

Our goal in the present essay is not to advance a new argument but to narrate the story of OpenText.org. This is important partly for the sake of documentation, as scholarly contributions to digital humanities projects do not necessarily culminate in traditional publications. We also intend for the present essay to serve as an invitation. The OpenText.org project, as a collaborative online endeavor, is only able to advance towards its stated aims with the assistance of interested scholars. For this reason, after surveying the origins of the project and some intervening developments in digital humanities research, we will discuss the current state of OpenText.org and the potential that remains for its further development.

THE VISION OF THE OPENTEXT.ORG PROJECT

The conception of the OpenText.org project involved the fusion of three distinct yet overlapping domains of research and innovation, each of which contributed to its early development, and each of which will remain an integral part of the project moving forward.

Most obviously, the project was launched by three New Testament scholars with the goal of producing resources that would aid in the study of the Greek New Testament. From its inception, therefore, the project has been associated with the field of biblical studies, and its primary participants have all been biblical scholars. The project—under its original name, the *Hellenistic Greek Text Annotation Project*—was first housed in the Centre for Advanced Theological Research at the University of Surrey Roehampton. Early presentations regarding the project were often given

---

2. Many smiles were exchanged among friends and colleagues when, at the 2014 annual meeting of the Canadian Society of Biblical Studies, Porter—as the sole CSBS member among the three OpenText.org partners—won the Norman E. Wagner Award for the innovative use of technology relating to biblical scholarship. He was undoubtedly a worthy recipient, as the OpenText.org project would never have launched or succeeded without his inspiration, direction, and ongoing support. It was good for everyone involved, however, that his receipt of this award did not require him to give a talk regarding the technological aspects of the project.

at society meetings related to biblical studies, including both annual and international meetings of the Society of Biblical Literature and the annual meeting of the Evangelical Theological Society.[3]

In fact, an entire series of publications was conceived in association with Sheffield Academic Press, with the idea being to supply tools and resources that would be not only linguistically and technologically sophisticated but also heuristically and pedagogically useful to biblical scholars.[4] In short, although the scope of the OpenText.org project was always much broader than the New Testament, it was viewed by its founders chiefly as a means by which to better understand the texts of the New Testament.

If biblical scholarship was the seedbed for OpenText.org, linguistics was the seed. For one thing, it was the application of linguistics to the study of the New Testament that first brought together the project's initial partners. In the early 1990s, Reed studied with Porter at Biola, using both GRAMCORD and the Thesaurus Linguae Graecae (TLG). Although some published work did come out of these early interactions,[5] there also emerged an underlying frustration with the technological limitations of the available resources, as well as a desire to move beyond the very limited information contained therein. For his part, O'Donnell opted to undertake doctoral studies with Porter in Roehampton after finding a copy of his *Idioms of the Greek New Testament* in a used bookstore. During the course of his doctoral research, which involved the application of corpus linguistics

---

3. Early presentations at biblical studies conferences in 2000 and 2001 include: Porter, "OpenText.org: Program and Prospects"; Porter, "Analyzing the Computer Needs"; Porter and O'Donnell, "Expanding the Boundaries of Grammar"; Porter et al., "OpenText.org: A Collaborative Internet-based Project"; Porter, "Who Owns the Greek Text?"; Porter and O'Donnell, "OpenText.org and Recent Developments." Some have since been published (see the bibliography).

4. Specifically, the Biblical Languages: Greek (BLG) series was envisioned as a six-volume set, together with complementary digital resources. BLG 1 was to be an introductory grammar composed by Porter and Reed (now published as Porter, Reed, and O'Donnell, *Fundamentals of New Testament Greek*); BLG 2 was an intermediate grammar (Porter, *Idioms*); BLG 3 was to be an advanced reference grammar undertaken in concert with Chrys Caragounis and Brook W. R. Pearson; BLG 4 was to be a corpus-based lexicon of Hellenistic Greek, derived from a digitally annotated corpus of Hellenistic texts by Porter, O'Donnell, and Pearson; BLG 5 was to be an advanced Hellenistic Greek reader undertaken by Porter and Pearson; BLG 6 was to be an instructor's guide to teaching Greek, together with software tools designed to aid both professors and students in the classroom.

5. See, e.g., Reed, "Infinitive with Two Substantival Accusatives," 1–27.

to the New Testament,[6] O'Donnell and Porter began work on a richly annotated corpus of Hellenistic Greek. Taking as a key inspiration the corpus-linguistic work being done at Lancaster University, and drawing heavily upon Systemic Functional Linguistics in order to isolate distinct annotation layers, they drafted an initial annotation scheme and then manually annotated all of Philemon.[7] Meanwhile, Reed had completed his doctoral work at the University of Sheffield, applying discourse analysis to the study of the New Testament.[8] Upon formally joining the project, Reed proposed the "open text" moniker by which the project is still known. Together, these three presented their research at linguistic society meetings, advocating for interdisciplinary work and advancing a strong case for the relevance of corpus linguistics to New Testament studies.[9]

Fifteen years ago (as still today), only a small minority of biblical scholars possessed any real expertise in linguistics. The interdisciplinary requirements of the OpenText.org project were even more specific than this, however, because the task of developing online digital resources demands technical expertise in computer programming and web development. Given the interdisciplinary and highly specialized nature of its ambitions, how could the OpenText.org project succeed in accomplishing its plans? Here OpenText.org took as its inspiration the open-source software movement, which in the 1990s was emerging as a significant force in the world of computer programming.[10] Its founders envisioned a small but collaborative community of technologically astute biblical scholars who would develop open-source tools. These tools would then be made available to a somewhat larger community of scholars, who would together annotate an entire corpus of Hellenistic Greek texts and thus produce the open annotation data so critical to the research opportunities being pursued by the project.

---

6. See O'Donnell, *Corpus Linguistics*.

7. Some of the early annotation guidelines can still be viewed at http://www.opentext.org/model/guidelines.html. Some of the early annotations of Philemon can be seen in O'Donnell et al., "OpenText.org: The Problems and Prospects," 421–22, and in the reprint, O'Donnell et al., "OpenText.org and the Problems and Prospects," 120–21. See also O'Donnell, *Corpus Linguistics*, 168–201, 253–72.

8. See Reed, *Discourse Analysis of Philippians*.

9. Key presentations and publications in linguistic forums include: Porter et al., "OpenText.org and the Problems and Prospects"; Porter and O'Donnell, "Theoretical Issues"; Porter et al., "OpenText.org: An Experiment."

10. See O'Donnell, "Open Text?"

In essence, this constituted an early pioneering attempt at crowd-sourcing, launched in the same year as Wikipedia.

Porter, O'Donnell, and Reed's goal of bringing together biblical scholarship, linguistics, and open-source web-development was highly ambitious for its time. Even fifteen years later, it remains ambitious, despite intervening developments in the digital humanities that have made it somewhat more feasible (see below). The goal also remains essential to the future development of biblical studies, inasmuch as there is a tremendous need for empirical research into the language of the New Testament. Scholars who wish to make well-founded claims regarding the Hellenistic Greek language need to have at their disposal the sorts of resources envisioned by OpenText.org. Moreover, the ethos of the original OpenText.org project continues to offer an antidote to both the isolation that has long characterized the humanities and the commercialization that continues to characterize the development of software resources related to the Bible.[11] We conclude this section, therefore, with a brief summary of the core values that motivated the original vision of OpenText.org and that continue to guide the project today.

First, OpenText.org prioritizes the use of unrestricted Greek texts (i.e., texts that are either in the public domain or freely licensed under a suitable Creative Commons license).[12] We believe that a good case can be made against the legality (to say nothing of the logic) of applying a restrictive copyright to what is purportedly the closest that modern scholarship can get to the wording of an ancient text.[13] But if modern eclectic editions *are* in fact legally protected by copyright, then it becomes wholly impractical to employ them in web-based resources meant to be freely available. In short, either the copyright of the standard eclectic editions needs to be challenged, or projects like OpenText.org need to employ an alternative base text.[14]

---

11. For an assessment along these lines, see Porter, "Analyzing the Computer Needs."

12. For information on Creative Commons licenses, see https://creativecommons.org/about.

13. See Porter, "Who Owns the Greek?"

14. In this respect, the SBLGNT is a step in the right direction, although its somewhat restrictive license is an unnecessary encumbrance. A better choice is perhaps the 1904 edition of the Nestle Greek New Testament, which has been made freely available in digital format by Diego Santos at https://sites.google.com/site/nestle1904/home. The OpenText.org project is also exploring the possibility of moving the project to a single manuscript (see Smith and O'Donnell, "Computer-Aided Linguistic Analysis").

Second, when markup is produced by scholarly annotators, it too should be made freely available to other researchers in a useable format.[15] After all, if the goal of annotating a Greek text is to advance knowledge of the text and its language, other scholars should be encouraged not only to examine the data in question but also to employ it in their own research and to incorporate it into newly created resources. Furthermore, interested scholars should be encouraged to alter the data in question by clarifying, correcting, or expanding it, thereby furthering the academic work of its originators. To the extent that this model of academic progress involves a vast and constantly changing scholarly community, the application of restrictive licenses to digital annotations is both impractical and counterproductive. To require attribution is sensible, since it is proper for academics to recognize the hard work carried out by predecessors; to require that other scholars make explicit requests for permission is to place a roadblock in the path of progress.

Third, the source code for resources related to the project should ideally be open and freely available. Because New Testament research projects are typically overseen by New Testament scholars—most of whom lack programming skills—it is paramount that willing programmers can quickly and easily make small contributions to the project. It is also vital to ensure that programming work is not wasted. Code should be recycled whenever possible, and ideally managed using a publicly available source code repository.[16]

Fourth, the project should be guided by sound linguistic principles. This encompasses everything from the selection of texts for annotation (i.e., the formation of a representative corpus),[17] to the definition of annotation layers (e.g., lexical, morphological, syntactic, discourse, contextual, etc.),[18] to the formulation of specific descriptive categories (e.g., Subject,

15. It is regrettable that the original OpenText.org annotations were not openly released. We are hopeful that new versions of the annotations will soon be released, provided that some outstanding issues can be resolved with regard to copyright restrictions. If a new XML format is successfully developed in conversation with BiblicalHumanities.org (see below), this will help to make the data accessible to both individuals and other related projects.

16. The BiblicalHumanities.org community has recently brought together a number of relevant repositories. They can be viewed at https://github.com/biblicalhumanities.

17. See esp. O'Donnell, *Corpus Linguistics*, 102–37; also O'Donnell, "Designing and Compiling"; and Pang, *Revisiting Aspect*.

18. Concerning the importance of moving beyond word-oriented morphological annotations, see Porter, "Analyzing the Computer Needs." For a discussion of annotation

Adjunct, etc.), to the design and use of tools for data analysis (e.g., tools for statistical analysis or even machine learning). Notably, this does not preclude the fact that the annotations themselves will almost certainly expose limitations or even flaws in the linguistic model that underlies them. Similarly, it does not entail the imposition of any particular linguistic theory or model. It does not even require that all elements of the project conform to a single theory or model. It entails only that linguistic theorization should accompany linguistic annotation, and that an informed team should guide the development of the OpenText.org resources so as to make them both reliable and useful.

THE LAUNCH OF THE OPENTEXT.ORG ANNOTATED GNT

The goals of the OpenText.org project were, unsurprisingly, difficult to realize. Nevertheless, owing to a few key individuals and organizations, important milestones were reached. A small community of collaborators was formed, a website was launched, and, for a brief time, an online discussion forum was maintained. The most significant milestone, however, was the production of the first syntactically-annotated electronic Greek New Testament.

Financially speaking, the development of the OpenText.org annotated GNT drew from three main sources. A special one-time grant was awarded to the project in the spring of 2000 by the Society of Biblical Literature, for the amount of $10,000 USD. In the same year, a private donor who believed strongly in the project contributed $22,500. With these two sources of money, O'Donnell was able to develop a web-based annotation tool and to begin the task of annotating grammatical units.[19] Subsequently, a third source of money emerged in the form of Logos Bible Software. After seeing successive presentations at SBL meetings, Logos became interested in the OpenText.org annotations.[20] Conversations ensued between Reed and Bob Pritchett, and in 2005 Logos committed $60,000 to the project, receiving exclusive rights to sell the OpenText.org annotations for a period of twelve

---

layers, see O'Donnell, *Corpus Linguistics*, 138–63. Regarding the use of XML for the encoding of ancient papyri, see also Land, "Digitizing Ancient Inscriptions."

19. O'Donnell's web-based annotation tool was written in JavaScript and included a (then very cutting-edge) drag-and-drop interface.

20. In addition to the earlier presentations cited above, we note also O'Donnell et al., "Discourse Grammar of Mark 13"; O'Donnell and Tan, "OpenText.org"; Tan, "Pauline Lexicon"; O'Donnell and Smith, "Caught in a Syn-Net."

years.[21] With this source of commercial funding, the first syntactically annotated Greek New Testament was completed in 2005, with most of the actual annotation work done by Randall Tan.[22]

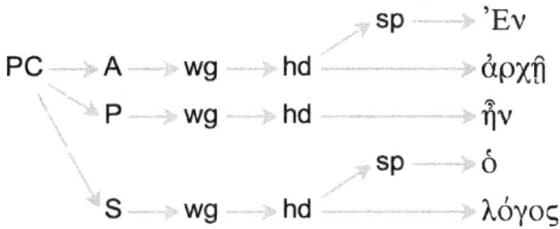

Figure 1: The Logos Bible Software Display

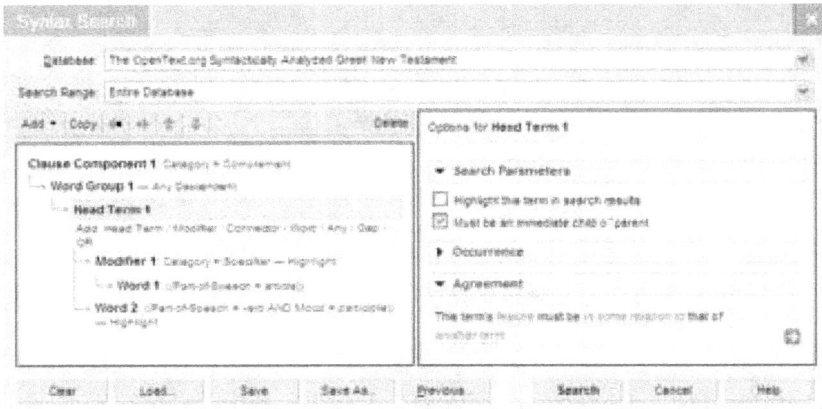

Figure 2: The Logos Bible Software Search Interface

---

21. The OpenText.org *Syntactically Annotated Greek New Testament* officially premiered in Logos Bible Software 3 0, released in 2006. Notably, the release of the annotations within Logos Bible Software was unhindered by copyright restrictions, because Logos had already licensed the use of the Nestle-Aland text.

22. O'Donnell did some of the annotation work himself. Also, Robert Picirilli took time to assist the project, working especially on Mark's Gospel. For his part, Tan began annotating Romans during the course of his doctoral work (see Tan, "Fulfilling the Law") and then completed the majority of the annotation work following the involvement of Logos. Because a manual annotation process was used, errors were inevitably made. Some of these have been found and corrected in the project XML, but the implementations of the XML—both in the Logos software and on the project website—have not been consistently updated to account for the corrections.

For their part, the Logos team reworked the initial data in order to produce a horizontal directed graph (see Figure 1: The Logos Bible Software Display).[23] In subtle ways, this display runs the risk of misrepresenting the linguistic model underlying the annotation; it does, however, consolidate multiple levels of annotation into a single graph, making it possible to see all of the annotation at once. Moreover, grammatical structures were made searchable in the Logos implementation, making it possible for the end user to find particular structures or to identify words occurring in certain structures. In our opinion, the original search interface supplied by Logos was a bit clunky and unwieldy (see Figure 2: The Logos Bible Software Search Interface), but it represented a crucial step forward in the history of biblical studies and it opened up avenues of research that would have been far less feasible without machine-readable annotations.

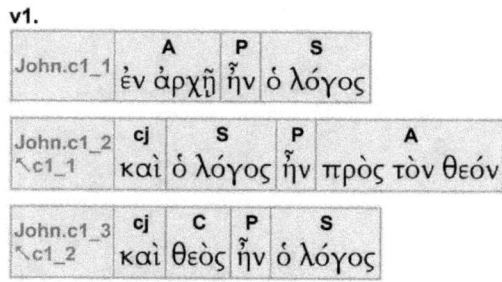

Figure 3: The OpenText.org Clause Display

Around the same time that the Logos implementation became commercially available, the OpenText.org team released freely-available HTML displays on the project website. These displays took the form of box diagrams, with separate visualizations for clauses and word groups (see Figure 3: The OpenText.org Clause Display and Figure 4: The OpenText.org Word Group Display).[24]

---

23. For a reflection on Logos Bible Software's decision to use a directed graph, see the brief account in Brannan, "Greek Linguistic Databases."

24. A third type of display, dubbed the functional clause display, was also produced. Unfortunately, this display was never made available for the entire New Testament.

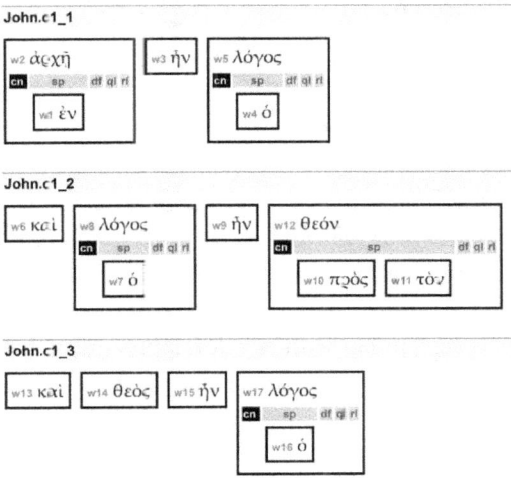

Figure 4: The OpenText.org Word Group Display

Although these displays were more legible than the Logos graphs, and although they better captured the underlying linguistic model of the annotation, the web displays provided on the OpenText.org website were static and non-searchable, which prevented scholars from making full use of the project resources. A web-based search interface was successfully developed by Catherine Smith as an MSc CompSci (Master of Science in Computer Science) dissertation project, but when issues surrounding the project's XML database made it difficult to immediately employ the interface on the OpenText.org website, work on implementing the web-based search interface languished and only a handful of individuals have benefited from Smith's efforts.[25]

Without at all downplaying the absolutely bold and progressive accomplishments attained in the initial launch of the OpenText.org project—many of which were on the cutting edge of corpus linguistics and web-development, to say nothing of biblical scholarship—we observe that the OpenText.org project, after reaching the crucial milestone of annotating the complete New Testament, failed to make rapid progress on its other stated aims. Its key players continued to work behind the scenes, with occasional presentations being made, but the initial momentum was lost.[26]

25. Smith, "Implementing a Corpus Browser."

26. For an example of work carried out in the intervening years, see Smith and O'Donnell, "Interactive Corpus Annotation."

INTERVENING DEVELOPMENTS IN THE DIGITAL HUMANITIES

Although progress slowed for the OpenText.org project following the completion of the initial New Testament annotations, the same cannot be said for progress in the digital humanities generally. To the contrary, numerous advances have been made in the area of digital humanities and web technology, and many of these relate directly to the goals of the OpenText.org project. In addition, other grammatical annotations of the GNT have been released during the last decade. Scholars who are actively involved in these areas will already be familiar with key developments, but we will nevertheless provide a brief recount for the sake of less well-acquainted readers. This should make it easier for New Testament scholars to understand the current status of the OpenText.org project and the opportunities that are available for its further development.

Most importantly, the past decade has seen an explosion of research in what was formerly known as humanities computing, so much so that the field now known as the digital humanities is becoming a significant player in academic research.[27] The digital humanities is an interdisciplinary field of study concerned with the relationships that exist between human knowledge and digital media. Notably, it does not merely study how scholars employ computational tools; it also studies how computational tools affect the scholarship of those who use them. Roberto Busa, who is sometimes called the father of humanities computing, writes that

> In this field one should not use the computer primarily for speeding up the operation, nor for minimizing the work of the researchers. It would not be reasonable to use the computer just to obtain the same results as before, having the same qualities as before, but more rapidly and with less human effort... Today's academic life seems to be more in favor of many short-term research projects which need to be published quickly, rather than of projects requiring teams of co-workers collaborating for decades... [But] it would be much better to build up results one centimetre at a time on a base one kilometre wide, than to build up a kilometre of research on a one-centimetre base.[28]

---

27. An early overview of the digital humanities is available online in Schreibman et al., *Companion to Digital Humanities*. A far more recent overview is Gardiner and Musto, *Digital Humanities*.

28. Busa, "Annals of Humanities Computing," 89.

The growth of the digital humanities is thus the growth of a community of scholars who seek to promote, and ultimately produce, research projects that are not only digital, but also visionary, long-term, collaborative, and open. Clearly, the growth of such a community represents a positive development for OpenText.org and for related projects within the field of biblical scholarship.

A simple example involves the use of XML (eXtensible Markup Language) as a serialization format. Already at its inception, the OpenText.org project was XML-based, despite the fact that XML was at that time a newly emerging standard.[29] Today, XML representation is the *de facto* standard within the digital humanities due to its human readability and the widespread availability of tools for machine processing.[30] Perhaps even more importantly, major steps have been taken within the past decade in the direction of XML-based text encoding standards, so that numerous humanities projects are not only using the same serialization format but also encoding their data using standardized markup. This standardization is meant to ensure that the data produced by contemporary digital humanities projects is not like the data of their predecessors, which very quickly became obsolete and was rarely compatible with the systems used by alternative projects. It is preeminently manifested in the guidelines of the Text Encoding Initiative (TEI), a member-funded non-profit corporation that aims "to develop, maintain, and promulgate hardware- and software-independent methods for encoding humanities data in electronic form."[31] The TEI guidelines encompass a wide range of markup, including structural and non-structural elements, unit boundaries, non-hierarchical structures, feature structure markup, and so on.[32] Not all projects follow these guidelines, but the prominence of the Text Encoding Initiative demonstrates that there is a vibrant and ongoing discussion within the digital humanities with

---

29. Initial conceptual work on OpenText.org was being carried out even as XML became a W3C Recommendation in February of 1998.

30. Crucially, an XML serialization of a data model can be employed as a pivot format, allowing annotations in one representation to be transformed into another representation. For example, an elaborate and complicated XML document can be very easily transformed into a simplified representation—or even into HTML—using either XSLT or XQuery.

31. TEI Consortium, "TEI: History." A number of large-scale collaborative projects use the TEI format, including the Oxford Text Archive and the Perseus Project. For a list of projects using TEI, see http://www.tei-c.org/Activities/Projects/.

32. The latest TEI guidelines (P5) are available at: http://www.tei-c.org/Guidelines/.

regard to XML and its effective use in annotation projects. This conversation was already underway at the time OpenText.org was founded, but it has grown and advanced considerably in the meantime.

Because the use of interoperable representation formats is just as vital in the case of linguistic annotations as in the case of text encoding, work continues on the establishment of standard formats for linguistic annotations.[33] The TEI guidelines encompass linguistic annotation, and, as Stührenberg points out, several of the more recently proposed linguistic annotation frameworks have been influenced by the TEI guidelines.[34] Yet here, more than in the area of text encoding, there are significant alternatives to TEI.[35] Notably, a subcommittee of the International Organization for Standardization (ISO) has been working to formulate *de jure* (i.e., obligatory) standards.[36] The objective of this group is to prepare standards and guidelines for effective language resource management by developing "principles and methods for creating, coding, processing and managing language resources."[37] Here again, therefore, the maturing of the digital humanities has provided the OpenText.org project with a vast and continually growing resource in the form of related projects working to address similar or identical issues.

In addition to these developments with respect to text encoding and linguistic annotation, there have been other developments related to web-development. In particular, the flowering of the collaborative software

---

33. Ide and Romary identify eleven general requirements aimed at ensuring interoperability among application-specific representations at various stages of implementation, including explicitness, uniformity and consistency, and support for partial results and ambiguities. See Ide and Romary, "International Standard"; Ide and Romary, "Towards International Standards." In addition to the Linguistic Annotation Framework (LAF) discussed by Ide and Romary, further examples include the Syntactic Annotation Framework (SynAF), the Penn Treebank, and the Morphosyntactic Annotation Framework (MAF). See Declerck, "SynAF"; Marcus et al., "Penn Treebank"; Abeillé, *Treebanks: Building*; Clément and Villemonte de la Clergerie, "MAF." We have also taken note of FoLiA (Format for Linguistic Annotation), available online at https://proycon.github.io/folia. See van Gompel and Reynaert, "FoLiA."

34. See Stührenberg, "TEI and Current Standards."

35. See, however, Bański, "Why TEI Stand-Off Annotation Doesn't Quite Work."

36. Subcommittee 4 (Language Resource Management) of the technical committee 37 (TerminologyandOtherLanguageandContentResources). See http://www.iso.org/iso/home/standards_development/list_of_iso_technical_committees/iso_technical_committee.htm?commid=297592 for more detail. For a discussion regarding the subcommittee, see Stührenberg, "TEI and Current Standards," 2–14.

37. Ide and Romary, "International Standard," 211.

development model and the open-source model have provided a more mature infrastructure for digital humanities projects, with numerous tools and platforms having been developed in the past decade. Github, for example, is a web-based software repository that offers distributed versioning control and source code management functionality, both essential to collaborative software development.[33] Open-source XML databases and application platforms such as eXist-db and BaseX have continued to mature, and they provide a stable and free platform on which scholars can develop XML resources. And of course, the emergence of so-called Web 2.0 technologies such as HTML5 and cross-platform JavaScript libraries (such as Prototype and jQuery) make it easier to handle graphical display and dynamic or interactive content, which is essential for creating the dynamic front-end interfaces and graphical displays originally envisioned by OpenText.org. Taken together, these new (or improved) technologies provide a more robust environment for collaborative digital humanities projects, and hence an improved environment within which the OpenText.org project can continue to pursue its original goals.

There is not just a changed technological environment, however. Changes have also taken place with regard to the digitization of the Greek New Testament and the creation of linguistic annotations.[39] Around the time that a commercialized version of OpenText.org was released by Logos Bible Software, the Perseus project launched their own endeavor to create treebanks for ancient Greek materials, and a number of non-biblical texts have now been analyzed.[40] A few short years later, Logos released both the Lexham Discourse Greek New Testament and the Cascadia Syntax Graphs of the New Testament, with the latter being derived from work by the Global Bible Initiative (GBI; formerly Asia Bible Society). A year later, in 2010, the PROIEL (Pragmatic Resources in Old Indo-European Languages) treebank was launched. Some of these resources are only available commercially, but the tide is slowly turning in favor of open source-code and open data, with Creative Commons licenses having been adopted by the Perseus Digital Library, the Penn Parsed Corpora of Historical Greek, the Global Bible Initiative, and the PROIEL project.[41]

38. See https://github.com.

39. For an overview, see Brannan, "Greek Linguistic Databases."

40. For a list of analyzed texts, see https://perseusdl.github.io/treebank_data/.

41. For the Penn Parsed Corpora of Historical Greek, see http://www.ling.upenn.edu/~janabeck/greek-corpora.html. Other projects have annotated parts of the Greek

For digital biblical scholarship, there is one additional development that is especially noteworthy. Together, Jonathan Robie and Randall Tan have launched BiblicalHumanities.org with the goal of bringing together like-minded computer scientists and biblical scholars.[42] With respect to each of the above areas, they are seeking to facilitate collaboration among diverse biblical studies projects, providing a hub around which communication can take place. Already, they have brought together a GitHub repository that provides easy access to various digital resources related to biblical studies (e.g., texts, syntactic treebanks, morphological analyses, lexicons, etc.), with multiple high quality treebanks of the Greek New Testament already available in XML format (including the aforementioned GBI syntax trees). In addition, talks have begun with regard to the use of a common interchange format for all of these projects, a step that would further encourage collaboration and hence overall progress. We are encouraged by all of these developments, since they serve to confirm that the OpenText.org vision is one shared by others within biblical scholarship.

THE CURRENT STATUS OF THE OPENTEXT.ORG PROJECT

Whereas the wider field of the digital humanities has been very active for the past decade and many crucial advances have taken place, progress for the OpenText.org project has been slow.[43] A handful of scholars have used the annotated GNT both in teaching and in research, with a number of publications explicitly citing the data or seeking to explore its possible expansion.[44] Moreover, interested scholars have continued to make

---

New Testament, such as the Accordance grammatical syntax database module (http://www.accor dancebible.com/store/details/?pid=gnt28-T.syntax).

42. The technical advisory board, headed by Jonathan Robie, is listed at http://biblicalhumanities.github. io/about/.

43. An important example of ongoing work is the aforementioned work on anaphora resolution. See Smith and O'Donnell, "Interactive Corpus Annotation."

44. See, for example, from those directly involved in the project: Porter and O'Donnell, "Conjunctions"; Porter and O'Donnell, "Comparative Discourse Analysis"; Porter and O'Donnell, "Building and Examining Linguistic Phenomena"; O'Donnell and Smith, "Discourse Analysis of 3 John"; Porter and Pitts, "Πίστις with a Preposition"; Pitts, "Greek Clause Structure." Many of Porter's works are related to the OpenText.org project, including Porter, "New Perspectives"; Porter, "New Testament Studies and Papyrology"; Porter, "Greek of the Gospel of Peter"; Porter, "Prolegomena"; Porter, "Buried Linguistic Treasure"; Porter, "Babatha Archive." See also, Lee, *Paul's Gospel in Romans*; Burggraff, "Corpus Linguistic Verb Analysis"; Peters, *Greek Article*; Dvorak and Walton, "Clause as Message"; Xue, *Paul's Viewpoint on God*, etc. James Libby has employed the

contributions to the OpenText.org corpus, despite the original annotation tools becoming unusable in current web browsers.[45] A number of project goals have not yet been accomplished, however, and it is fair to say that the number of active contributors to the project has not grown enough to warrant the epithet *crowd-sourced*.

Notwithstanding these realities, we are convinced that a great deal of life remains in the OpenText.org project and that it may yet succeed in accomplishing its initial aims. A new affiliation has been established between OpenText.org and the Centre for Biblical Linguistics, Translation, and Exegesis (CBLTE) at McMaster Divinity College in Hamilton, Ontario, and within the context of the Centre, we have been working together in order to assess the current status of OpenText.org and to chart a course for further progress. In the process, we have renewed some of the technological infrastructure of the project and created some working prototypes that will eventually form the basis for an upcoming relaunch of the OpenText.org website.

In what follows, we will describe the current status of the OpenText.org project by tracing some of the key steps that we ourselves have taken in recent years.[46] Because most of our efforts have taken place "under the hood," so to speak, they will perhaps be of little direct interest to the majority of biblical scholars. Our discussion, therefore, will aim to highlight how the culmination of these efforts will make the OpenText.org website more useful. We will include just enough detail to satisfy the interest of technologically-oriented biblical scholars who might consider participating in a project of this sort.

OpenText.org annotations in various computational projects: Libby, "Demonstrating an Advanced Computational Linguistics Software Tool"; Libby, "Disentangling Authorship and Genre"; Libby, "Pauline Canon."

45. Andrew W. Pitts and Sean A. Adams implemented an algorithm for detecting paragraph divisions in narrative Greek discourse using the OpenText.org database, presenting their findings at the Society for Textual Scholarship 14th Biennial International Interdisciplinary Conference, New York, NY, March 14–17, 2007. We are also grateful for the work of Mark Proctor and his students at Lee University, who on their own initiative produced an annotation of the Gospel of Peter during the summer of 2012. A handful of additional annotation efforts were also made by a variety of others, and we are cautiously hopeful that the results of these efforts will eventually be publicly released.

46. For recent work by others involved in the project, see Smith and O'Donnell, "Computer-Aided Linguistic Analysis."

New XML Working Format

As already mentioned above, the initial annotation produced by OpenText.org was encoded in XML. One of the many advantages of using the XML encoding format is that an XML representation can be easily transformed into another XML representation. Moreover, the XML language is very tightly integrated with the HTML used to create web pages, so that XML can be very easily transformed into a web page using a style sheet language called eXtensible Stylesheet Language (XSL). The core of the original OpenText.org website, therefore, consisted of HTML displays generated by means of XSL from underlying XML data.

Although different XML formats were employed in the OpenText.org project at different times for different purposes, the XML that was used for the original web displays was organized in such a way that each annotation layer for each chapter in the New Testament was stored in a separate XML document. This permitted the data to be updated easily, because the files were of a small size and were easy to manage without a version control system. Within each annotation layer, information was encoded in keeping with an explicit annotation specification. Moreover, different XML elements were used for each annotation layer in order to isolate the relevant units and components defined by each layer.[47]

Inasmuch as the OpenText.org project was, from the outset, oriented towards the study of texts rather than merely grammatical units, the annotation specifications also made room for additional information as well. This information was typically assigned to one or another of the grammatical annotation layers and then incorporated by way of attributes and/or empty elements. For instance, information regarding Louw and Nida's semantic domains was included for each word in the corpus.[48] Preliminary work was also carried out with respect to such things as the semantic roles performed by clausal participants (e.g., agent, patient, etc.), the various ways in which adjuncts could supply circumstantial information (e.g., *where*, *when*, *what*, and *how*), the ways in which different clauses related to one another,[49] and

---

47. Initially, the higher levels of annotation (i.e., paragraph, clause, and word group) were each assigned to a distinct XML namespace, although this approach was later abandoned.

48. For a discussion of semantic domains and the (now dated) theoretical framework behind Louw and Nida's lexicon, see Louw, *Semantics of New Testament Greek*; Nida and Louw, *Lexical Semantics*.

49. In this respect, the initial OpenText.org annotations distinguished between primary, secondary, and embedded clauses according to their function within a discourse.

the different ways that entities are introduced and/or tracked within Greek discourses (i.e., grammaticalized, reduced, implied).[50] Only some of this information was actually annotated for the entire GNT, but it is important to understand that the original plan was to incorporate a range of additional linguistic features into the core grammatical, morphological, and lexical annotation.

At the outset of our recent efforts to prepare for a relaunched OpenText.org website (see below), we assessed the XML format used to generate the original web displays and found that it was not well-suited for the work we intended to do. It did not straightforwardly permit the range of interfaces we saw ourselves designing, and some of its strengths made it less accessible to biblical scholars lacking computer programming experience.[51] We therefore devised a new XML format, and this new format is the working format that is employed in our current web prototypes.[52]

In developing our XML format, we chose to rigidly maintain the canonical word order of the base texts being annotated. This complicates the annotation in cases where grammatical units or components are discontinuous, because the words of a discontinuous unit or component cannot be brought together into a single XML element. With canonical word order preserved, however, the complexity in the XML annotation mirrors the complexity in the underlying text, making it very intuitive both to read and to query. In technical terms, we have moved away from a standoff format and towards an inline format, and as part of this move, we have moved away from the use of separate XML documents for each annotation layer in favor of a single XML document comprising all of the annotations. In upcoming presentations and publications, we will present this new working format and explain its design. Here, it must suffice to say that we have taken

---

For each primary and secondary clause, the annotation also identified a nearby clause to which the clause in question was related.

50. See O'Donnell, *Corpus Linguistics*, 156–58.

51. Given that so few skilled computer programmers bought into the initial OpenText.org launch, one of our current goals is to develop efficient resources that can be customized and extended by any motivated biblical scholar with a technological bent, even if the scholar in question does not have any formal training in computer science.

52. When we discuss the work that we have been doing for the OpenText.org project in connection with a new annotation format and some new web displays, it should be understood that this represents only an initial proof of concept. Our efforts have culminated in a working prototype, but the final implementation (if there is such a thing in the digital humanities) will no doubt vary from our prototype due to the input of others.

steps to make the OpenText.org code easier to work with and hence more accessible to biblical scholars interested in using and improving the XML.

The (Re-)Launch of the OpenText.org Website

As mentioned above, we are presently formulating plans for a re-launch of the OpenText.org website, including some new web-based resources that expand on the functionality of the earlier website. Given the nature of the work, these new resources will be released gradually over a period of time. It should not be very much longer before a new OpenText.org website will be in place. This will provide the project with a new public face, in order to reflect the fact that the project remains an active one. It will serve as a central hub and will bring together interested parties, including not only scholars, students, and programmers but also anyone else who is interested in the Greek New Testament. In the immediate future, it will allow us to consolidate our existing resources and to unveil prototypes of the new resources that we are developing; eventually, it will host a suite of web-based tools that will enable the production, correction, visualization, and analysis of diverse linguistic annotations. The amount of time that intervenes between the launch of the new website and the launch of the new resources will be determined by the extent to which the requisite people and resources are made available to the project.

At the time of writing, we have designed a working prototype to facilitate multiple display options, and these new displays will—for now, at least—serve as the backbone of the new OpenText.org website. Whereas the earlier website presented either a static clause display or a static word-group display, the user of the new interface is presented with a single viewing area within which the properties of the display can be toggled (see Figure 5: The New Display Prototype). For instance, if the clause display setting is activated, the display presents clause tables with internal cells for each structural component; if it is not selected, the text still displays but as plain flowing text. Along the same lines, the user can choose whether or not to display word group structures, with each unit type being controlled independently of the others in real-time. With respect to grammatical structures, our new prototype allows users to show and hide specific structural components within each of the different grammatical units, with the display indicating hidden components by means of solid bands of varying thicknesses.[53] Users can choose to display full or abbreviated labels—or no

---

53. To cite a simple example, a user might choose to hide all of the Adjuncts in a

labels at all, which is useful for pedagogical purposes—and they can decide whether the labels should distinguish between component subtypes if the annotation offers them (e.g., direct vs. indirect object). We have made it possible for users to choose whether or not they wish to display structures for embedded grammatical units, as it is sometimes only necessary to view the structure of a single top-level unit. Finally, we have included chapter and verse references even when they occur within a grammatical unit, as this facilitates working with extended passages (as opposed to just query hits).

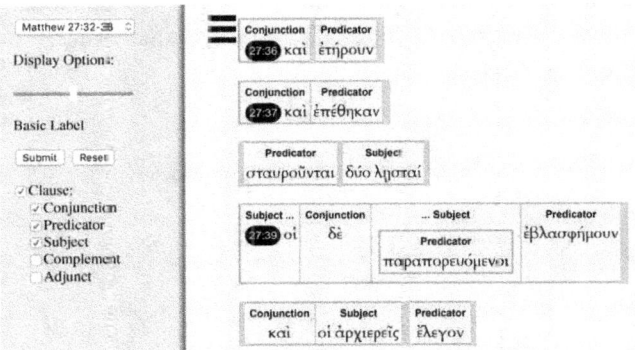

Figure 5: The New Display Prototype

Implicit in the above discussion is the fact that our new prototype allows its users to view all of the annotation layers in a single display. In developing this functionality, we have identified some weaknesses in the earlier annotation scheme, and we have taken the opportunity to develop newer strategies that we find preferable. When the Greek article specifies a participial clause, for example, the resulting unit contains a clause but is itself a word group. The original OpenText.org annotation, however, analyzes the article as part of the participial clause, placing it within the Predicator component (see Figure 6: Three Renderings of Gal 2:9).[54] This is

---

passage in order to focus specifically on core transitivity structures. Our prototype implements this by having checkboxes for each of the structural components. When a checkbox is unchecked, the relevant components are eliminated from the display along with all of their contents. In their place, however, orange bands are displayed, alerting the user in a non-intrusive manner to the fact that some of the text has been hidden. These bands vary in thickness depending on the number of structural components that have been hidden at a particular point in the overarching structure.

54. In context, this wording is a part of the grammatical subject of an overarching clause, being the last of a series of four word groups (Ἰάκωβος | καὶ Κηφᾶς | καὶ Ἰωάννης

undesirable from a theoretical and pedagogical point of view, since it obscures the fact that the article specifies the entire clause without itself being a component within it. It also obscures the very close relationship between the participle δοκοῦντες and the infinitival clause στῦλοι εἶναι, since the wording οἱ δοκοῦντες has the appearance (at a quick glance) of being a complete word group. Keeping issues like this in mind, we designed our prototype display so that the article is consistently kept out of the Predicator component. When both layers of structure are shown, the article is placed in a distinct word group component; when the word group structure is hidden, the article is still kept outside of the participial clause so that the user can more clearly see the internal structure of that clause.

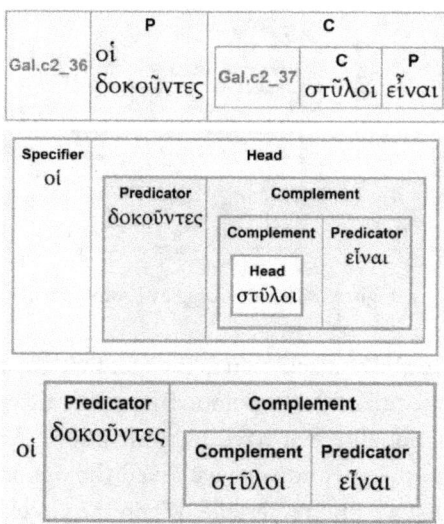

Figure 6: Three Renderings of Gal 2:9

Another challenge that we have addressed in our new prototype involves the annotation of discontinuous units. Our prototype uses the same table structure for displaying grammatical units that was employed in the original clause displays. Now, however, the words of the text proceed consistently from left to right and top to bottom in their canonical order, and the

---

| οἱ δοκοῦντες στῦλοι εἶναι). Whereas the original OpenText.org does not clarify that the word group οἱ δοκοῦντες στῦλοι εἶναι is related to all three of the preceding groups, this sort of information is integrated into the new XML format, with sympathetic highlighting allowing the display to reveal that the final group elaborates on the previous three groups.

structural components of a unit are consistently displayed with their cells and labels vertically aligned in a single row. These changes should help to avoid some recurring misunderstandings that we have repeatedly needed to clear up when using the OpenText.org displays in Greek classrooms.

A simple example can be seen in Matt 14:16, where the conjunction δέ is not a part of the Subject comprising the words ὁ Ἰησοῦς (see Figure 7: Displaying Discontinuity in Matt 14:16). The old web displays present the conjunction within the discontinuous Subject component, preserving the word order by using a top-to-bottom flow within the Subject. In the case of postpositives, this is fairly transparent, but in more complex cases, the presentation confuses the end user, causing many of our students to think that the vertically embedded wording is a sub-component of the Subject rather than an intervening component belonging to the overarching clause. Our prototype avoids this confusion by keeping all of the components of the overarching clause aligned. It inserts ellipses before and after the component label of any discontinuous component, and it uses a dotted line for the left or right border of any discontinuous grammatical unit.

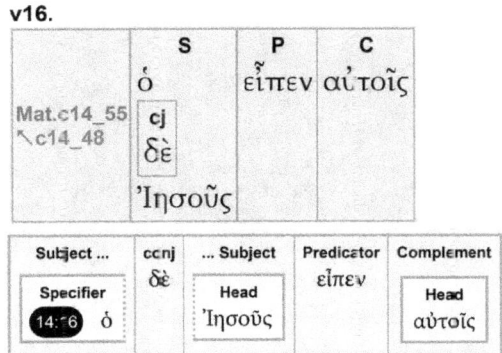

Figure 7: Displaying Discontinuity in Matt 14:16

When we turn to even more complicated instances of discontinuity, the advantage of a single display with all annotation layers becomes even more readily apparent. Consider the opening clause in Heb 10, with its fairly complex initial Adjunct (see Figure 8: Two Displays of Heb 10:1). In the original OpenText.org web display, it is only the absence of an identifier that enables the user to discern that the Predicator ἔχων is an intervening component in the overarching clause Heb.c10_2 whereas the Predicator μελλόντων is part of the embedded clause Heb.c10_3. The display also departs from the canonical word order owing to the complexity of the various discontinuities, obscuring the canonical location of both γάρ and ὁ νόμος. Our new prototype display is still complex and difficult to read at first glance, but it is consistent in preserving the canonical word order, consistent in horizontally aligning the various components of a unit, and consistent in using nested boxes only for embedded structures. Accordingly, it is possible to see that γάρ and ὁ νόμος are both components of the top-level clause, and also to see that these two wordings separately interrupt the linear expression of the participial clause constructed around ἔχων, producing a circumstantial clause with three discontinuous segments.

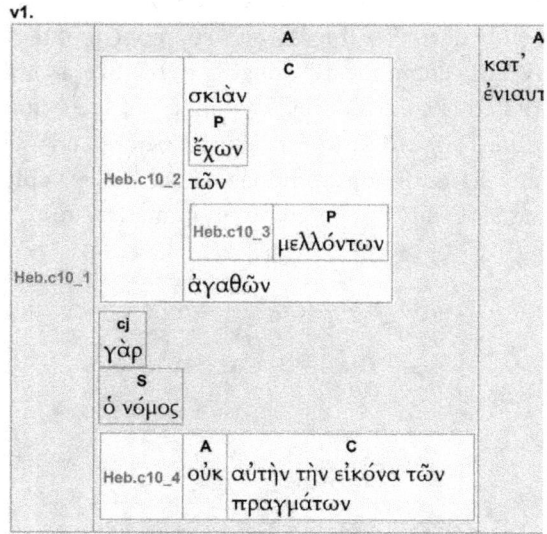

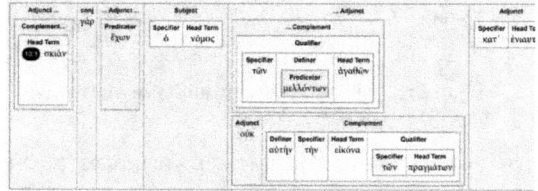

Figure 8: Two Displays of Heb 10:1

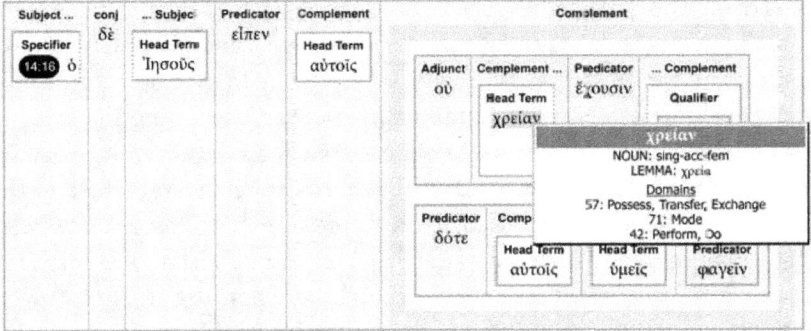

Figure 9: Matthew 14:16 with Lexical Pop-Up

To conclude this section, we present our new display of Matt 14:16 (see Figure 9: Matthew 14:16 with Lexical Pop-Up). This screenshot captures many of the developments on which we have been working, as well as the potential that exists for real-time features such as pop-up windows and sympathetic highlighting.[55] This final figure also provides a glimpse of an embedded text, in that it displays some of the words of Jesus. We encode embedded texts in the same manner as the New Testament texts themselves, except that we annotate each text as a first-, second-, or third-order text (i.e., a text, or a text-within-a-text, or a text-within-a-text-within-a-text, etc.). Then, for all of the texts in our corpus, we supply information regarding their context of situation (e.g., who is speaking, to whom, in speech or writing, etc.). This will facilitate, for example, analyses of spoken conversations within narrative texts, or analyses that wish to extract or exclude quotations from Paul's letters.

Authoring of Companion Handbook

In tandem with the original launch of the OpenText.org website, a number of guides were written by individuals associated with the project and then

---

55. Whenever a user hovers over a word, for instance, the prototype supplies a pop-up display with lexical information about that word, with the information being customizable in various ways. This has been available on the original OpenText.org website, but only for certain parts of the New Testament. In releasing the new prototype, we will extend this very useful functionality to the entire corpus. Eventually, we hope to expand the prototype so that non-hierarchical relations can be displayed via highlighting (e.g., when a user hovers over an appositional component, we might highlight the earlier wording with which it is in apposition).

posted to the website.⁵⁶ These brief introductions sought to explain the goals of the project, the data available in the annotations, and the visual displays made available on the website. They also sought to give some guidance for people interested in either annotating new texts or using the existing displays in classroom contexts. Despite these efforts, however, it remained difficult for people to understand what exactly was being represented by the annotations. Reflecting on various confusions, we see at least two obstacles that will need to be addressed as the OpenText.org project moves forward. In the first place, many users approached the OpenText.org annotations with little to no familiarity with linguistics. Admittedly, we are basing this claim on anecdotal evidence, but we have heard such a wealth of testimony to this effect that it seems safe to make a cautious generalization. For these users, the brevity of the online web articles was an impediment to clear understanding. Simply put, they needed more documentation than the OpenText.org project was able to provide on its website. They needed a basic introduction to linguistics and grammar, an introduction to the issues involved in explicitly modeling grammatical structures, and some additional help understanding the various labels and conventions used on the OpenText.org website. While we do not suppose that all of this information needs to be directly composed by the OpenText.org project, we take seriously the fact that students and scholars need some additional help in becoming familiar with our annotations, and we plan to substantially increase the amount of introductory documentation that accompanies the project.

Whereas for some, the general idea of grammatical modeling was itself an obstacle, for others the devil was in the details. These users of OpenText.org already knew about linguistics and grammar, but they nevertheless failed to fully appreciate why certain decisions were made in the process of designing the annotations and the accompanying displays. Much of their confusion, we suggest, can be chalked up to the (understandable but nonetheless misguided) expectation that XML encodings and HTML displays should transparently mirror one (and only one) theoretical model of language. According to this assumption, if Subject, Predicator and Adjunct elements are encoded as the children of a clause element, or else displayed as the three cells of a clausal box diagram, then the Subject,

---

56. For instance, the articles included O'Donnell, "OpenText.org Syntactically Analyzed Greek New Testament"; Tan, "Introduction to the OpenText.org Annotation Model"; Tan, "OpenText.org Clause Annotation Process"; Tan, "OpenText.org Word Group Annotation Process"; Pitts, "Semantic Domain Theory"; and Adams and Burggraff, "Using Linguistic Features."

Predicator, and Adjunct are being explicitly modeled as daughter constituents and hence as grammatical siblings in a hierarchical tree. Notably, it follows from this premise that the annotation underlying the Logos graphs is a complete theoretical muddle, given that these graphs include such bizarre representations as Figure 10. In this display, nodes and branches are displayed identically, and there would appear to be a strange fusion of constituency and dependency (e.g., with each word group having as its sole *constituent* the head of an apparent *dependency* structure).[57]

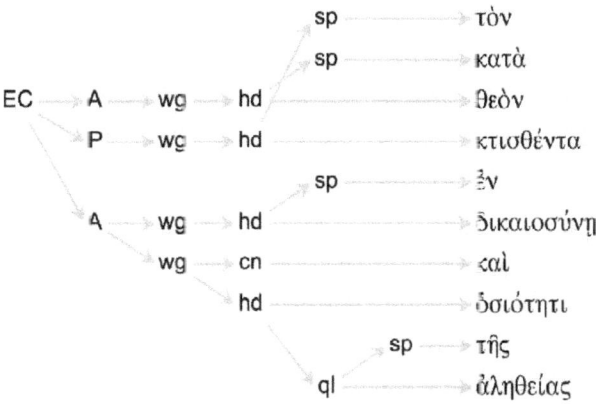

Figure 10

The short explanation of this confusion is that there need not be a simplistic one-to-one correspondence between: (a) the encoding scheme used to represent grammatical phenomena in XML; (b) the visual representations used to display grammatical units in HTML; and (c) the theoretical model of grammar being employed by an annotator or end user. To the contrary, XML by its very nature imposes a hierarchical tree structure, yet this tree can be used to represent diverse data models in various different ways. Similarly, the horizontal box diagram displays employed on the OpenText.org website are an extremely useful convention because of their flexibility and legibility, yet they do not necessarily entail a (fairly flat) constituent structure. They indicate that certain linguistic tokens are interrelated in a recurring way, but there is nothing to prevent a user from interpreting an S–P–A box diagram to entail: (1) that the wording in the

---

57. Evidence of the confusion that this display prompted can be seen in the effort exerted by Michael Aubrey in his attempts to make theoretical sense of the Logos graphs (see Aubrey, "New Testament Greek Syntax Databases").

Subject box is an argument of the verb in the Predicator box, and (2) that the wording in the Adjunct is an adjunct of the same verb. Granted, these relations will, for some theories, involve only the grammatical heads of the wordings in the respective various boxes, but here again, if lower level annotations consistently allow the end user to identify whatever part of the component's wording is regarded as its grammatical head, then the annotation has succeeded in encoding and representing the information that is needed by the user who wishes to study the relevant grammatical relations using a dependency model.

As mentioned above, the new OpenText.org resources that we are developing will differ from the earlier resources in various ways, with some of these changes involving the XML format and the HTML displays and other changes involving the annotation model itself (e.g., the extraction of Greek articles from the Predicator component of substantive participles). In tandem with these changes, we are preparing an extensive annotation handbook that will document our descriptive categories. This handbook will provide a detailed introduction to OpenText.org for users who are unfamiliar with linguistics and uncertain how to understand the web displays. Similarly, it will draw connections between our annotations and a number of different linguistic models currently in use, so that linguistically-informed users can better understand how annotation decisions were made and how the relatively flat descriptions provided by the annotations can be leveraged by analysts of diverse theoretical persuasions. One of us (Chris) has already written a draft of the handbook, and we are exploring how best to proceed with its release.

Collaboration with BiblicalHumanities.org

As mentioned above, several open-source and open-data projects are now annotating Hellenistic Greek texts, and BiblicalHumanities.org is working to bring these projects together. By the time this essay is in print, initial progress will have been made in the direction of common data formats for linguistic annotations, with the idea being to make it possible for the OpenText.org annotations to incorporate data from other projects (and vice versa) and for various projects to use some of the same tools and graphic user interfaces. The different voices participating in these talks represent distinctive perspectives on Hellenistic Greek, but the idea is not to efface these distinctives. Rather, the goal is to encourage the shared development of core resources, even if those resources are customized in certain ways when implemented by a particular project. We are excited to be participating in these discussions, and we anticipate that they will enable OpenText.org to release its annotations in a shared XML format in the not-too-distant future.

In addition to these preliminary conversations regarding grammatical annotation formats, we see three areas where the work of BiblicalHumanities.org will have a significant impact on OpenText.org and its annotation efforts. First, in the area of textual criticism and the establishment of the text(s) of the Greek New Testament (and eventually other texts as well), BiblicalHumanities.org is pursuing a shared infrastructure that will enable digital projects to base their annotations on standard texts and to use standard references for defined segments within those texts. Second, in the area of morphology, we are interested in the continued development of the MorphGNT, another project affiliated with BiblicalHumanities.org. We are interested not only because of the information MorphGNT has produced with respect to the New Testament, but because of its potential to supply morphological analyses for other texts within our planned corpus.[58] Third, in the related area of lexicography, we are interested in how BiblicalHumanities.org will standardize the identification of lexical items, as we anticipate the development of lexical resources and wish to ensure that any efforts in this respect will interface as fully as possible with work being done by others.

Perhaps most of all, this last development gives us hope for the future of OpenText.org, as it indicates a growing interest in the development of open-source biblical resources and hence a growing community within which OpenText.org can continue to mature and expand. We unashamedly invite interested readers to visit BiblicalHumanities.org and OpenText.org and to consider the possibility of becoming involved.

FUTURE PROSPECTS

Biblical scholars who find it useful to employ grammatical displays in research or teaching will perhaps be interested in a new OpenText.org website with new interactive web displays. And those who are actively interested in the digital humanities will be pleased to hear that OpenText.org aims to release its data and its source code and to do so in ways that will make the data and the code easy to access and use. For everyone else, we will

---

58. The home of the MorphGNT project, which is carried out by James Tauber and Ulrik Sandborg-Petersen, can be found at http://morphgnt.org.

conclude by mentioning two additional resources that we are now beginning to design. These resources seek to address some very pressing needs—namely, the need for a user-friendly annotation and editing interface, and the need for a user-friendly search and analysis interface.[59] Certainly, we would welcome input and assistance from interested biblical scholars.

Designs for a New Editor

As mentioned above, the initial annotation tool designed by O'Donnell was, for its time, a cutting-edge example of web-development, employing an early drag-and-drop interface long before HTML5. Today, there remains a need for a similarly user-friendly annotation tool that can facilitate the production of manual annotations by scholars who lack technical expertise, including not only grammatical annotations but also pragmatic or discourse-related annotations. Such a tool, we suggest, should seek not only to facilitate the initial process of annotation, but also the subsequent processes of correction and revision, inasmuch as these have similar requirements.[60] At one time, OpenText.org began to develop such an editor, but it never reached maturity and was never released for public use.

The dynamic visual displays that we have been developing provide an important resource for the development of an annotation editor, and we have intentionally designed both our XML and our HTML displays so that a web-based editor can effectively leverage the XQuery Update Facility, which is now a W3C Recommendation. Moreover, by employing a fairly flat inline markup influenced by TEI, we have succeeded in producing a very straightforward correspondence between our logical data model and our visual displays. At present, we are focusing our attention on designing intuitive visual interfaces both for the editing of unit and component boundaries and for the editing of component labels.

Designs for a New Interface

As already explained, when Logos released the OpenText.org Syntactically Analyzed Greek New Testament, they included a search interface that allowed Logos users to search the annotations using grammatical search

---

59. See Brannan, "Greek Linguistic Databases," 4.

60. For an interesting and somewhat related development along these lines, see the Son of Suda On Line, which "enables multi-author, version controlled, peer reviewed scholarly curation of papyrological texts, translations, commentary, scholarly metadata, institutional catalog records, bibliography, and images" (www.papyri.info).

criteria. The web-based search interface developed by Smith, however, was never widely announced or made easily accessible on the OpenText.org website, with the result that scholars interested in the OpenText.org annotations were forced to purchase the Logos implementation or else manage without any search functionality.

Along with the design of a new annotation editor, work is once again underway on the development of a web-based search interface. In keeping with our underlying linguistic model, we envisage an interface that uses both structural components and systemic features as search criteria, with the two being integrated for complex searches.[61] One of our current interface designs, for instance, involves the creation of a search query through the drawing of a box diagram, with systemic features being added in pop-up boxes. This simplifies the process of designing a query, because the user defines the query using graphic conventions with which he or she is already familiar. Along with simple search results, we would also like to provide end users with some analyses of their search results. For instance, hits might be ordered in flexible ways (e.g., not only by canonical order, but by sub-corpus, or by a chosen grammatical system, etc.), or statistics might be shown for particular systemic features associated with the search results (e.g., the proportion of the retrieved clauses that are transitive vs. intransitive).

CONCLUSION

One of our goals in this essay has been to document various ways in which the OpenText.org project has had a significant past. Another has been to present some of the work that we are currently undertaking and to extend an invitation to anyone who is interested in collaborating on this sort of work. Our final goal has been to communicate the fact that the OpenText.org project continues to have a bright future.

BIBLIOGRAPHY

Abeillé, Anne, ed. *Treebanks: Building and Using Parsed Corpora*. Dordrecht, Netherlands: Kluwer Academic, 2003.

---

61. The present essay is chiefly concerned with the annotation of grammatical structures. The annotation of grammatical features, while important to our overall aims, is thus peripheral to our concerns here and not something we can discuss extensively.

Adams, Sean, and Philip Burggraff. "Using Linguistic Features to Analyze Romans 5: An Application of the OpenText.org Discourse Model." http://opentext.org/resources/articles.html.

Aubrey, Michael. "New Testament Greek Syntax Databases: Retrospect and Prospect." Paper presented at BibleTech 2010, San Jose, CA, March 26–27, 2010. https://www.academia.edu/12073252/New_Testament_Greek_Syntax_Databases_Retrospect_and_Prospect.

Bański, Piotr. "Why TEI Stand-Off Annotation Doesn't Quite Work: And Why You Might Want to Use It Nevertheless." Paper presented at Balisage: The Markup Conference 2010, Montréal, Canada, August 3–6, 2010. *Proceedings of Balisage: The Markup Conference 2010* (Balisage Series on Markup Technologies 5): http://www.balisage.net/Proceedings/vol5/html/Banski01/Balisage Vol5-Banski01.html.

Brannan, Rick. "Greek Linguistic Databases: Overview, Recent Work, and Future Prospects." Paper presented at the Lorentz Center Workshop in Biblical Scholarship and Humanities Computing: Data Types, Text, Language and Interpretation, Leiden, Netherlands, February 8, 2012. https://www.academia.edu/1481766/Greek_Linguistic_Databases_Overview_Recent_Work_and_Future_Prospects.

Burggraff, Philip D. "A Corpus Linguistic Verb Analysis of the Pauline Letters: The Contribution of Verb Patterns to Pauline Letter Structure." PhD diss., McMaster Divinity College, 2011.

Busa, Roberto. "The Annals of Humanities Computing: The Index Thomisticus." *Computers and the Humanities* 14 (1980) 83–90.

Clément, Lionel, and Éric Villemonte de la Clergerie. "MAF: A Morphosyntactic Annotation Framework." In *Proceedings of the 2nd Language and Technology Conference (LT '05)*, 90–94. Poznan, Poland, 2005.

Declerck, T. "SynAF: Towards a Standard for Syntactic Annotation." In *Proceedings of the 5th Conference on International Language Resources and Evaluation Conference*, edited by N. Calzolari et al., 229–32. Genova: European Language Resources Association, 2006.

Dvorak, James D., and Ryder Dale Walton. "Clause as Message: Theme, Topic, and Information Flow in Mark 2:1–12 and Jude." *BAGL* 3 (2014) 31–85.

Gardiner, Eileen, and Ronald G. Musto. *The Digital Humanities: A Primer for Students and Scholars*. Cambridge: Cambridge University Press, 2015.

Ide, Nancy, and Laurent Romary. "International Standard for a Linguistic Annotation Framework." *Journal of Natural Language Engineering* 10 (2004) 213–15.

———. "Towards International Standards for Language Resources." In *Evaluation of Text and Speech Systems*, edited by Laila Dybkjær et al., 263–84. Text, Speech and Language Technology 37. Dordrecht, Netherlands: Springer, 2007.

Land, Christopher D. "Digitizing Ancient Inscriptions and Manuscripts: Some Thoughts about the Production of Digital Editions." *JGRChJ* 9 (2013) 9–41.

Lee, Jae Hyun. *Paul's Gospel in Romans: A Discourse Analysis of Rom 1:16—8:39*. LBS 3. Leiden: Brill, 2010.

Libby, James A. "Demonstrating an Advanced Computational Linguistics Software Tool Applied to the Text of the Greek New Testament." Paper presented at the Annual Meeting of the Society of Biblical Literature, Boston, MA, November 22, 2008.

———. "Disentangling Authorship and Genre in the Greek New Testament: History, Method and Praxis." PhD diss., McMaster Divinity College, 2014.

———. "The Pauline Canon Sung in a Linguistic Key: Visualizing NT Text Proximity by Linguistic Structure, System, and Strata." *BAGL* 5 (2016) 122–201.

Louw, J. P. *Semantics of New Testament Greek*. Semeia Studies. Philadelphia: Fortress, 1982.

Marcus, Mitch, et al. "The Penn Treebank: Annotating Predicate Argument Structure." In *Proceedings of the Workshop on Human Language Technology*, edited by Clifford Weinstein, 114–19. Stroudsburg, PA: Association for Computational Linguistics, 1994.

Nida, Eugene A., and J. P. Louw *Lexical Semantics of the Greek New Testament*. SBLRBS 25. Atlanta: Scholars, 1992.

O'Donnell, Matthew Brook. *Corpus Linguistics and the New Testament*. NTM 6. Sheffield: Sheffield Phoenix, 2005.

———. "Designing and Compiling a Register-Balanced Corpus of Hellenistic Greek for the Purpose of Linguistic Description and Investigation." In *Diglossia and Other Topics in New Testament Linguistics*, edited by Stanley E. Porter, 255–97. JSNTSup 193. SNTG 6. Sheffield: Sheffield Academic, 2000.

———. "Introducing the OpenText.org Syntactically Analyzed Greek New Testament." http://opentext.org/resources/articles.html.

———. "Open Text? What Can Corpus-Based Projects Learn from the Open-Source Software Movement?" In *Digital Evidence: Selected Papers from DRH2000, Digital Resources for the Humanities Conference, University of Sheffield, September 2000*, edited by Marilyn Deegan et al., 207–28. London Office for Humanities Communication, Kings College, 2001.

O'Donnell, Matthew Brook, et al. "OpenText.org and the Problems and Prospects of Working with Ancient Discourse." In *A Rainbow of Corpora: Corpus Linguistics and the Languages of the World*, edited by Andrew Wilson et al., 109–21. Munich: Lincom, 2003.

———. "OpenText.org: The Problems and Prospects of Working with Ancient Discourse." In *Proceedings of the Corpus Linguistics 2001 Conference*, edited by Paul Rayson et al., 413–22. Lancaster: Lancaster University, 2001.

———. "A 'Discourse Grammar' of Mark 13." Paper presented at the Annual Meeting of the Society of Biblical Literature, San Antonio, TX, November 20, 2004.

O'Donnell, Matthew Brook, and Catherine J. Smith. "'Caught in a Syn-Net': Using the Louw-Nida Lexicon in the Computational Analysis of Hellenistic Greek." Paper presented at the Annual Meeting of the Society of Biblical Literature, Philadelphia, PA, November 21, 2005.

———. "A Discourse Analysis of 3 John." In *The Linguist as Pedagogue: Trends in the Teaching and Linguistic Analysis of the Greek New Testament*, edited by Stanley E. Porter and Matthew Brook O'Donnell, 127–45. NTM 11. Sheffield: Sheffield Phoenix, 2009.

O'Donnell, Matthew Brook, and Randall K. Tan. "OpenText.org: Introducing a New Syntactically-Tagged Greek New Testament." Paper presented at the International Meeting of the Society of Biblical Literature, Singapore, June 29, 2005.

Pang, Francis G. H. *Revisiting Aspect and* Aktionsart: *A Corpus Approach to Koine Greek Event Typology*. LBS 14. Leiden: Brill, 2016.

Peters, Ronald D. *The Greek Article: A Functional Grammar of ὁ-items in the Greek New Testament with Special Emphasis on the Greek Article*. LBS 9. Leiden: Brill, 2014.

Pitts, Andrew W. "Greek Clause Structure and Word Order: A Synchronic Study of the New Testament Corpus." In *The Language of the New Testament: Context, History and Development*, edited by Stanley E. Porter and Andrew W. Pitts, 311–46. LBS 6. Leiden: Brill, 2013.

———. "Semantic Domain Theory: An Introduction to the Use of the Louw-Nida Lexicon in the OpenText.org Project." http://opentext.org/resources/articles.html.

Porter, Stanley E. "Analyzing the Computer Needs of New Testament Exegetes." Paper presented at the Annual Meeting of the Society of Biblical Literature, Nashville, TN, November 18–21, 2000. Published in Stanley E. Porter, *Linguistic Analysis of the Greek New Testament: Studies in Tools, Methods, and Practice*, 29–46. Grand Rapids: Baker, 2015.

———. "The Babatha Archive, the Egyptian Papyri and Their Implications for Study of the Greek New Testament." In *Early Christian Manuscripts: Examples of Applied Method and Approach*, edited by Thomas J. Kraus and Tobias Nicklas, 213–37. TENTS 5. Leiden: Brill, 2010.

———. "Buried Linguistic Treasure in the Babatha Archive." In *Proceedings of the Twenty-Fifth International Congress of Papyrology, Ann Arbor July 29–August 4, 2007*, edited by Traianos Gagos, 623–32. American Studies in Papyrology Special Edition. Ann Arbor: Scholarly Publishing Office, University of Michigan Library, 2010.

———. "The Greek of the Gospel of Peter: Implications for Syntax and Discourse Study." In *Das Evangelium nach Petrus: Text, Kontexte, Intertexte*, edited by Thomas J. Kraus and Tobias Nicklas, 77–90. TUGAL 158. Berlin: de Gruyter, 2007.

———. *Idioms of the Greek New Testament*. 2nd ed. BLG 2. Sheffield: Sheffield Academic, 1994.

———. "New Perspectives on the Exegesis of the New Testament: Anglo-American Insights." In *Herkunft und Zukunft der neutestamentlichen Wissenschaft*, edited by Oda Wischmeyer, 63–84. Neutestamentliche Entwürfe zur Theologie 6. Tübingen: Francke, 2003.

———. "New Testament Studies and Papyrology: What Can We Learn from Each Other?" In *Akten des 23. Internationalen Papyrologenkongresses, Wien, 22–28. Juli 2001*, edited by Bernhard Palme, 559–72. Papyrologica Vindobonensia 1. Vienna: Verlag der Oesterreichischen Akademie der Wissenschaften, 2007.

———. "OpenText.org: Program and Prospects." Paper presented at the Annual Meeting of the Society of Biblical Literature, Nashville, TN, November 17, 2000.

———. "Prolegomena to a Syntax of the Greek Papyri." In *Proceedings of the 24th International Congress of Papyrology, Helsinki, 1st–7th of August 2004*, edited by J. Frösén et al., 921–33. Helsinki: Societas Scientiarum Fennica, 2007.

———. "Who Owns the Greek Text of the New Testament? Issues that Promote and Hinder Further Study." Paper presented at the Annual Meeting of the Society of Biblical Literature, Denver, CO, November 17–20, 2001. Published in Stanley E. Porter, *Linguistic Analysis of the Greek New Testament: Studies in Tools, Methods, and Practice*, 17–28. Grand Rapids: Baker, 2015.

Porter, Stanley E., and Matthew Brook O'Donnell. "Building and Examining Linguistic Phenomena in a Corpus of Representative Papyri." In *The Language of the Papyri*, edited by T. V. Evans and D. D. Obbink, 282–311. Oxford: Oxford University Press, 2010.

———. "Comparative Discourse Analysis as a Tool in Assessing Translations Using Luke 16:19–31 as a Test Case." In *Translating the New Testament: Text, Translation, Theology*, edited by Stanley E. Porter and Mark J. Boda, 185–99. MNTS. Grand Rapids: Eerdmans, 2009.

———. "Conjunctions, Clines and Levels of Discourse." *FN* 20 (2007) 3–14.

———. "Expanding the Boundaries of Grammar, Exploring the Word." Paper presented at the Annual Meeting of the Evangelical Theological Society, Colorado Springs, CO, November 14–16, 2001.

———. "OpenText.org and Recent Developments in Greek Textual Studies." Paper presented at the International Meeting of the Society of Biblical Literature, Berlin, July 19–22, 2002.

———. "Theoretical Issues for Corpus Linguistics and the Study of Ancient Languages." Paper presented at the Corpus Linguistics 2001 Conference, Lancaster University, Lancaster, March 29–April 2, 2001. Published in *Corpus Linguistics by the Lune: A Festschrift for Geoffrey Leech*, edited by Andrew Wilson et al., 119–37. Lodz Studies in Language 8. Frankfurt am Main: Peter Lang, 2003.

Porter, Stanley E., and Andrew W. Pitts. "Πίστις with a Preposition and Genitive Modifier: Lexical, Semantic, and Syntactic Considerations in the πίστις Χριστοῦ Discussion." In *The Faith of Jesus Christ: Exegetical, Biblical, and Theological Studies*, edited by Michael F. Bird and Preston M. Sprinkle, 33–53. Peabody, MA: Hendrickson, 2009.

Porter, Stanley E., et al. *Fundamentals of New Testament Greek*. Grand Rapids: Eerdmans, 2010.

———. "OpenText.org: A Collaborative Internet-Based Project for the Linguistic and Literary Analysis of the Greek New Testament." Paper presented at the Annual Meeting of the Society of Biblical Literature, Denver, CO, November 17–20, 2001.

———. "OpenText.org and the Problems and Prospects of Working with Ancient Discourse." Paper presented at the Corpus Linguistics 2001 Conference, Lancaster University, Lancaster, March 29–April 2, 2001. http://ucrel.lancs.ac.uk/publications/cl2003/CL2001%20conference/papers/odonnell.pdf

———. "OpenText.org: An Experiment in Internet-Based Collaborative Humanities Scholarship." Paper presented at the Association for Computers and the Humanities and Association for Literary and Linguistic Computing Conference, New York University, NY, June 13–16, 2001.

Reed, Jeffery T. *A Discourse Analysis of Philippians: Method and Rhetoric in the Debate over Literary Integrity*. JSNTSup 136. Sheffield: Sheffield Academic, 1997.

———. "The Infinitive with Two Substantival Accusatives: An Ambiguous Construction?" *NovT* 33 (1991) 1–27.

Schreibman, Susan, et al., eds. *A Companion to Digital Humanities*. Oxford: Blackwell, 2004. Online: http://www.digitalhumanities.org/companion.

Smith, Catherine J. "Implementing a Corpus Browser for the OpenText.org Database." Paper presented at the Linguistics Institute of Ancient and Biblical Greek, McMaster Divinity College, Hamilton, ON, August 25, 2006.

Smith, Catherine J., and Matthew Brook O'Donnell. "Computer-Aided Linguistic Analysis for a Single Manuscript Witness: Preparing to Map the OpenText.org Annotation." In *The Language and Literature of the New Testament: Essays in Honor of Stanley E. Porter's 60th Birthday*, edited by Lois K. Fuller Dow et al., 106–37. BibInt 150. Leiden: Brill, 2016.

———. "Interactive Corpus Annotation of Anaphor Using NLP Algorithms." In *Proceedings of the Corpus Linguistics Conference: CL2007*, edited by Matthew Davies et al. Birmingham: University of Birmingham, 2007. http://ucrel.lancs.ac.uk/publications/CL2007/paper/191_Paper.pdf.

Stührenberg, Maik. "The TEI and Current Standards for Structuring Linguistic Data: An Overview." *Journal of the Text Encoding Initiative* 3 (2012) 2–14.

Tan, Randall K. "Fulfilling the Law apart from the Law: A Discourse Approach to Paul and the Law in Romans." PhD diss., Southern Baptist Theological Seminary, 2004.

———. "Guide through the OpenText.org Clause Annotation Process." http://opentext.org/resources/articles.html.

———. "Guide through the OpenText.org Word Group Annotation Process." http://opentext.org/resources/articles.html.

———. "Introduction to the OpenText.org Annotation Model from a Pedagogical Perspective." http://opentext.org/resources/articles.html.

———. "The Pauline Lexicon: Developing a Lexical Profile of Paul's Vocabulary." Paper presented at the International Meeting of the Society of Biblical Literature, Singapore, June 27, 2005.

TEI Consortium. "TEI: History." n.p. Online: http://www.tei-c.org/About/history.xml.

Van Gompel, Maarten, and Martin Reynaert. "FoLiA: A Practical XML Format for Linguistic Annotation: A Descriptive and Comparative Study." *Computational Linguistics in the Netherlands Journal* 3 (2013) 63–81.

Xue, Xiaxia E. *Paul's Viewpoint on God, Israel, and the Gentiles in Romans 9–11: An Intertextual Thematic Analysis.* Carlisle: Langham Monographs, 2015.

3

Clause Structuring and Transitivity
Advantages of OpenText.org and Its Prospects

CHRIS S. STEVENS

INTRODUCTION

OVERCOMING THE SOCIO-POLITICAL GAP between ancient authors and modern interpreters is a difficult task. In the case of biblical studies, two millennia separate ancient authors from modern interpreters, resulting in much cultural distance. In recent decades, advances in linguistic tools for biblical studies have helped overcome many hurdles in this regard. While interpretation does not have to be limited solely to the authorial horizon, an appropriate way to begin the exegetical process is by giving primary attention to the linguistic features of the text. The linguistic tools presented here help examiners focus on author-created focality and prominence. These tools and methods are particularly useful in the formal analysis of a "text-based discipline—which, after all, is what biblical studies is supposed to be."[1]

Computers present a significant advantage for using complicated linguistic methods. However, no tool is perfect and only through use and critique will computer programs be improved. The focus of this paper is to evaluate the current abilities and future applications of OpenText.org for biblical studies.[2] As a test case, clause structuring and transitivity patterns, a

---

1. Porter, "Linguistic Issues," 51.
2. In this essay I will primarily be using OpenText.org through Logos Bible software.

method developed by Martín-Asensio, will be applied to Phil 2.[3] I will show there are many advantages to using OpenText.org, but there are also many areas requiring improvement for implementing it into biblical studies.

APPROACHING INTERPRETATION

Albert Schweitzer once protested that it has "always been a weakness of theological scholarship to talk much about method and possess little of it."[4] This critique is true a century later. There are many approaches to biblical interpretation with varying emphasis on textual analysis. In the case of ideological interpretations, proponents are often explicit about a reader-centered hermeneutic.[5] However, some interpretive approaches can unintentionally fall victim to the biases of those doing the interpretation due to a lack of formal and consistent methods of textual analysis.[6] In effect, the result yields whatever the interpreter finds to be significant.

Admittedly, it is impossible to be free from all subjectivity. As Bultmann put it, there is no "*such thing as presuppositionless exegesis.*"[7] This does not imply everyone can do whatever they wish; rather "exegesis of the biblical writings, like every other interpretation of a text, must be unprejudiced."[8] Students and scholars will benefit from incorporating methods that examine a text while not being overly dominated by prejudices of their own or of secondary literature.

LINGUISTIC FOCUS ON THE TEXT

The use of linguistic tools and methods admittedly does not eliminate all presuppositions. Choices about what linguistic methods to use and how to implement them are still subjective decisions. Linguistics does, however,

---

3. Martín-Asensio, *Transitivity-Based Foregrounding*. The work on Phil 2 was originally explored in Stevens, "Clause Structure and Transitivity," 327–49.

4. Schweitzer, *Paul*, 34.

5. These approaches have varying degrees of merit by offering unique ways to read ancient texts. Well-known approaches include, but are not limited to, postcolonial, feminist (e.g., Schüssler Fiorenza, *Memory of Her*), and Marxist approaches, as well as liberation theology (e.g., Gutiérrez, *Theology of Liberation*).

6. Traditional exegetical handbooks prescribe overt subjectivity into the initial steps. Gordon Fee tells students to read in English, make a translation, and use secondary literature, from the very beginning (*NT Exegesis*, 28–30). See also Conzelmann and Lindemann, *Interpreting the New Testament*, 36.

7. Bultmann, "Exegesis," 195, emphasis original.

8. Bultmann, "Exegesis," 199.

postpone the task of content interpretation until after a thorough analysis of how the author has crafted the text. With OpenText.org, there is no need to reference resources on content interpretation, since at this stage of study the text alone is the focus of investigation.

An advantageous aspect of OpenText.org concerns its delicacy to separate features into distinguishable categories. Consider that in 1992, Helen Dry, noting the terminological ambiguity and difficulty of linguistic prominence, concluded that, "in the absence of an agreed-upon definition of the central concept, we may identify as foreground *whatever* textual feature *strikes us* as prominent."[9] Similarly, Kathleen Callow defined prominence as "any device whatsoever which gives certain events, participants, or objects more significance than others in the same context."[10] In contrast, Martín-Asensio finds that functional linguistics, which is the method of OpenText.org, is capable of integrating the most fruitful insights from literary criticism, psycholinguistics, and discourse analysis into one coherent theory of linguistic foregrounding.[11] Importantly, the functional model gives primary attention to the linguistic features rather than assessing and interpreting the content. In opposition to a reader-centered understanding of prominence, Martín-Asensio concludes, "I define foregrounding as linguistic prominence which is consistent and motivated, and can be seen to cohere with the overall theme(s) of the text in which it is found . . . (and it) provides a link between stylistic and functional analysis and is capable of revealing important insights into the writer's agenda."[12]

For the purpose of analyzing style, theme, and prominence, OpenText.org helps one to focus on the authorial choices in the structuring of clauses as a means for communication. The structural selections are significant in light of the non-configurational character of Koine Greek that allows for great flexibility in the order of linguistic constituents. To be sure, there are certain rules to Koine word order, such as an article or preposition preceding its noun. Within the typological categories of Hale, however,

---

9. Dry, "Foregrounding," 447, emphasis mine.

10. Callow, *Discourse Considerations*, 49. Cynthia Westfall finds that terms such as importance, causality, emphasis, salience, unexpectedness, figural properties, highlighting, and prominence have all been muddled together ("Analysis of Prominence," 76).

11. Martín-Asensio, *Transitivity-Based Foregrounding*, 79. Martín-Asensio is using the methods developed by M. A. K. Halliday demonstrated in the literary analysis of William Golding's *The Inheritors*. See Halliday, "Linguistic Function," 88–125.

12. Martín-Asensio, *Transitivity-Based Foregrounding*, 17, 90.

Koine would be considered to have relatively "free word order."[13] This is on account of the flexible ordering of the grammatical subject, object, and verb.[14] In the case of Philippians, even the first few verses demonstrate this fact with Phil 1:1 being subject-object-verb, 1:3 verb-object, and 1:8 object-subject. One realizes that the order from the unrestricted options is a product of multiple, simultaneous, and interdependent authorial choices. Since human language can only select a single linguistic item at a time, the selection of order is a meaningful representation of prioritization and a means of highlighting.[15]

Through these linear structural choices the author construes experience, gives indications of their appraisal and attitude, and packages the linguistic material in a rhetorical manner.[16] The realization of one clause order over another is, therefore, a representation of the author's presentational decisions. The variation in the linear order of linguistic elements is a matter of markedness.[17] The more common orders are less marked, and the more infrequent are more marked. Studying the clause order will draw attention to the authorial markedness and OpenText.org helpfully displays the clause ordering visually better than other programs.

OpenText.org Annotation Software

OpenText.org is a textual markup that annotates Koine texts, specifically the New Testament, in a functional syntactic manner according to Systemic Functional Linguistics (SFL).[18] The texts are tagged for lexical and grammatical functional information built around the clause, which Halliday explains is the "central processing unit in the lexicogrammar."[19] The approach

---

13. Hale, "Warlpiri," 5.

14. Two further characteristics of non-configurational languages, which Koine also has, are the "use of syntactically discontinuous expressions" and "use of null anaphora" (Hale, "Warlpiri," 5).

15. Brown and Yule, *Discourse Analysis*, 125–40.

16. Following Martín-Asensio, the term "rhetorical" is used in the "widest sense of *ars bene dicendi*, the art of addressing a situation effectively by means of speech" (*Transitivity-Based Foregrounding*, 51). Furthermore, rhetoric in epistles is "not dependent upon rhetorical theory; they more likely represent a type of 'universal' rhetoric prevalent at the time" (Reed, "Epistle," 189).

17. For markedness theory see Battistella, *Markedness*; Andrews, *Markedness*; Fleischman, *Tense*.

18. Porter et al., "OpenText.org."

19. Halliday, *Introduction to Functional Grammar*, 10. OpenText.org also does

is to focus upon grammatical function rather than grammatical form and phrase-structures.[20] Consider an example from Phil 2:1–2, which contains clauses 2.4–5 in OpenText.org:

||[cj] εἴ |[S] τις σπλάγχνα καὶ οἰκτιρμοί ||

||[P] πληρώσατέ |[C] μου τὴν χαρὰν ||[21]

The first clause, which is indented to indicate that it is a dependent clause, only contains a conjunction and a subject component (cj-S).

OpenText.org provides users with a lot of information while utilizing minimal bracketing and labels. The text is tagged according to the functions of Subject (S), Predicator (P), Complement (C), Adjunct (A), Conjunction (cj), and Address (add). Also, three distinct clause levels are recognized: Primary, Secondary, and Embedded. Furthermore, one of the advantages over other bracketing and labeling models is in the visual presentation of the text. OpenText.org preserves the linear order so the analyst can read the text. Other approaches have a vertical text and maximal bracket lines labeling individual linguistic elements. The layout makes it visually difficult if not entirely unreadable; the layout is for data purposes only.[22] Best of all, the OpenText.org annotation is free online with the statement that "the project aims both to serve, and to collaborate with, the scholarly community."[23]

OpenText.org and Transitivity

The popular understanding of grammatical transitivity is whether or not a verb takes an object. In SFL, transitivity concerns the lexicogrammatical network occurring at the clause level, specifically the interaction between persons, processes, and things. In other words, it is an analysis of "who does

---

word-group annotation with the four types of modification: Specifiers (sp), Definers (df), Qualifiers (ql), and Relators (rl). While also a helpful approach, the word-group level will not be explored in this paper as the focus is on transitivity occurring on the clause level.

20. For an introduction to the difference between functional and grammatical analysis, see Thompson, *Introducing Functional Grammar*, 18–26; Halliday, *Introduction to Functional Grammar*, 1–36.

21. "Clause 2.4–5" refers to numbering in OpenText.org and not verse numbers. Also, readers will note the shorthand: S = Subject, C = Complement, P = Predicator, A = Adjunct, cj = Conjunction, and add = Address. The double bars indicate the start and end of a clause, and the single bars indicate where one word-group ends and the next begins.

22. The layout of OpenText.org is different in the online and the Logos representation of the model, but both are linear and readable.

23. Online: opentext.org/about/overview.

what to whom."²⁴ Transitivity analysis concentrates on the verbal process extending from one participant, the actor, to another participant, the goal. To be a transitive clause, there must be at least two participants and a process. The endless options of clauses can be organized into three primary process types: Material, Mental, and Relational.²⁵

OpenText.org is designed to be immediately applicable to clausal transitivity, since the very "annotation scheme reflects Halliday's conception of the grammar of a clause (i.e., the transitivity system at the level of a clause)."²⁶ OpenText.org also handles the particulars of Koine flexibility regarding the participants. Consider clause 2.81 at Phil 2:29a:

||ᴾ προσδέχεσθε |ᶜʲ οὖν |ᶜ αὐτὸν |ᴬ ἐν κυρίῳ |ᴬ μετὰ πάσης χαρᾶς ||

This is a transitive clause, and though OpenText.org does not annotate for process types, it is a mental process. The OpenText.org presentation handles the Koine grammar of not having an explicit subject. The inflectional nature of Koine encodes the second person plural into the verb, which in English is expressed as "You (pl.) (Actor) receive (Process-Mental)²⁷ him (Goal), in the Lord with all joy (Adjunct-Manner)." The Actors extend through the process to the Goal. Consider another example in clauses 2.47–48 at Phil 2:17–18:

||ᶜʲ καὶ |ᴾ συγχαίρω |ᶜ πᾶσιν ὑμῖν ||
||ᶜ τὸ ···ᶜ |ᶜʲ δὲ |···ᶜ αὐτὸ |ᶜʲ καὶ |ˢ ὑμεῖς |ᴾ χαίρετε ||

The first clause is like the one above. It is a transitive mental clause with the participants encoded in the verb. The latter clause does have an independent grammaticalized subject, ὑμεῖς (i.e., the Philippians). Notice the three examples have differing clause orders. The first is P-cj-C-A-A, the second

---

24. Martín-Asensio, *Transitivity-Based Foregrounding*, 10.

25. Halliday, *Introduction to Functional Grammar*, 213–15. Material processes are external to the Actor/Agent, Mental are internal senses, and Relational concern processes of being. Additional labels of increased delicacy include Behavioral, Verbal, and Existential, but for our purposes here can be subsumed under the primary categories.

26. Opentext.org/model/introduction. See Tan, "Transitivity," on the OpenText.org website for a brief presentation of transitivity.

27. Process types often require interpretation. However, OpenText.org does not label for process types at this time. Further discussion is not necessary for the purposes of this paper.

is cj-P-C, and the third is C. . .(cj). . .C-cj-S-P. However, the free order does not disrupt transitivity analysis.[28]

What exactly does transitivity analysis indicate about the structural selections of the author? At the clause level, many interdependent choices are made by the author to create a particular type of transitivity structure. Martín-Asensio contends that through these selections the author guides the reader and the "transitivity choices have to do with the representation of experience, and are realized by the functional elements of process, participants, and circumstances."[29] As Halliday explains, "transitivity is really the cornerstone of the semantic organization of experience" and the "particular transitivity patterns that stand out in the text contribute to the artistic whole."[30] Consequently, attention to transitivity is an analysis of the ideational metafunction of language, namely viewing the clause as the means by which the author construes experience.

SEARCHING AND USING OPENTEXT

The format and design of OpenText.org annotation are eminently suitable for clause structuring and transitivity analysis. The freely available online annotation by OpenText.org is a valuable resource for looking at individual clauses, verses, or even pericopae. It visually represents the linguistic organization and indicates how linguistic items relate to one another. But if an analyst wants to examine patterns and anomalies, especially across whole letters, then searchability becomes a necessity. Unfortunately, the online version is not yet searchable. Searchability is a goal for the future, but currently the only way to search OpenText.org is by using Logos software.[31] Unfortunately, the current state of the search functionality in Logos is quite complicated and the results are sometimes erroneous.[32]

---

28. There is an additional and specialized way of looking at transitivity. While transitivity concerns the extension of an Actor to a Goal, ergativity analysis looks at causation. As Halliday puts it, "the ergative is a nuclear rather than a linear interpretation" (*Introduction to Functional Grammar*, 347–48). Grammatical voice in Greek can likely be better categorized with transitivity and ergativity, with the middle voice being ergative. See O'Donnell, "Some New Testament Words," 156–60.

29. Martín-Asensio, *Transitivity-Based Foregrounding*, 55. Martín-Asensio is building upon the SFL work in Halliday, "Linguistic Function," and the typological approach in Hopper and Thompson, "Transitivity."

30. Halliday, "Linguistic Function," 119.

31. This paper was written using Logos 6.11 to search OpenText.org.

32. To perform the following search inquiries, I read and watched everything Logos

Previously Andrew Pitts used Logos 3.0 to search OpenText.org and offered an explanation of his search strings.[33] In one search, he wanted to find all P-C clauses that allowed for the presence of adjuncts and addressees, excluded subject components, and required the complement in the final position (e.g., APC, addCPC, but not SPC, nor PCadd). When his search is reproduced exactly, the results contain false positives in Philippians. On the primary level, the program returns 30 hits. However, Phil 2:28, 4:3, and 4:17 are all inaccurately counted three times.[34] Plus clauses 3.17 and 4.61 are counted twice. Worse yet, clause 4.46 is counted six times instead of once.[35] Therefore, of the 30 hits, only 19 are correct, representing 63 percent accuracy.

The results for the secondary clause level are correspondingly inflated. For instance, Phil 1:27, clauses 1.66–74, is counted nine times instead of four. Of the reported twenty-nine results, only twelve are correct, a 41 percent accuracy. The multiple readings render the numbers inaccurate for statistical purposes. The results must be scrutinized and pruned. Therefore, while searching in Logos does speed matters up, the effort to check accuracy is a hindrance to overall usability.

In another search, consider a step-by-step process that a user might make for S-initial clauses. To begin, it is helpful to know the number of subject components to establish a base for calculating percentages. Thankfully, there is a preset string for subject components, which returns eighty-nine hits in Philippians. However, in pruning the data one immediately recognizes that Phil 1:1 and 1:2 display two hits each, likely because of the discontinuous subject.[36] The double count inflates the numbers since it is in

---

offered on OpenText.org. I also read the forums at community.logos.com/forums and other blogs on how to use the syntactical search functions. Multiple search strings were created for every inquiry with only the most helpful presented here. I am a competent user of Logos, and, therefore, any errors in use reflect the challenges that would be faced by any typical user.

33. Pitts, "Greek Word Order," especially 331–36.

34. To explain, Logos returns with "30 results" at the top of the search return. However, Phil 2:28 is counted as two, but there is only one P-C on the primary level. Also, Phil 4:17 is counted three times but there are only two in clauses 4.60 and 4.61. Again, Phil 4:3 is counted three times while only clauses 4.5 and 4.6 are actual instances. Furthermore, the Logos order is sometimes wrong. For instance, it counts clause 4.2 as cj-C-C[CPA]-P, when the NA28 presents the order as cj-C-P-C.

35. The four embedded clauses might be the cause of the program miscalculating results, even though the embedded clauses are cj-P.

36. For instance, the S component in Phil 1:1 is Παῦλος καὶ Τιμόθεος δοῦλοι

fact one functional subject comprising two word groups, not two distinct subject components. So the preset search needs to be adjusted. I guessed that removing the word-group category might help to only search the clause rank. Oddly, instead of reducing the number of hits by subsuming multiple word groups into a single functional unit, it actually increased the result to ninety-three. Upon examination, Phil 1:1 and 1:2 are each counted as a single hit and so is the discontinuous subject in 1:13. I do not know the reason for the increase in the number of hits; one would expect a decrease.

A second step, and seemingly a logical one, taken to find S-initial clauses on the primary level is to select two further search options in the search interface: (1) "Appears at the beginning" for the Subject and (2) "Clause level primary." The result is twenty-nine hits, but it did not find all S-initial clauses. Clause 1.46 was not found on account of the conjunction initial position,

||^{cj} καὶ |^S [[^{P} τὸ ἀποθανεῖν]] |^C κέρδος ||^{37}

How to nuance the string to account for the cj-initial clauses is not straightforward. I guessed an easy solution would be to toggle the "may or may not appear" option for a conjunction preceding the subject. Unfortunately, the result is zero because it contradicts the selection of the subject "appears at the beginning." For newer users, there is no easy way to find the S-initial components, and getting around the problem encounters further challenges.

Trying to work within the parameters of the program, the search string below would seem like a logical choice. It is a primary level search with an optional conjunction and no add, A, C, or P, preceding the subject.

Χριστοῦ Ἰησοῦ, but Logos is counting the two head terms Παῦλος and Τιμόθεος as individual hits. The same goes for χάρις and εἰρήνη in 1:2.

37. The double square brackets indicate an embedded clause. In this case the embedded clause consists of a single word-group, an article, and a participle, which has been rank-shifted down to function as the subject of the main clause.

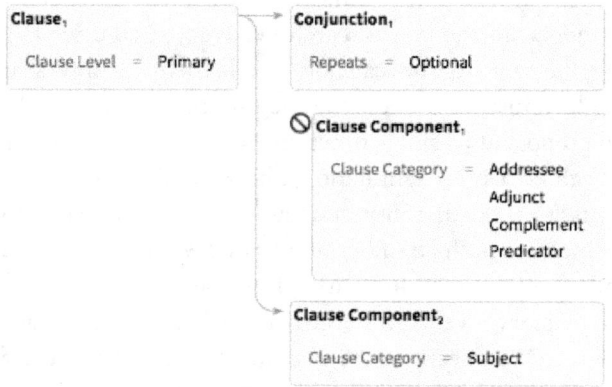

The search only returns six hits. However, four are incorrect as they have C, P, A, or add preceding the S. Thus the search is 67 percent inaccurate. In fact, although the search looks like a logical choice, the query string does not work in a linear fashion. Rather, negated features must be indicated at the front of the search. Furthermore, the search misses many clauses. The way to find clause-initial subjects, ignoring conjunctions, is to remove the negated components and turn off the search option "Appears at the beginning."[38]

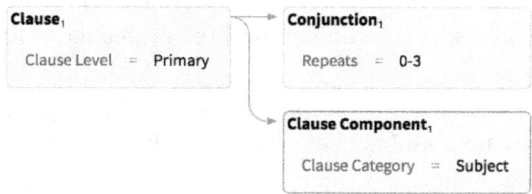

Notice the conjunction is allowed to repeat. Without the repeating option, there are only five results. With the repeating option, the analyst receives fifty-one results to work through, including thirty-five legitimate S-initial clauses. Among the results that have to be removed are five subject-only clauses, clause 1.13 (C-cj-S), and clause 2.13 (A-C-S-P). Thus, after trying numerous search strings, I was unable to obtain results that did not require pruning.[39]

    38. Perhaps Logos could have an "Ignore Conjunctions" option similar to Bible-Works graphical searching engine that can "Allow," "Exclude," or "Require" punctuation. It would bypass the difficult search string creation and enable users to quickly focus on large component patterns.

    39. Pitts ("Greek Word Order," 331) also reports the selection of "May Repeat"

On the other hand, finding S-final clauses is far easier, since there are no concerns about conjunctions. Of the ten results, consider the only wrong occurrence in clause 3.8:

||^S ἡμεῖς $^{...S}$ |^{cj} γάρ |^P ἐσμεν |^C ἡ περιτομή |$^{...S}$ [[^{P} οἱ $^{...P}$ |^A πνεύματι θεοῦ |$^{...P}$ λατρεύοντες] [[^{cj} καὶ |^P καυχώμενοι |^A ἐν Χριστῷ Ἰησοῦ]] [[^{cj} καὶ |^A οὐκ |^A ἐν σαρκὶ |^P πεποιθότες]] ||

The subject component is in the initial position but the search counts it as being in the final position. The problem is likely because of three embedded clauses that serve as further defining ἡμεῖς. Table 1 charts the locations of all subjects, predicators, and complements in primary and secondary clauses that appear in either the initial or final word-groups of clauses.

Table 1: Locations of Subject, Predicator, and Complement[40]

Structure	Location	Philippians	Philippians 2
Subject	Initial	Prim: 1:1, 2, 15(2x), 16, 17, 18, 21(2x), 22; 3:1, 3, 4, 7, 13, 15, 18, 20; 4:5(2x), 7, 8(5x), 9, 11, 19, 23 Sec: 1:6, 9–10, 12, 13(2x), 19–20, 22, 26, 28; 3:4, 12, 19(3x), 21; 4:3, 8(2x)	Prim: 2:4–5, 21 Sec: 2:1, 5, 6, 9, 11, 19, 20, 24, 27, 28
Subject	Final	Prim: 1:8; 4:21, 22 Sec: 1:22	Prim: 2:13 Sec: 2:11
Predicator	Initial	Prim: 1:3, 18, 19, 23; 3:2(3x), 12, 17; 4:3, 4, 9(3x), 10, 12(2x), 15, 17, 18(2x), 21(2x), 22 Sec: 1:7, 8, 9, 25(2x), 27, 29; 3:4, 9	Prim: 2:2, 19, 24, 29 Sec: 2:9, 15, 17, 18, 26(2x), 27, 30.
Predicator	Final	Prim: 1:9, 15, 18(2x), 22, 25, 27; 3:12(2x), 13, 15(2x), 16(2x), 18, 20; 4:2, 4, 6, 8, 9(2x), 11 Sec: 1:12, 16, 20; 3:8(2x), 15, 18; 4:10, 16	Prim: 2:4, 12, 21, 22, 29 Sec: 2:9, 16(2x), 18, 20, 24, 26, 27, 28

---

inaccurately inflates the results.

40. Prim = Primary Level; Sec = Secondary Level.

Comple-ment	Initial	Prim: 1:8, 9, 22; 3:1(2x), 7(2x), 15, 16, 17; 4:2(2x), 9, 13, 20 Sec: 1:29, 30; 3:8, 15; 4:15	Prim: 2:3, 4, 13, 20, 22, 23, 25, 29 Sec: 2:2, 7, 11, 18, 26, 27
Comple-ment	Final	Prim: 1:21(2x), 22, 23; 3:1(2x), 2(3x), 5, 7(2x), 8, 15, 17; 4:3, 5(2x), 8(6x), 17(2x), 18(2x) Sec: 1:27, 28; 3:18, 19(2x), 20, 21; 4:8(2x)	Prim: 2:2, 3, 4, 19, 20, 21, 25, 28 Sec: 2:6, 9, 15, 18, 23, 26, 27, 30

Though time consuming, locating the individual constituents is worthwhile for the information they provide. In Philippians, clauses are more likely to begin with a subject or predicate than a complement. Clauses are also more likely to end with a complement or predicate rather than a subject. Concerning Phil 2, there is a concentration of S-initial components in 2:4–11.[41] The section opens with one of only two primary S-initial clauses, 2:4–5. It ends with the only secondary S-final clause, 2:11. Also, Phil 2:5, 6, 9, and 11 all have a secondary S-initial clause, which is the highest concentration in Phil 2.

Component Ordering

OpenText.org is useful for more than simply locating and analyzing clausal components. OpenText.org is also useful for finding the order of clauses. However, the difficulties encountered in finding the location of a single component are exponentially increased when trying to find the order of clauses such as C-S, P-C, S-P-C, S-C-P, P-C-S, etc. A few examples will suffice to show the challenge of the searches. To begin, a search string for S-P-C clauses with no adjuncts is given below.

---

41. Porter contends the choice of the S-initial structure is to mark or highlight a clause in Philippians. Porter, "Word Order," 194, 200–201.

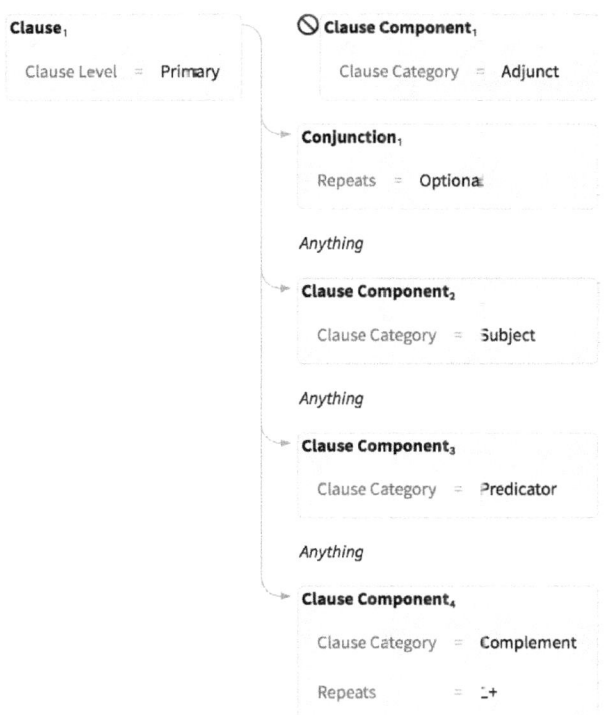

The adjunct is negated at the front. Anything is allowed to intervene, such as repeated conjunctions or addresses. Also, the complement is allowed to repeat, as in the case of clause 3.20 (S-P-C-C). The search returns twenty-four hits, though only clauses 3.20, 4.12, and 4.29 are among the desired clauses. Consequently, writing even a lengthy search still necessitates extensive pruning of the results. What is worse, the search did not find S-P-C clause 3.8.

A second example is a search for S-C-P clauses that allows for adjuncts. The search allows for repeating conjunctions and the presence of adjuncts. Also, the "Anything" element has been toggled for "may or may not appear," to further broaden the search. Again the numbers are conflated. At the top of the search return, it reports there are 64 results for the primary and secondary level; however, it only lists Phil 1:17 (eight times), 1:19–20 (54 times), and 2:4–5 (two times). Why it counts them multiple times is inexplicable to me.[42]

42. In other instances of miscounting there appears to be a simple answer. For instance, clause 3.20, ||cj ἀλλὰ |S ἅτινα |P ἦν |C μοι |C κέρδη ||, is counted as having two P-C constructions. The occurrence of a second complement explains the double count. However, I have no explanation for Phil 1:19–20 being counted 54 times.

Thankfully, all three results are correct—however, the query did not find clause 2.26. Clearly the search needs to be adjusted for greater inclusion as presented in the next example.

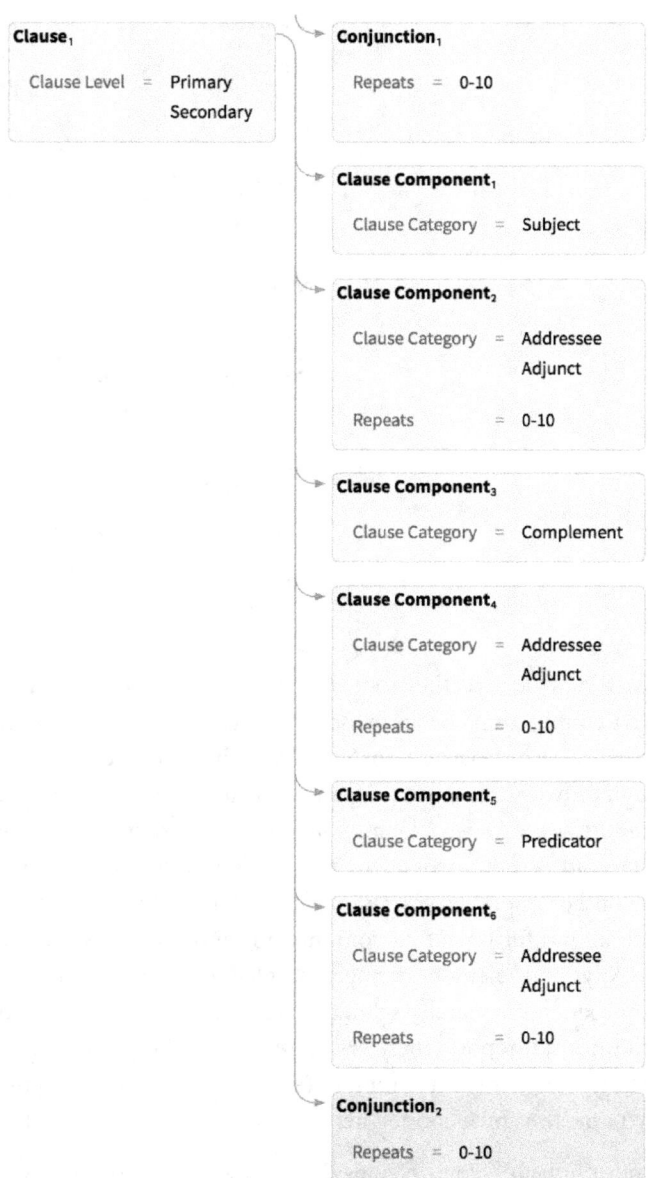

The adjusted search produces 16 hits on both primary and secondary levels, though again it only pulls up six locations. Thankfully, this search did find 2.26 and additionally 1.41, 2.55, and 2.80, but there are problems. First, primary clause 3.48 is actually C-S-C-P and thus not an accurate hit. Second, the query no longer finds clause 1.33 (S-cj-A-C-P-A-A), which should be a hit. Therefore, casting the net wider does find more hits, but it still does not find them all. And much to the dismay of any prospective user, a wider net also requires more time spent correcting the inaccuracies.

My last search example involves S-P-C clauses allowing for adjuncts. The string below allows for initial conjunctions, addresses, and adjuncts. It also allows for initial subjects with a postpositive conjunction. All appropriate parameters are toggled, but still not everything is found. The search finds clause 4.39, but it does not find clause 3.8—yet they are both primary clauses in the form of S-cj-P-C, so the search should find them both. The problem is likely the embedding. In clause 4.39, the complement contains an embedded clause A-C-F, with the adjunct itself containing a further embedded clause. This should not render the search deficient, but it does.

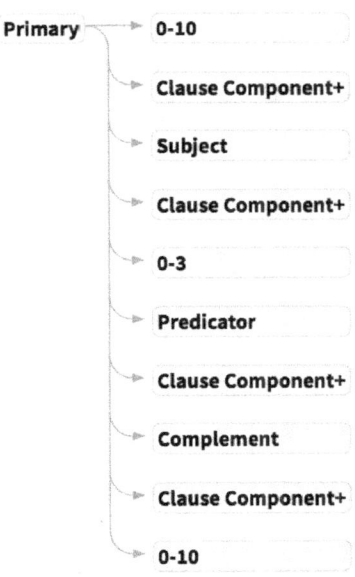

Table 2: Clause Order Results for Philippians

Structure	Including Adjuncts and Address		No Adjuncts or Address	
	Phil	Phil 2	Phil	Phil 2
C (only)	Prim: 1:23; 3:1, 5–6	Prim: 2:3, 21 Sec: 2:27	Prim: 3:1 Sec: 1:28; 3:19	Prim: 2:4 Sec: 2:27
C-S	Prim: 4:20	0	Prim: 1:8; 3:15	Sec: 2:11
C-P	Prim: 1:9, 12, 22; 4:13 Sec: 1:30; 3:8, 15; 4:16	Prim: 2:12, 14 Sec: 2:2, 7, 27	Prim: 1:12; 3:15, 16, 17; 4:2, 8, 9(2x)	Prim: 2:20, 22
C-P-C	Prim: 2:19, 23	0	Prim: 4:2	0
P (only)	Prim: 1:18, 23, 25, 27; 3:1, 12(2x), 13–14, 16; 4:1, 4(2x), 6, 9, 10, 11, 14, 18 Sec: 1:16, 20, 27–28, 30; 3:9–10, 11, 18; 4:10, 15	Prim: 2:24 Sec: 2:12, 15–16, 16(2x), 17, 22, 27(2x), 28, 30	Prim: 1:18, 19; 3:12; 4:4, 9(2x), 18 Sec: 1:25; 4:10	Sec: 2:17, 26(2x)
P-C	Prim: 1:3; 3:8(2x); 4:3, 12, 17, 21 Sec: 1:8, 10, 14, 25, 27; 3:18; 4:3, 10	Prim: 2:19, 28, 29 Sec: 2:7–8, 9, 15, 17, 18, 23, 30	Prim: 3:2(3x), 17; 4:3, 12(2x), 18	Prim: 2:2 Sec: 2:8
P-S	Prim: 4:15 Sec: 1:20	0	0	0
S (only)	Prim: 1:15, 16; 3:4; 4:23 Sec: 1:22, 28; 3:12, 19; 4:3, 15	Sec: 2:5	Prim: 1:18; 3:13 Sec: 1:22	Sec: 2:1(3x)
S-P	Prim: 1:18; 3:20; 4:6, 9 Sec: 1:6, 9, 12, 26	Sec: 2:10, 11, 19, 24	Prim: 3:18	0

S-C	Prim: 1:1, 2, 24; 3:1	0	Prim: 1:21(2x), 22; 3:15; 4:5, 8(5x) Sec: 3:19(2x); 4:8(2x)	0
S-C-P	Prim: 1:17 Sec: 1:19	Prim: 2:4–5 Sec: 2:20	0	Sec: 2:9, 28
S-P-C	Pri: 4:7, 8, 19 Sec: 1:14, 28; 3:4 21; 4:3	0	Prim: 3:3, 7; 4:5; 11	Sec: 2:27
P-S-C[A]	0	0	0	0
P-C-S	0	0	Prim: 1:7; 4:21, 22	0
C-P-S	Sec: 1:29	0	0	Prim: 2:13
C-S-P	0	Prim: 2:4 Sec: 2:18	0	0

A. The P-S-C structure does appear in a few embedded clauses; see 1:7, 1:10, and 3:21.

RESULTS OF CLAUSE AND TRANSITIVITY IN PHILIPPIANS 2

Once the data is compiled, the analyst can look for patterns or anomalies. Without discussing every piece of information, there is one linguistically intriguing portion of Phil 2. Both the structure and transitivity of Phil 2:4–11 indicates the author has made specific selections to draw attention to the so-called "Hymn of Christ."[43] The main indicators are the structural choices. First, Phil 2:4 has three S-initial clauses in a row (clauses 2.15, 16, 17) with the last dependent clause also being S-initial (clause 2.29).[44] Secondly, 2:4 contains the only primary-level C-S-P in all of Philippians. Third, 2:4–5 is one of only two primary S-C-P clauses in all of Philippians. And lastly, 2:4 has one of only two primary C-only clauses in Philippians. Thus, all three clauses in Phil 2:4 are structurally distinctive for Philippians.

---

43. This represents an adjustment from a previous published paper of mine that found that the peak began in 2:5 (Stevens, "Clause Structure and Transitivity," 349). For a discussion on this important pericope, see Hooker, "Philippians 2 6–11," 88–102; Martin, *Hymn of Christ*.

44. The only other place with more S-initial clauses is 4:8. There are seven in a row, with two being dependent. Phil 2:1 has four S-initial clauses in a row but three are S-only.

Additionally, there are 15 clauses dependent upon Phil 2:4–5, which is by far the most in Phil 2.[45]

The transitivity analysis also indicates Phil 2:4–5 contains anomalous features. There are 85 clauses in Phil 2—62 primary or secondary and 23 embedded. Only 22 are intransitive. There are six different Actors of transitive clauses: Paul, the Philippians, God, Christ, Epaphroditus, and a universal reference to people (clauses 2.13, 15, 55, 56). That Paul and the Philippians are Actors is no surprise as the letter is from Paul as author to the Philippians as recipients. It is likewise not surprising that Epaphroditus functions as Actor in clause 2.85, since he is a primary character within the latter part of the chapter. What does stand out is the section consisting of clauses 2.13–29, Phil 2:4–11.

Interestingly, neither Paul nor the Philippians are Actors or Goals in this section. The Philippians are absent for 22 clauses, 2.11–33. The section starts off with an indefinite adjective, ἕκαστος, and ends with an indefinite adjective, πᾶσα γλῶσσα. The transitive Actors refer to all humanity. Furthermore, Christ is the Actor in clauses 2.20, 23, and God (ὁ θεός) is Actor in 2.26, 27. The section is marked out as being presented before the Philippians to receive information. They are not direct Actors or Goals, but are exhorted to become participants who adopt the mindset and ethic presented (Phil 2:2–5).

Consequently, Phil 2:4–11 contains a number of unique and rare authorial choices for the letter of Philippians. The authorial choices of the S-initial concentration, the selection of infrequent clause orders, the multiple clausal dependencies, and the transitive Actors make the section linguistically distinct relative to the co-text. The result is a high concentration of unique elements.

The syntactically dissimilar features do not alone prove—or even suggest—that the section is the macro-theme of Philippians. Such a conclusion is arrived at by analysis of many other discourse features.[46] However, if prominence is defined as "a general name for the phenomenon of linguistic highlighting," as Halliday does, then one can expect some "quantitative turbulence, if a particular feature is felt to be prominent."[47] The linguistic

---

45. Primary clause 2.38 is followed by eleven dependent clauses.

46. Jeffrey Reed finds prominence is the result of suprasentential arrangements (*Discourse Analysis*, 111). See also Westfall, "Analysis of Prominence," 77; Longacre, *Grammar of Discourse*, 38.

47. Halliday, "Linguistic Function," 93, 103.

makeup of Phil 2:4–11 is statistically anomalous and, therefore, is found to have linguistic or syntactic prominence. Such prominence deserves extra attention in subsequent interpretative tasks.

The advantage of using a linguistic tool like OpenText.org to analyze Phil 2:4–11 is that its location in the letter and its relative prominence are found and explored by linguistically marked features prior to any interpretation of the content. Claiming that Phil 2:4–11 is relatively prominent within its co-text has no dependency on questions regarding Paul's use of previous literary material or the theological interpretation of the content.[48] My claim would, however, support the impression that it is an important section. Other tools used for interpretation can make use of the data examined here.

STATE OF OPENTEXT.ORG AND FUTURE NEEDS

In conclusion, there are many strengths and weaknesses of the current usability of OpenText.org in Logos. Its most advantageous feature for a text-based discipline like biblical studies is its linguistic grounding. The advantages to using a linguistic method try to avoid, at least initially, the pitfalls of subjectivity that Schweitzer critiqued. OpenText.org specifically offers the analyst a way of scrutinizing many details of the text without interpreting the content. The engagement with the text examines the very foundation of the authorial choices in crafting the text.

In the examination of Phil 2, the linguistic evidence indicates 2:4–11 is crafted in a manner distinct from its immediate co-text and even from the rest of Philippians. Such a conclusion, while abstract, is statistically defensible and useful for subsequent content interpretation. The content of 2:5–11 is notorious in biblical studies, but through the use of OpenText.org it is shown that 2:4 ought to be used as a significant feature in the interpretation of the section.[49]

---

48. Martin contends there is "almost universal agreement" that Phil 2:6–11 was a pre-Pauline hymn (*Philippians*, 93–100). Opposing voices are few, but Strimple ("Phil 2:5–11," 250) says there is "no *a priori* theological" reason for requiring a prior history. Also, Fee ("Philippians 2," 43) doubts there was prior history, but if so it has "been so thoroughly taken over by Paul" that its history is a moot point.

49. While modern commentaries claim 2:5–11 are "the most important section of [Philippians]," there is not much discussion concerning how the grammar of 2:4 draws attention to the pericope. See O'Brien, *Philippians*, 186; see also Hansen, *Philippians*, 116–17.

Furthermore, with OpenText.org, linguistic elements are explored that might otherwise be missed. The chart of clause ordering above points to patterns that are not seen by simply reading the text. And in no way would a theological reading of Philippians ever realize that the three clauses in Phil 2:4 are all linguistically unique in Philippians. Simply put, OpenText.org gives students and scholars tools to mine for rich linguistic data that has not often been used in biblical studies.

Despite its strengths, there are significant weaknesses to the current state of OpenText.org. The major challenge is searchability within the Logos platform. If the quality of a tool is measured by its ability to maximize user effort to accomplish a task, then OpenText.org within Logos is a failure. For even a motivated user such as myself, it takes more time to create and prune searches than it would to manually use the free online version. While some of the search examples above can be and were improved through trial and error, the difficulties faced will make broad appeal improbable.

I offer a few key suggestions for improving OpenText.org. First, the most pressing need is a drastic development in intuitive usability. Searching for results should not require a degree in computer technology. The ability to develop straightforward search strings, such as those found in BibleWorks software, is the only way the program will gain wider use. A program with a months-long learning curve will not be incorporated into scholarly research. Of course, "intuitive" does not necessarily mean "easy." Complex tools understandably take effort to learn. However, to drive a car, a learner practices; they do not undergo courses in the intricacies of the modern internal combustion engine or aerodynamics. Biblical scholars are interested in the results, not in the internal workings of the system.

Second, OpenText.org searching must be accurate. Embedded clauses and further defining word-groups should not cause search confusion concerning component location and order of a clause (as evidenced in clause 3.8). Also, high levels of inflation of results and searches often being more than 50 percent inaccurate render the system almost unusable. The time involved in confirming search results must be reduced greatly. A search for S-P-C clauses should find all and only S-P-C clauses. If it is not accurate, then the query engine cannot be trusted and should, therefore, not be used.

In addition to searches becoming more user-friendly, the OpenText.org annotations could someday function more like an interactive research assistant than an archive for retrieval only. Consider by analogy the process of using a library. Sometimes a person knows exactly what they are looking for, a certain book or article with a known author and title. Other times, perhaps most of the time, research involves looking for the unknown. The inquiring mind visits the library to explore the available resources. Researchers do not always know what to look for, or how to go about finding the unknown. Similarly, the current state of OpenText.org in Logos operates solely on prior knowledge. The user must know the types of things to look for and how to search for them, which is not easy. A truly innovative step would be if information were graphed in various ways to automatically highlight patterns and anomalies. For instance, seeing transitive patterns plotted over clause structures, simultaneously interweaving tense-form patterns, could reveal linguistic patterns that would require hours of manual work.[50] Also, multiple pre-set searches would save a lot of time for the user. These pre-set searches would also guide newer users to important elements of a text to consider, similar to a librarian directing someone where to go. Additionally, it would be advantageous for the tagging to include more information. For instance, the predicator could include process types. Searching for patterns of mental or material processes could very well reveal matters of interest.

Beyond these improvements, there are also potential ways to apply the program in entirely different directions. In the future, users should be able to create their own texts. The tools for tagging and blocking could be freestanding, allowing users to tag and search any text they create.[51] It could be similar to the sentence-diagramming modules in BibleWorks and Logos. I suggest this because users would significantly benefit from having personalized texts to study. For instance, Phil 4:3 in Sinaiticus reads ||^A ναὶ |^P ἐρωτῶ |^{cj} καὶ |^C σέ |^{add} γνήσιε σύζυγε ||, but in P46 the text is ||^A ναὶ |^P ἐρωτῶ |^{cj} καὶ |^{add} γνήσιε σύνζυγε ||. The absence of a complement in P46 is interesting and worth exploring. A textual critic would be interested to know if P46 has a propensity for dropping pronouns before direct addresses. If that were the case it would be considered a scribal style rather than an error in the transmission history.

A free standing, user model would open up numerous other opportunities in textual criticism of papyri and manuscript research. Consider that Philippians in Sinaiticus is different in seven clause-level locations than the

---

50. The three-layered approach is the basis of analysis by Martín-Asensio, *Transitivity-Based Foregrounding*, 61.

51. Beyond the canonical texts, only the Gospel of Peter is currently online.

text in Alexandrinus (1:8, 10; 2:17, 24; 4:15, 18).[52] If both texts could be tagged a thorough comparison could be made to try and explain the differences. Further comparing Alexandrinus, Vaticanus, Claromontanus, and others directly with one another would enable all sorts of explorations.[53] For instance, does the scribe of Vaticanus have a tendency to front subject components more than the scribe of P46? Tagging and searching would be the way to find out.

CONCLUSION

Today OpenText.org is a demonstrably useful tool. It offers some distinctive capabilities for linguistic inquiry that can enhance biblical studies richly. However, the current online version is unsearchable and the flaws in the Logos search features severely hamper its usefulness.[54] The future design of the program should be mindful of the program's learnability, efficiency, and accuracy. Furthermore, if users could tag and search their own texts, OpenText.org would be used in new and significant ways. The progenitors of the program are on the right path, and all the contributors are to be thanked for their work. There is a solid base for the next group of volunteers "to serve, and to collaborate with, the scholarly community" in order to address weaknesses and to develop new strengths.[55] If an accurate, searchable, user-friendly version of OpenText.org were created, I believe it would gain wide appeal within biblical studies.

BIBLIOGRAPHY

Andrews, E. *Markedness Theory: The Union of Asymmetry and Semiosis in Language*. Durham, NC: Duke University Press, 1990.
Battistella, Edwin L. *Markedness: The Evaluative Superstructure of Language*. SUNY Series in Linguistics. Albany: State University of New York Press, 1990.
Brown, Gillian, and George Yule. *Discourse Analysis*. CTL. Cambridge: Cambridge University Press, 1983.
Bultmann, Rudolf. "Is Exegesis without Presuppositons Possible?" *Encounter* 21 (1960) 194–200.

---

52. This is excluding obvious scribal errors such as Sinaiticus Phil 3:4, 10; 4:20.

53. Online there is a document titled, "Character Level (Diplomatic) Papyrus Encoding" from February 2001, opentext.org/model/guidelines/papyrus. But that idea concerns analysis of physical features of papyrus and parchment rather than the text only.

54. This paper was originally presented at the Bingham Colloquium in June 2016. In the final stages of editing, the Logos program has shown some signs of improvement. However, search results are still numerically inflated and still yield inaccurate hits.

55. Opentext.org/about/overview.

Callow, Kathleen. *Discourse Considerations in Translating the Word of God*. Grand Rapids: Zondervan, 1974.

Conzelmann, Hans, and Andreas Lindemann. *Interpreting the New Testament: An Introduction to the Principles and Methods of N.T. Exegesis*. Peabody, MA: Hendrickson, 1988.

Dry, Helen A. "Foregrounding: An Assessment." In *Language in Context: Essays for Robert E. Longacre*, edited by Shin Ja J. Hwang and William R. Merrifield, 435–50. Dallas: The Summer Institute of Linguistics, 1992.

Fawcett, Robin P. *Invitation to Systemic Functional Linguistics through the Cardiff Grammar: An Extension and Simplification of Halliday's Systemic Functional Grammar*. 3rd ed. Equinox Textbooks and Surveys in Linguistics. London: Equinox, 2008.

Fee, Gordon D. *New Testament Exegesis: A Handbook for Students and Pastors*. Philadelphia: Westminster, 1983.

———. "Philippians 2:5–11: Hymn or Exalted Pauline Prose?" *BBR* 2 (1992) 29–46.

Fleischman, S. *Tense and Narrativity: From Medieval Performance to Modern Fiction*. London: Routledge, 1992.

Gutiérrez, Gustavo. *A Theology of Liberation: History, Politics, and Salvation*. Translated by C. Inda and J. Eagleson. London: SCM, 1973.

Hale, Ken. "Warlpiri and the Grammar of Non-Configurational Languages." *Natural Language and Linguistic Theory* 1 (1983) 5–47.

Halliday, M. A. K. *Halliday's Introduction to Functional Grammar*. Revised by Christian M. I. M. Matthiessen. 4th ed. London: Routledge, 2014.

———. "Linguistic Function and Literary Style: An Inquiry into the Language of William Golding's *The Inheritors*." 1971. Reprint. In *Linguistic Studies of Text and Discourse*, edited by Jonathan J. Webster, 88–125. Collected Works of M. A. K. Halliday 2. New York: Continuum, 2002.

Hansen, G. Walter. *The Letter to the Philippians*. PNTC. Grand Rapids: Eerdmans, 2009.

Hooker, Morna Dorothy. "Philippians 2.6–11." In *From Adam to Christ: Essays on Paul*, 88–102. Cambridge: Cambridge University Press, 1990.

Hopper, Paul J., and Sandra A. Thompson. "Transitivity in Grammar and Discourse." *Language* 56 (1980) 251–93.

Longacre, Robert E. *The Grammar of Discourse*. 2nd ed. Topics in Language and Linguistics. New York: Plenum, 1996.

Lukaszewski, Albert, et al. *The Lexham Syntactic Greek New Testament, SBL Edition: Sentence Analysis*. Bellingham, WA: Lexham, 2011.

Martin, R. P., and Gerald F. Hawthorne. *Philippians*. WBC 43. Dallas: Word, 2004.

Martin, Ralph P. *A Hymn of Christ: Philippians 2:5–11 in Recent Interpretation and in the Setting of Early Christian Worship*. 3rd ed. Downers Grove, IL: InterVarsity, 1997.

Martín-Asensio, Gustavo. *Transitivity-Based Foregrounding in the Acts of the Apostles: A Functional-Grammatical Approach to the Lukan Perspective*. JSNTSup 202. Sheffield: Sheffield Academic, 2000.

O'Brien, Peter T. *The Epistle to the Philippians: A Commentary on the Greek Text*. NIGTC. Grand Rapids: Eerdmans, 1991.

O'Donnell, Matthew Brook. "Some New Testament Words for Resurrection and the Company They Keep." In *Resurrection*, edited by Stanley E. Porter et al., 136–65. LNTS 186. London: T. & T. Clark, 1999.

Pitts, Andrew W. "Greek Word Order and Clause Structure: A Comparative Study of Some New Testament Corpora." In *The Language of the New Testament: Context,*

History, and Development, edited by Stanley E. Porter and Andrew W. Pitts, 311–46. LBS 3. Leiden: Brill, 2013.

Porter, Stanley E. "Linguistic Issues in New Testament Lexicography." In *Studies in the Greek New Testament: Theory and Practice*, 49–74. SBG 6. New York: Peter Lang, 1996.

———. "Word Order and Clause Structure in New Testament Greek: An Unexplored Area of Greek Linguistics Using Philippians as a Test Case." *FN* 6 (1993) 177–205.

Porter, Stanley E., et al. "The OpenText.org Syntactically Analyzed Greek New Testament." Logos Bible Software, 2006.

Reed, Jeffrey T. *A Discourse Analysis of Philippians: Method and Rhetoric in the Debate over Literary Integrity*. JSNTSup 136. Sheffield: Sheffield Academic, 1997.

———. "The Epistle." In *Handbook of Classical Rhetoric in the Hellenistic Period: 330 B.C.–A.D. 400*, edited by Stanley E. Porter, 171–93. Leiden: Brill, 1997.

Schüssler Fiorenza, Elisabeth. *In Memory of Her: A Feminist Theological Reconstruction of Christian Origins*. London: SCM, 1983.

Schweitzer, Albert. *Paul and His Interpreters: A Critical History*. Translated by W. Montgomery. London: Adam and Charles Black, 1912.

Stevens, Chris S. "Clause Structure and Transitivity: Objective Grammatical Means for Beginning Exegesis Using Philippians 2 as a Test Case." *Conversations with the Biblical World* 35 (2015) 327–49.

Strimple, Robert B. "Philippians 2:5–11 in Recent Studies: Some Exegetical Conclusions." *WTJ* 41 (1979) 247–68.

Tan, Randall. "Transitivity." 2005. Online: opentext.org/resources/articles/a6.

Thompson, Geoff. *Introducing Functional Grammar*. 2nd ed. London: Hodder Education, 2004.

Westfall, Cynthia Long. "A Method for the Analysis of Prominence in Hellenistic Greek." In *The Linguist as Pedagogue: Trends in the Teaching and Linguistic Analysis of the Greek New Testament*, edited by Stanley E. Porter and Matthew Brook O'Donnell, 75–94. NTM 11. Sheffield: Sheffield Phoenix, 2009.

Wu, Andi, and Randall Tan. *Cascadia Syntax Graphs of the New Testament: SBL Edition*. Bellingham, WA: Lexham, 2010.

4

The Future of New Testament Lexicography
Remodeling Relational Semantics and Componential Analysis through Distributional Corpus Analysis

Ryder A. Wishart

INTRODUCTION

Lexical semantics over the last quarter century has been marked by significant developments in various directions, including a number of approaches that Dirk Geeraerts has termed neostructuralist. Neostructuralist lexical semantics attempts to maintain structuralist insights, while exploring new methods of qualitative and quantitative analysis. When it comes to lexical semantics of an epigraphic language, qualitative methods have always been the norm. However, in light of new developments in corpus analysis, new avenues of quantitative research have become available. Not only are new tools available, but there are also opportunities to make use of past methods that have shaped the discipline of New Testament lexicography, such as componential analysis and relational semantics. A neostructuralist approach to both of these methods could, I would argue, avoid common methodological pitfalls while building on past achievements in New Testament lexicography. Therefore, I argue the following thesis: biblical studies ought to take a quantitative approach to lexicography using distributional corpus analysis as a framework within which both componential analysis and relational semantics can be remodeled.

Before describing in more detail how these methods could be remodeled, I will first offer a generalized description of both methods and their roles in New Testament lexicography. Next, I will explain the key obstacles in New Testament lexicography and how distributional corpus analysis can overcome these obstacles, with special reference made to word space models. Finally, I will propose a distributional, corpus-based remodeling of componential analysis and relational semantics in a way that upholds the motivating values of qualitative structuralist semantics.

COMPONENTIAL ANALYSIS AND RELATIONAL SEMANTICS[1]

Componential analysis and relational semantics have played important roles in shaping the direction of Greek New Testament lexicography, despite significant drawbacks with each method. I will first describe lexical semantics as it pertains to biblical studies, followed by an outline of the problems typically associated with componential analysis and relational semantics.

Lexical Semantics and Biblical Studies

Following more general trends in lexical semantics, lexicography of the Greek New Testament has shown significant development since the advent of modern linguistics. Whereas semantics is more generally the study of meaning, lexical semantics is the more specific study of the meaning of lexemes, that is, the headwords one might find in a dictionary. Lexical semantics has played a key role in biblical studies, especially over the last century as linguistics has grown into a discipline capable of standing on its own. Dirk Geeraerts describes the history of lexical semantics as a series of movements beginning with historical-philological semantics. Historical-philological semantics focused largely on identifying authorial intention in the analysis of epigraphic languages.[2] Geeraerts explains,

---

1. The following accounts of both componential analysis and relational semantics are not exhaustive or comprehensive. Information on either method can be found in numerous places; the following are some examples. For more detailed information about componential analysis, see Murphy, *Lexical Meaning*, 43–79; Wierzbicka, *Lexicography and Conceptual Analysis*, 59–69; Nida, *Componential Analysis*; Hanks, *Lexical Analysis*, 70–72; Saeed, *Semantics*, 259–304; Lyons, *Linguistic Semantics*, 107–17; Lyons, *Semantics*, 1:317–35; Ruhl, *Monosemy*, 181–82. For more detailed information about relational semantics, see Lyons, *Semantics*, 270–317; Cruse, *Lexical Semantics*; Murphy, *Semantic Relations and the Lexicon*, 133–236; Croft and Cruse, *Cognitive Linguistics*, 141–92; Storjohann, "Sense Relations," 248–65.

2. In this paper an epigraphic language, also called a "dead" language, is one that no longer has native speakers, restricting linguistic analysis to the texts and records of

> Because [historical-philological] linguistic semantics is a historical discipline, its primary material consists of texts from dead languages or from previous stages in the development of a living language. Its basic methodological procedure is therefore the *interpretation* of those texts. Only afterwards can changes between periods (and the mechanisms guiding them) be recognized, classified, and explained. The primary methodological step of the historical semantician is that of the historical lexicographer and the philological scholar: to interpret historical texts against the background of their original context by trying to recover the original communicative intention of the author.[3]

Because the texts were ancient artifacts, historical semanticists needed first to interpret the texts, and only then could they do the work of lexicography.

The second movement Geeraerts describes is the rise of structuralist semantics. Building largely upon insights from the father of modern linguistics, Ferdinand de Saussure, structuralist semantics views language as a system governed by an autonomous set of rules. That is, meaning is generated in language by means of a set of rules. Just like the pieces on a chess board may be carved into virtually any set of distinguishable shapes, it is not the real-life features of the pieces, but the rules governing them that determine their relative values. As Geeraerts explains regarding language as a system, "the fact that we describe the linguistic sign as being part of such a system implies that we characterize the sign *within* the system, in its relations to other signs in the system."[4] Structuralism, therefore, changed the way many researchers analyzed lexical semantics. This change in theory about language inspired the development of new tools and methods of analysis. Two of these in particular, relational semantics and componential analysis, will be discussed further in this paper.[5]

Structuralist semantics has also had a significant impact on biblical studies, though the impact was not immediate. As one surveys key works such as Moisés Silva's *Biblical Words and Their Meaning*, or Peter Cotterell

---

that language. For information about the unique challenges attending corpus analysis of epigraphic languages, see Bamman and Crane, "Structured Knowledge," 1–2.

3. Geeraerts, *Theories of Lexical Semantics*, 14.

4. Ibid., 49.

5. For a discussion of the role of relational semantics in the broader movement of structuralist semantics, see ibid., 80–91. Geeraerts's discussion of componential analysis is primarily located in his discussion of generative semantics (101–17) and neostructuralist semantics (esp. 124–56).

and Max Turner's *Linguistics and Biblical Interpretation*, the structuralist approach to lexical semantics stands out as an important factor for biblical studies. In 1961, James Barr's *The Semantics of Biblical Language* directly challenged the way biblical theologians of his day were doing lexical semantics. He argued that they made use of a faulty method, beginning with untested hypotheses and allowing those to dominate the data.[6] In an attempt to remedy popular views of word meaning and introduce those in biblical studies to the field of linguistics, Cotterell and Turner, Silva, and David Black created introductions to linguistics meant to help students and scholars in biblical studies to adopt methods that avoided the pitfalls of the Biblical Theology Movement so severely criticized by Barr.[7] In seeking to adopt a more structuralist approach to language analysis, these authors argue for a relational semantics approach to word meaning, and describe the benefits of componential analysis in determining the exact relationships that hold between word senses. These methods constitute significant advances in methodology, and should be considered indispensable tools for biblical studies today. These two tools, relational semantics and componential analysis, provide useful conceptual frameworks by which we can think about and articulate key aspects of lexical semantics, such as the relatedness of word meanings. However, one of the drawbacks of both structuralist and historical-philological semantics has been the over-reliance on intuition or introspection; all too often, conclusions are drawn from insufficient data. This problem, though, is remedied by more recent developments in what Geeraerts describes as neostructuralist semantics.

Neostructuralist semantics represents a cluster of approaches that maintain the basic insights of structuralist semantics—and most specifically the choice to view language as a system. Geeraerts divides these neostructuralist approaches into decompositional approaches to meaning and relational approaches.[8] Decompositional approaches assume that meaning, for example word meaning, is composed of smaller building blocks, variously referred to as primes, primitives, or components. Relational approaches, on the other hand, claim that meaning is a matter of paradigmatic contrast. A linguistic feature, for example a word, has meaning only in relation to its near-neighbours—its synonyms, antonyms, hyponyms,

---

6. Barr, *Semantics*, 22.

7. Cotterell and Turner, *Linguistics and Biblical Interpretation*; Silva, *Biblical Words*; Black, *Linguistics for Students*. Cf. Barr, *Semantics*.

8. Geeraerts, *Theories of Lexical Semantics*, 124–25.

etc. Both the decompositional and relational approaches that characterize neostructuralist semantics have direct ties to structuralist semantics, and both have played a significant role in the development of New Testament lexicography, especially in Louw and Nida's lexicon based on semantic domains.[9]

Louw and Nida's lexicon based on semantic domains makes use of these two tools of analysis—relational semantics and componential analysis. The lexicon is organized into clusters of words that correspond to 93 domains of meaning, which include subdomains under each category. Within a single domain Louw and Nida placed words that have related meaning, whether synonyms or antonyms. The use of terms such as synonymy, antonymy, as well as others, reflects an attempt to describe the relational semantics of the lexicon by categorizing words into paradigmatic relationships. That is, words with related meanings can be said to share a paradigm, and users of the language select words on the basis of (among other considerations, such as syntax) their paradigmatic contrast to other words. Louw and Nida's lexicon, however, does not describe these relationships directly, but rather the categories or domains by virtue of which words have these relationships—thus a lexicon "based on semantic domains." Their task is one of classification, as they explain, "A dictionary based on semantic domains is in many ways like a classification of flora or fauna based on families, genera, and species. One may say that the domains constitute families of meanings, the subdomains are the genera, and the individual entries are the species."[10] The decompositional approach of Louw and Nida is evident, in that the "primary basis for classification of meanings into domains," is componential analysis (see below). If a set of words shares a feature or set of features, they can be said to occupy a similar domain of meaning. However, the relational approach is also evident, because the lexemes are grouped together with words that they relate to paradigmatically. In a review of the lexicon, Lyons claims that their lexicon can better be described as a "bilingual thesaurus (organized conceptually . . .)."[11]

One of the problems with Louw and Nida's use of semantic domain theory is its subjectivity in actually identifying and classifying domains. They explain that "certain distinctions in classification are always subject

---

9. Louw and Nida, *Greek-English Lexicon*.
10. Ibid., 8.
11. Lyons, "Review," 204.

to possible differences in treatment."[12] For example, it is unclear just how specifically lines of distinction should be drawn. The nature and extent of semantic distinctions in Hellenistic Greek is difficult to establish with certainty for the simple reason that lexicographers have no way to elicit information from native speakers.[13] What Louw and Nida attempt to do is to classify the thought patterns of ancient Greeks, the cognitive structure of a language for which we have only written texts. They therefore admit, "There is no easy way to resolve such [problems] of classification, since we really do not know precisely how native speakers of Hellenistic Greek thought about such matters."[14] Louw and Nida's lexicon represents an important step forward for New Testament lexicography, however. They not only acknowledge the insights and advances of structuralist linguistics, but they attempt to actually incorporate those insights into the very structure of their lexicon.[15] Thus, to attempt to create a new lexicon or lexical database that does not explicitly incorporate the relational semantics of Hellenistic Greek would be an unfortunate step backward. Louw and Nida's lexicon is doubtless the most significant advance in recent lexicography of the Greek New Testament.[16] Thus, it follows that some of the most noteworthy achievements in this area have been the result of a structuralist/neostructuralist approach to linguistics, including both a relational view of meaning and a componential approach to word meaning. Next, I will briefly outline some of the critiques levelled against both of these methods.

Critiques of Componential Analysis and Relational Semantics

Though their impact on biblical studies has nevertheless been substantial, both componential analysis and relational semantics have been strongly criticized. Both methods exhibit diversity as actually implemented by linguists, yet some general issues can be identified that apply to most implementations of these methods.

---

12. Nida and Louw, *Lexical Semantics*, 112.
13. Ibid., 109–10.
14. Ibid., 114.
15. Lee, *History of New Testament Lexicography*, 177–78.
16. Ibid., 155. Or "one of the most significant," according to Porter, *Linguistic Analysis*, 47.

Componential Analysis

There are two important critiques of componential analysis: (1) the use of an arbitrary descriptive metalanguage and (2) a reductionist approach to meaning. Componential analysis is a decompositional method of analyzing lexical meaning. A good example is furnished by contrasting the English words *girl*, *woman*, and *man*. These words can be analyzed on the basis of whether certain marked features—components—are present or not in the semantics of a lexeme.

Girl	– adult	+ female	+ human
Woman	+ adult	+ female	+ human
Man	+ adult	– female	+ human

On the basis of these marked features or components of these lexemes, these words could be defined as follows:

Girl: female human non-adult

Woman: female human adult

Man: non-female human adult

Obviously, the number of components could be easily multiplied. In fact, one suspects that the process happens in reverse most of the time. As Riemer points out, "anything that can appear in a definition can be converted into a component, and . . . there are therefore no a priori constraints on components other than constraints on what can be expressed in a metalanguage."[17] Most linguists who attempt componential analysis claim that the components only superficially mirror English terms—by intent they are actually meant to represent language-neutral concepts. However, because these terms almost always correspond to the target language (whether that be English, German, Spanish, etc.), the alleged metalanguage appears to be an arbitrary imposition on the lexis of the source language. There is no way to prove that the components are actually metalinguistic rather than simply words in English (or some other modern language).

The second issue has to do with the theory of meaning motivating componential analysis—namely, decompositional semantics. According to Riemer, "Decompositional approaches to lexical content, which proceed by analysing meanings into smaller components, are a highly common

---

17. Riemer, "Lexical Decomposition," 214.

explanatory strategy in semantics."[18] Despite this commonality, there are significant problems; as Riemer explains, "The considerable heuristic utility of decompositional approaches to meaning is offset by the no less significant problems that attach to decomposition as a theory of underlying semantic structure."[19] He outlines a number of difficulties inherent in a decompositional approach to lexical meaning. First, "There are, in particular, numerous areas of the vocabulary which seem ill-suited to a decompositional approach."[20] Second, it is likely that any semantic information associated with a lexeme is revisable under the right circumstances, which means that components cannot, after all, be truly necessary or even criterial (in a prototype view). Third, it has so far proved impossible to create paraphrases of any kind that are completely substitutable for the words they purport to define. That is, each lexeme in a vocabulary is a prime, not precisely reducible to a set of components.[21] Fourth, there is a lack of constraints on the use of metalinguistic terms. As he explains,

> We can only apply primitive metalinguistic terms objectively (or, at least, in a manner that commands intersubjective agreement) by *identifying* them with the object-language terms whose meaning we want an account of—and we do not get one simply by reinstating these very object-language terms in the metalanguage, even if we dress them up in small capitals, surround them with brackets, or employ other kinds of typographical signal to designate them as metalanguage terms.[22]

Fifth, word meaning typically seems to exhibit Gestalt phenomena. That is, we perceive word meaning not by seeing the parts and then deducing the whole but rather by first grasping the whole, which then enables us to infer the parts. "In other words," Riemer says, "identification of the *component* seems to depend on prior identification of the *whole concept* . . . but this is exactly the opposite of the direction required by a decompositional approach."[23] While decompositional semantics are useful and popular,

---

18. Ibid., 213.

19. Ibid.

20. Ibid., 221. Silva also points out that "componential analysis . . . works better for some portions of the vocabulary than others" ("Review," 166).

21. Cf. Ruhl, *Monosemy*, 201, who says, "What is often overlooked is that each word is a primitive: posited primitives are often simply English words."

22. Riemer, "Lexical Decomposition," 225.

23. Ibid., 226.

they tend to inaccurately reduce lexical meaning in another language to nothing more than a set of words in English (or German, Spanish, etc.).

In sum, a remodeling of componential analysis should at least be able to explicitly justify the descriptive metalanguage, or—even better—operate without a metalanguage at all, and should also provide meaningful descriptions of lexical meaning that are not reductionist but instead take into account the semantic complexity of utterances and contexts.

Relational Semantics

Regarding relational semantics, one issue stands above the rest: the semantics–pragmatics divide.[24] Semantics, typically, is understood as intralinguistic, stable, or context-independent meaning.[25] The semantics of a word can be thought of as its meaning apart from any contextual modulation. Pragmatics, on the other hand, generally refers to extralinguistic, transient, or contextually-dependent meaning. This distinction becomes a matter of much debate when it comes to creating definitions for lexemes. How much contextual or pragmatic information should be included in a definition? This difference can also be described as the semantic–encyclopedic divide.

In lexical semantics, it is typical to describe two opposite ends of a spectrum when it comes to defining words: on one side is the dictionary approach; on the other is the thesaurus approach. The dictionary approach tends to include more encyclopedic information, including, often, many of the real-life references made with the lexeme. By contrast, the thesaurus approach does not include encyclopedic information, defining words instead on the basis of their near neighbors. A word and its neighbors are said to occupy a paradigm, domain, or field. The thesaurus approach reflects most clearly the insights of relational semantics. A clear distinction between semantics and pragmatics is assumed, insofar as the relationships between lexemes are intralinguistic and make no necessary reference to extralinguistic reality or encyclopedic information—thesaurus entries are constrained by semantics. However, lexical semantics has by and large abandoned such a tidy distinction, opting instead for a functionalist approach to meaning.[26]

---

24. Because this is such a highly debated issue, there are bound to be divergences in terminology. The definitions offered here are not meant to be representative of the numerous perspectives, but rather generally valid construals for the sake of situating the following critique.

25. For this definition of *semantics*, which is characteristic of Systemic Functional Linguistics, see Fawcett, *Theory of Syntax*, 38.

26. On the rejection of the semantics–pragmatics divide in cognitive semantics,

Croft and Cruse, for example, claim that pragmatics are integral to sense relations. They reject construing hyponymy, incompatibility, and antonymy as logically transitive or entailment relationships.[27] That is, they deny that sense relations are a stable feature of lexemes. As an alternative they hold a "dynamic construal approach," and claim that "sense relations do not hold between words as such, but between specific construals of words."[28] Their position entails, therefore, that "while the paradigmatic viewpoint is accepted as valid, the items in the paradigm are not lexical items but contextual construals of lexical items, and the relationships are relations between a particular construal of the item actually chosen and potential construals of other items that might have been chosen in that context."[29]

In summary, componential analysis has over time become a more strongly polarizing issue, though its appeal for lexicography is understandable due to its intuitive methodology. While relational semantics, in turn, has not become obsolete, the tidy semantic descriptions of a thesaurus approach have come into question. However, I would argue that both of these methodological approaches to analysis can be helpfully remodeled within a distributional corpus framework. Before examining how this might take place, though, I will first describe the main obstacles faced by New Testament lexicographers.

OBSTACLES IN NEW TESTAMENT LEXICOGRAPHY

New Testament lexicography faces three key obstacles, which correspond to the main problems with lexicons outlined by John Lee.[30] First there has always been an undue reliance on previous lexicographical work. Lee meticulously traces the histories of many modern lexicons, identifying in every case liberal recycling of previous material. "The whole history of New Testament lexicography," says Lee, "is one of reliance on predecessors and transmission of older material with varying degrees of revision. If all were well with the tradition, there would be no cause for concern. . . . But this

---

see Geeraerts, *Theories of Lexical Semantics*, 182. Halliday and Matthiessen describe the same phenomenon in Systemic Functional Linguistics (*Construing Experience*, 12). A functionalist approach to meaning is introduced in Thompson, *Introducing Functional Grammar*, 1–13.

27. Storjohann, "Sense Relations," 260–61.

28. Croft and Cruse, *Cognitive Linguistics*, 143.

29. Ibid., 145.

30. Lee, *History of New Testament Lexicography*, 40–41.

is hardly the case."[31] Lexicographers, however, can hardly be blamed for this. Lee points out that if one were to fully analyze one word each day, every day of the year, it would still take roughly 13.7 years to cover even the roughly 5000 lexemes contained in the New Testament, and even that time frame is idealistic.[32] Second, the material itself, which has been transmitted from revision to revision for centuries, "has employed a method of indicating meaning, the archaic gloss method, that is intrinsically weak and deceptive."[33] Offering glosses, which are effectively translation substitutes, has been the dominant practice of lexicons, though this situation is changing.[34] Third, as Lee demonstrates, there are numerous instances where either Latin or vernacular translations have exercised undue influence on the glosses included in lexicons. There is a cyclical process at work (which Lee refers to as "a clandestine affair")[35] between translations and lexicons, each providing the other with justification for particular glosses. Thus, from Lee's analysis, it is clear that there is a need for original research that does not simply reformat the glosses of previous lexicons and translations. However, such a research project is not without its own potential problems, but faces the following obstacles: inconsistency, subjectivity, and logistics.

Inconsistency

When it comes to offering definitions, there is a lack of controls and hence an unacceptable degree of inconsistency involved in the creation of definitions.[36] Porter offers an extended discussion of this inconsistency in BDAG. First, Porter notes that BDAG sometimes has a wrong meaning for a lexeme. (However, apart from examples of actual usage, there is very little objective data that can be pointed to, such as the quantified vectors mentioned below, in order to justify or overturn a given definition.) Second, some entries are unclear in their distinctions or ordering, sometimes apparently reflecting the divergent shades of nuance in the English glosses, rather than the actual Greek term. Data that strictly reflects usage of the

---

31. Ibid., 11.
32. Ibid., 5.
33. Ibid., 40–41.
34. Porter, *Linguistic Analysis*, 49–50.
35. Lee, *History of New Testament Lexicography*, 31.
36. As Lee says, "Not that everything in the tradition is wrong: much of the material, certainly much of what is vital, is sound. But consistent reliability is what we seek" (ibid., 178).

Greek terms would help remedy this problem. Third, words of the same part of speech are often treated in very different ways.[37] "What seems to be lacking," explains Porter, "is any kind of a systematic way of quantifying meaning [within the definitions]. There is no apparent means by which components of meaning are defined and articulated."[38] There are other issues identified by Porter, but these suffice to illustrate the nature of the problem.

Greater consistency could, I suggest, be obtained by subsuming lexis—and lexical semantics—within grammar. That is, a lexicon cannot continue to focus merely on words as if they operate in isolation. A myopic focus on words as isolated units of meaning is likely part of the problem. What I am suggesting is a serious rethinking and expansion of the categories by which we conceptualize the language of the New Testament, one that incorporates lexicography, yet much more besides, including what is traditionally called grammar, and all of that within the larger world of Hellenistic Greek usage.[39]

Distributional corpus analysis, however, does not necessitate a hard distinction between lexis and grammar, viewing both systems as statistical patterns.

Subjectivity

One of the ways subjectivity becomes a problem is in theoretical disagreement, which introduces a unique set of issues. Investing in the production of a new lexicon or lexicogrammatical database is a huge undertaking and requires alignment between researchers regarding how lexical semantics is to be approached. For example, there is disagreement as to what is the difference between homonymy and polysemy, or whether words should be treated as monosemous signifiers. Because there are many different ways to do linguistic analysis there are bound to be theoretical differences and disagreements as to the best way to structure and produce a lexicon. Disagreements about theory cannot be totally eliminated; however, radical divergence need not be the final word when it comes to creating tools that everyone can use. For instance, automatically generating the data may relieve some of the tension, because there is less time and money at stake. In the past, lexicographers would find their data by reading and interpreting

37. In BDAG, for example, under ὅτι, the fifth sense is not a meaning at all, but simply a catch-all category of usages that do not seem to fit under the first four meanings.

38. Porter, *Linguistic Analysis*, 69.

39. Ibid., 80.

individual instances of words. However, automated statistical natural language processing (NLP) will make the task of gathering data more objective. While it will still be necessary to interpret automatically generated data, the data itself is significantly more objective and theory-independent than simply relying on individual interpretations of single passages.

Logistics

Finally, original lexicographical work faces the not-insignificant obstacle of logistics. As mentioned above, the creation of a lexicon is an enormous task. It is one thing to suggest ways that lexicography can be done rightly; it is quite another to actually undertake the task. While corpus-based methods of analysis provide substantial advantages for lexicography, the task of compiling and especially of annotating corpora is quite literally compendious. For these reasons, it would be expedient to automate as much of the process as possible. As Ravin explains,

> It has recently become clear, however, that if machines are to "understand" natural language, they must have recourse to extensive lexical databases, in which a wealth of information about the meaning of words and their semantic relations is stored. To create such databases manually is not feasible. The task is too time consuming and labor intensive. Instead, current research in lexical semantics concentrates on the extraction of semantic information from sources available on-line, such as dictionaries and thesauri in machine-readable form. . . . This information is then being used to create lexical databases for NLP systems.[40]

Although currently the tools for doing this kind of work require knowledge of programming languages and use of command line tools that most people are unfamiliar with, "automated lexicon construction," McEnery and Wilson point out, "is a goal which seems increasingly realistic thanks to corpus-based n[atural] l[anguage] p[rocessing] systems."[41] Statistical NLP, as will be seen below, is capable not only of providing syntagmatic information, like a "key word in context" concordance search, but also of providing paradigmatic information about related lexemes such as synonyms, and, theoretically, hyponyms and hypernyms.

In the following section, I will describe distributional corpus analysis and its potential for avoiding the problems just outlined.

40. Ravin, "Synonymy," 397.
41. McEnery and Wilson, *Corpus Linguistics*, 144.

DISTRIBUTIONAL CORPUS ANALYSIS AND WORD SPACE MODELS

Due to the difficulties and pitfalls of New Testament lexicography, new approaches need to be explored. One such approach, which builds upon the insights of structuralism/neostructuralism, is distributional corpus analysis.[42] Distributional corpus analysis, while avoiding key obstacles to New Testament lexicography, provides promising new directions for automated or semi-automated lexicography using word space models.

Distributional Corpus Analysis

Distributional corpus analysis is part of a broader movement of neostructuralist semantics and maintains some of the key values of structuralist semantics. This approach views lexical meaning as a set of discernible patterns mined from large text corpora, and it represents a more rigorous and data-driven approach to relational semantics, using NLP.

Geeraerts describes two different types of NLP, symbolic NLP, which was more prominent from the 1950s until the 1990s, and statistical NLP, which became dominant during the 1990s.[43] Symbolic NLP uses a formal or logical metalanguage to encode language for computer processing. In this approach words, phrases, and constructions are generalized and then replaced with variables. For example, all noun phrases might receive the symbolic designation NP, all predicators might receive the designation P, etc.; other grammatical features such as clause types or dependency relationships might be replaced with other types of designations. Once the language data is translated into a metalinguistic symbolic language, it becomes easily readable by machines. By contrast, statistical NLP eliminates the intermediate step of translating language into a symbolic metalanguage. This latter approach is represented by the methods of distributional corpus analysis. Statistical NLP is a diverse set of approaches to corpus analysis, including a wide variety of methods which open up many new possibilities. Below, I will discuss one of these methods (i.e., word space modeling).

Distributional semantics was not entirely novel in the 1990s; it reflects the intuitions of earlier thinkers. Zellig Harris, for example, in a 1954 article, outlines a number of points about distributional structure: (1) distribution patterns are meaningful, (2) such patterns are consistent, (3) description

---

42. Geeraerts, *Theories of Lexical Semantics*, 165–78.
43. Ibid., 157.

of this kind can be entirely intralinguistic as distribution of a given element can be described relative to another element without reference to "outside" information, and (4) distributional restrictions can be described by a network of generalized rules. "In other words," Harris says, "difference of meaning correlates with difference of distribution."[44] Harris's views are similar to Firth's notion of collocation,[45] which has played a significant role in corpus linguistics in general, and has been incorporated into models of Systemic Functional Linguistics.[46]

Geeraerts explains that while symbolic NLP focuses primarily on the paradigmatic relations within a lexicon, statistical NLP, by contrast, focuses more specifically on the syntagmatic relationships within texts. However, the combination of multiple complementary tools within a distributional approach can be used to provide both syntagmatic and paradigmatic information. Because statistical NLP provides a more rigorously empirical basis for analyzing large corpora and does so at speeds that no lexicographer could have matched in the past, there is new potential for generating accurate information that can be used for semantic description of lexemes.

Geeraerts describes distributional corpus analysis as a convergence of neostructuralist and cognitive semantics. That is, this approach to linguistic analysis attempts to maintain some of the key insights of structuralism—for example, a systemic view of language—while also maintaining the view that meaning is a psychological phenomenon.

This convergence makes distributional corpus analysis a useful tool for biblical studies. On the one hand, semantic analysis need not be reductionist, attempting to account for all meaning according to strictly formal analysis. Meaning is fuzzy and transient in many ways, and a code view of language does not adequately account for all of the data.[47] Yet taking a psychological view of meaning presents certain difficulties for the study

44. Harris, "Distributional Structure," 156.

45. Cf. Sinclair, *Corpus, Concordance, Collocation*.

46. For bibliographic references see Halliday and Matthiessen, *Introduction to Functional Grammar*, 60 n. 2. For discussion, cf. Fewster, *Creation Language*, 58–68. The potential of corpus linguistics for biblical studies has been systematically outlined in Matthew Brook O'Donnell (*Corpus Linguistics*), and his discussion of the requirements for both a balanced and representative corpus should be duly applied in any distributional semantic analysis of Hellenistic Greek. However, word space models work better with higher amounts of data, and so experimentation should be done to determine the ideal number of words to include in a corpus for a given study.

47. On the distinction between code and inference, see Clark, *Relevance Theory*, 14–18.

of epigraphic languages. For example, attempting to discern prototypical meaning or prove sense differentiation within a lexeme is problematic, as we cannot sample or elicit data from native speakers, and thus we cannot "check" our results when we try to identify the cognitive structure of meaning in Hellenistic Greek. In the face of such difficulties, distributional corpus analysis provides an objective analysis, not of the ancient Greek mind, but of actual instances of linguistic usage. We can only conjecture as to why certain language was used, but we can nevertheless mine the language itself for information. On the other hand, using distributional corpus analysis provides us with concrete data regarding the formal side of language. Using computational analysis of large samples of data, we can actually generate meaningful data and draw accurate generalizations about the systems at work in the extant texts. While we must still interpret the data we generate, the data itself tends to be much more objective.

In short, automated or semi-automated lexicography needs to be considered as a more objective alternative to prevalent word study methods. Automation tools are already developed for a number of different processes for Modern Greek, such as lemmatization, morphological tagging, syntactical annotation of dependency relationships, as well as several others.[48] However, I want to describe one method in particular that should be further developed: word space tools.

Word Space Modeling

Distributional semantics recognizes the key role of collocation in word meaning. A word's syntagmatic relationships create the meaning of that word in a context. Thus, the rationale behind the computational approach of distributional semantics is that two words that have similar meanings will have similar contexts. To put it conversely, similar distribution equals similar meaning. We can tell that *run* and *walk* are similar because they are often used in the same kinds of sentences: "I'm going to *run* to the store"; "I'm going to *walk* to the store." Rather than seeing these words as possessing the absolute value of synonymy, however, it is far more useful to compute the degree of similarity between them.

Where analysis of collocations has always played a role in corpus-based studies, pointwise mutual information (PMI) can be used to simply and automatically calculate the significance of a given collocation, what

---

48. Prokopidis et al., "Natural Language Processing Tools," 511–19.

Church and Hanks call "the *association ratio*" between two words.[49] They explain, "mutual information compares the probability of observing x and y together (the joint probability) with the probabilities of observing x and y independently (chance). If there is a genuine association between x and y, then the joint probability $P(x,y)$ will be much larger than chance $P(x) P(y)$, and consequently $I(x,y) \gg 0$ [i.e. the mutual information of x and y will be greater than zero]."[50] However, when it comes to identifying and quantifying synonyms or related words, not only collocations but more specifically colligations are an important piece of data.[51] Whereas collocations are words that typically co-occur, colligations are grammatical patterns that typically co-occur with given words.

Usually, both collocations and colligations are identified using a key word in context, concordance search. However, the basic key word in context analysis, while useful for some tasks, cannot tell us about words or constructions that, though they may be similar, never actually occur together in the data. Instead, we can use a statistical NLP tool typically referred to as a word space or vector space model.[52] One can think of a word space model as a large network of connections, which is a matrix of extremely high dimensionality. Each word is like a point or node in the network, and each word is related to each other word; every word is connected to every other word in the network. In this network, each word is treated as a vector—that is, a value with magnitude and direction. By vectorizing words, they can be meaningfully compared to one another. There are a wide variety of variables in vector space models, including: (1) type of matrix, (2) method of weighting the data, (3) method of reducing the dimensionality of the matrix, and (4) method of comparing the resulting vectors.[53] I will briefly explain each of these variables, and the corresponding steps involved in such an analysis.

---

49. This method was first developed in Church and Hanks, "Word Association Norms," 22–29.

50. Ibid., 23. Note, however, that they do draw a distinction between mutual information, which is symmetrical, and association ratio, which is asymmetrical (i.e., the order of the collocations matters in the latter).

51. Halliday and Matthiessen, *Introduction to Functional Grammar*, 59–61; Thompson, *Introducing Functional Grammar*, 40.

52. Geeraerts, *Theories of Lexical Semantics*, 174–76. For a general introduction to the word space approach (specifically latent semantic analysis), see Landauer et al., "Introduction," 259–84.

53. For an overview, see Geeraerts, *Theories of Lexical Semantics*, 174–76.

1. The first step in generating a vector space is creating a word-by-feature matrix. This is essentially a table where rows represent individual words and columns represent "features." These features can be words, documents, contexts or search proximities (such as sets of ten adjacent words), or even dependency relationships. Each word is counted up based on its occurrence within each context. Different features are used for different purposes. If one wants to summarize a document based on its key concepts, a word-by-document matrix works best.[54] If one wants to analyze the relationships between lexemes, a word-by-context matrix can provide the needed data.

2. The second step involves weighting the data. Common methods include an analysis of the term-frequency in relation to the inverse-document-frequency (TF-IDF) when using a word-by-document matrix, and PMI when looking at the relationships between words. What these methods accomplish is the assignment of a value to the words; tabular word counts are turned into statistical probabilities.

3. The third step is to reduce the dimensionality of the matrix. In such a large analysis, using perhaps thousands of documents and tens of thousands of words, there is bound to be a lot of blank spaces in the table—that is, the matrix is sparse. In order to isolate the most relevant or significant information, the matrix must have its number of dimensions reduced. This can be accomplished in a number of ways while still maintaining the integrity of the data in the matrix, such as, for example, using singular value decomposition (SVD).

4. Now that the data has been rendered down to a manageable size, the values of each word, the vectors, can be compared using a variety of methods. The most popular method is calculating the cosine relationship between two vectors. Imagine the vectors are like lines on a graph, and the angle of their relationship is the relationship between the words in the word space. The higher the cosine value (1.0 indicating identify and 0 indicating non-similarity), the more similar the contexts of the words are, and thus the more similar the words themselves are according to a distributional view of meaning.

The key to this analysis is that it is automatically generated by computers with only minimal user input. Performing a very large analysis may take a computer a number of hours, but as a corpus typically consists of tens of

---

54. Landauer et al., "Introduction," 19–20.

millions of word occurrences, a similar analysis would take a lexicographer a lifetime. Thus, word space models have potential for overcoming the key obstacles of New Testament lexicography. They can be used for automating many of the tasks of lexicography and doing so in a more objective and consistent way than was possible in the past.

Word space modeling of Hellenistic Greek would have a not inconsiderable impact on New Testament studies. Imagine a database that provides consistent information regarding the relationships between lexemes, as well as relevant syntactic information based on the dependency relationships those lexemes participate in.[55] In the next section, I will describe how the structuralist methods of componential analysis and relational semantics can be remodeled to interface with distributional corpus analysis.

REMODELING COMPONENTIAL ANALYSIS AND RELATIONAL SEMANTICS DISTRIBUTIONALLY

Although componential analysis and relational semantics are generally out of favor, they have played an important role in biblical studies, and with some modifications their underlying structuralist values could be fruitfully interfaced with distributional corpus analysis.[56] These tools, I would argue, should be considered important assets for answering research questions about the Greek of the New Testament, because they are motivated by two of the key values of structuralism, systematicity and decompositionality.

A central goal of lexicography is the compilation of lexical entries that express the semantics of lexemes. Distributional corpus analysis, as we have seen, can be used to identify the near neighbors of words as they

---

55. Kintsch and Mangalath outline a two-tiered method of analyzing both the generalized meaning of a lexeme, the "gist," and the syntactic information. They demonstrate how different word space models may be combined to compound the results ("Construction of Meaning," 346–70).

56. Componential analysis shows up in many of the introductory books on linguistics and biblical interpretation. Black (*Linguistics for Students*, 120), for instance, claims that "through the principles of componential analysis, linguistics can provide a rational and demonstrable basis for the understanding of the crucial components that constitute the meanings of key terms." Cotterell and Turner (*Linguistics and Biblical Interpretation*, 173) explicitly promote Nida's method of componential analysis (Nida, *Componential Analysis*). Silva's (*Biblical Words*, 134) discussion of componential analysis describes its roots in phonological analysis, but he also raises some important concerns. Specifically, he points out that by using componential analysis it is difficult to avoid encyclopedic (rather than semantic) definitions, because components typically reflect the features of referents, rather than lexical units

are actually used in the corpus (i.e. those words that share the closest vectors). Since statistical distributional models of meaning do not attempt to describe the lexical content of items, however, but only their distributional facts, these models can hardly be called semantic. It would therefore seem that a distributional approach would not be useful for compiling semantic lexical entries. By contrast, componential analysis is a tool that is ideally suited to this task. As Riemer notes, "As long as one approaches semantic analysis with the aim of distinguishing a variety of semantic properties within a lexeme, some form of decomposition is the most likely theoretical model."[57] Both tools, componential analysis and relational semantics, are tightly connected in Louw and Nida's lexicon; componential analysis determines the domains into which words are placed, and thus it also determines the relational semantics of the lexicon.[58]

The question, then, is how to incorporate componential analysis into a distributional corpus analysis, given that componential analysis provides useful semantic information regarding lexemes, and distributional analysis provides a more objective method of assessment. What I propose is that we remodel componential analysis as a tool to aid in the process of generating lexical entries on the basis of distribution. The way we should remodel componential analysis is by viewing the vocabulary of a language as a hierarchy: the more abstract or general lexemes occupy the upper regions of the hierarchy, and the more concrete or specific lexemes occupy the lower.[59] Lexemes can then be partly defined on the basis of their near neighbours. A given lexeme will have, among its near neighbours, hypernyms, that is, words with similar but more general meaning, and it will also likely have hyponyms, which are words with similar but more specific meaning.[60] A lexeme's semantic meaning can be partly derived on the basis of its hypernyms. For example, car>Toyota>Corolla: a Corolla is a type of Toyota, which is a type of car. Viewed in this way, a lexeme's components of meaning are specifically its hypernyms.[61] This approach to componential

57. Riemer, "Lexical Decomposition," 229.

58. Nida and Louw note, "The primary basis for classification of meanings into domains and subdomains is the existence of shared features" (*Lexical Semantics*, 109).

59. This perspective on the lexicon is based on the pioneering work in monosemy by Charles Ruhl. See esp. Ruhl, *Monosemy*, 173–206.

60. Calculating specificity of meaning would be an interpretive step based on the data, although there may be ways of automating this task as well.

61. There have been a number of studies attempting to automate the identification of hyponyms and hypernyms from a corpus. For example, Zhou et al. have proposed

analysis is actually a certain perspective on hyponymy and the way lexemes relate to one another.[62] Viewing hyponymy this way, then, allows us to take a componential approach to semantic meaning, but to do so on the basis of the distributional facts present in the corpus.

There is another benefit to this type of componential analysis, in that the components of a word are not postulated as metalinguistic wordings, but rather as semantic features from the same language as the word. In other words, the components of a lexeme's meaning are restricted to lexicogrammatical features of the language itself. A word's components are the more abstract forms it shares a lexical field with, as indicated through its distributional similarity with those forms. Typically, decompositional approaches to lexical semantics "do not necessarily presuppose that the semantic components into which meanings are analysed are themselves lexicalized in individual words."[63] That is, the components are assumed to be metalinguistic. However, if a word's components are specifically its hypernyms—actual words in the lexicon—there can be more consistency in the types of features used to decompose the meanings of lexemes. While this approach would not describe what it is that makes a lexeme more specific than its hypernyms, it would provide a parsimonious description of some key semantic information about a lexeme.

---

a semi-automatic method for extracting hyponymous relationships between concepts, which they call lexical hyponymy relationships, in Chinese using very large web corpora ("Learning Hierarchical Lexical Hyponymy," 206). Acosta et al. note that most methods of extracting hyponym-hypernym relationships rely on a predetermined set of lexico-syntactic data that is provided by lexicons, thesauri, or direct input. They therefore propose a method of automatically extracting this "seed set" from a specialized corpus, such as medical texts, in order to expedite and improve the results when analyzing other corpora ("Extracting Definitional Contexts," 50).

62. Automatic extraction of lexical relations is not limited to hyponymy, either. Recent work in antonymy of the English language by Jones et al. (*Antonyms in English*) has proven to generate highly precise results. However, Jones's original work relied on a corpus of 280 million words, and in Jones et al. (*Antonyms*) this data base was supplemented with other corpora as well as data gathered through elicitation (Jones et al., *Antonymy*; Jones et al., *Antonyms in English*, 17). By comparison, the TLG corpus, when limited in range to the centuries 400 BC through 400 AD consists of just over 49 million words. Jones's work, however, has demonstrated the potential of identifying antonyms through syntactic frames, or typical contexts in which antonyms co-occur (such as "*x* as well as *y*").

63. Riemer, "Lexical Decomposition," 219. However, he points out that Natural Semantic Metalanguage theory assumes this very thing.

Statistical natural language processing, a sub-field of distributional corpus analysis, then, provides an avenue for analysis that is likewise motivated by the values of structuralism. As mentioned, two key values are (1) systematicity and (2) decompositionality. When it comes to systematicity, a distributional or statistical approach requires no semantic content to be contributed to the analysis by the user; all of the data comes directly from the corpus itself. Words are quantified and treated as vectors related by statistically deduced patterns. The vectors relate to one another within a vector space, which is a purely intralinguistic representation. Thus, on a distributional model of componential analysis the relationship between the two tools is reversed. Whereas in Louw and Nida's lexicon componential analysis determines the relational semantics, in a distributional approach the quantified vector relationships between lexemes determine their components, which are viewed as inheritance relationships where hyponyms inherit the semantics of their more general hypernyms.

Therefore, when it comes to the second value, decompositionality, word space models are ideal tools of analysis, as these models are explicitly based on the assumption that the meaning of a given context is composed of the smaller meaningful units it contains. As Landauer et al. explain, "LSA [latent semantic analysis, a word space method] represents the meaning of a word as a kind of average of the meaning of all the passages in which it appears, and the meaning of a passage as a kind of average of the meaning of all the words it contains."[64]

In summary, distributional relational semantics views lexical relations as statistical regularities that hold between vectors. Distributional componential analysis, in turn, views the decomposition of lexemes as a matter of semantic inheritance within a hierarchical, lexicogrammatical network.

FUTURE DIRECTIONS

To my knowledge the tools of NLP have yet to be applied systematically to analysis of Hellenistic Greek.[65] Nevertheless, statistical NLP holds promise for biblical studies because it evades many of the typical problems associated with the word studies that populate most commentaries. As men-

---

64. Landauer et al., "Introduction," 6. For a more recent discussion of how LSA and topic modeling can be integrated, see Kintsch and Mangalath, "Construction of Meaning," 346–70.

65. However, there has been some work regarding Classical Greek. See the Classical Language Tool Kit (CLTK): http://docs.cltk.org/en/latest/greek.html.

tioned above, using word space models of analysis provides consistency and objectivity to the data: all words can be included in a word-by-feature matrix; the process can be partially or even fully automated as more tools are developed; and divergent theoretical positions can be accommodated as different types of word space analysis can answer different questions about meaning. One of the obstacles faced in this respect, however, is the difficulty of obtaining access to the corpus itself. While *Thesaurus Linguae Graecae* can be accessed online, word space analysis cannot be performed on the corpus because the data needs to be processed through separate software. It would therefore be advantageous to develop a lexicogrammatical database that is freely accessible, where word space tools could be compiled and prepared, facilitating new research and answering new questions for New Testament studies. Unfortunately, even though the texts in question are simply digitized reproductions, issues of licensing remain a problem.[66]

CONCLUSION

Quantitative approaches to lexical semantics have made valuable advances over the last quarter century. This paper outlines the potential of a distributional approach to both componential analysis and relational semantics. This neostructuralist approach to both methods, I argue, avoids the common methodological issues of past achievements without dispensing with those achievements in New Testament lexicography. Biblical studies, to reiterate, ought to take a quantitative approach to lexicography using distributional corpus analysis as a framework within which both componential analysis and relational semantics can be remodeled. One of the first and most important steps in this direction will be the compilation and organization of a representative word space for Hellenistic Greek, to the end that many previously unanswerable questions may then be explored in a more objective, consistent, and logistically feasible way.

BIBLIOGRAPHY

Acosta, Olga, et al. "Extracting Definitional Contexts in Spanish through the Identification of Hyponymy-Hyperonymy Relations." In *Modern Computational Models of Semantic Discovery in Natural Language*, edited by Jan Žižka and František Dařena, 48–69. Hershey, PA: IGI Global, 2015. http://services.igi-global.com/resolvedoi/resolve.aspx?doi=10.4018/978-1-4666-8690-8.

---

66. For more on this discussion, see the chapter "Who Owns the Greek Text of the New Testament?" in Porter, *Linguistic Analysis*, 17–28.

Bamman, David, and Gregory Crane. "Structured Knowledge for Low-Resource Languages: The Latin and Ancient Greek Dependency Treebanks." In *Proceedings of the Conference on Text Mining Services*, edited by Gerhard Heyer, 1–10. Leipzig: Springer-Verlag, 2009.

Barr, James. *The Semantics of Biblical Language*. London: Oxford University Press, 1961.

Black, David Alan. *Linguistics for Students of New Testament Greek: A Survey of Basic Concepts and Applications*. 2nd ed. Grand Rapids: Baker Academic, 1995.

Church, Kenneth Ward, and Patrick Hanks. "Word Association Norms, Mutual Information, and Lexicography." *Computational Linguistics* 16 (1990) 22–29.

Clark, Billy. *Relevance Theory*. CTL. New York: Cambridge University Press, 2013.

Cotterell, Peter, and Max Turner. *Linguistics and Biblical Interpretation*. Downers Grove, IL: IVP Academic, 1989.

Croft, William, and D. Alan Cruse. *Cognitive Linguistics*. CTL. Cambridge: Cambridge University Press, 2004.

Cruse, D. A. *Lexical Semantics*. CTL. Cambridge: Cambridge University Press, 1986.

Fawcett, Robin P. *A Theory of Syntax for Systemic Functional Linguistics*. Amsterdam Studies in the Theory and History of Linguistic Science 206. Amsterdam: Benjamins, 2000.

Fewster, Gregory P. *Creation Language in Romans 8: A Study in Monosemy*. LBS 8. Leiden: Brill, 2013.

Geeraerts, Dirk. *Theories of Lexical Semantics*. Oxford: Oxford University Press, 2010.

Halliday, M. A. K., and Christian M. I. M. Matthiessen. *Construing Experience through Meaning: A Language-Based Approach to Cognition*. Open Linguistics. London: Cassell, 1999.

———. *Halliday's Introduction to Functional Grammar*. 4th ed. London: Routledge, 2014.

Hanks, Patrick. *Lexical Analysis: Norms and Exploitations*. Cambridge, MA: MIT Press, 2013.

Harris, Zellig S. "Distributional Structure." *Word* 10 (1954) 146–62.

Jones, Steven, et al. *Antonyms in English: Construals, Constructions and Canonicity*. Studies in English Language. Cambridge: Cambridge University Press, 2012.

———. *Antonymy: A Corpus-Based Perspective*. Abingdon, UK: Taylor & Francis, 2002. http://www.tandfebooks.com/action/showBook?doi=10.4324/9780203166253.

Kintsch, Walter, and Praful Mangalath. "The Construction of Meaning." *Topics in Cognitive Science* 3 (2011) 346–70.

Landauer, Thomas K., et al. "Introduction to Latent Semantic Analysis." *Discourse Processes* 25 (1998) 259–84.

Lappenga, Benjamin J. *Paul's Language of Ζῆλος: Monosemy and the Rhetoric of Identity and Practice*. BibInt 137. Leiden: Brill, 2015.

Lee, John A. L. *A History of New Testament Lexicography*. SBG 8. New York: Peter Lang, 2003.

Louw, Johannes P., and Eugene A. Nida. *Greek-English Lexicon of the New Testament Based on Semantic Domains*. 2 vols. New York: United Bible Society, 1988.

Lyons, John. *Linguistic Semantics: An Introduction*. 1995. Reprint. Cambridge: Cambridge University Press, 1996.

———. Review of *Greek-English Lexicon of the New Testament Based on Semantic Domains*, edited by Johannes P. Louw and Eugene A. Nida. *International Journal of Lexicography* 3 (1990) 204–11.

———. *Semantics*. 2 vols. Cambridge: Cambridge University Press, 1977.

McEnery, Tony, and Andrew Wilson. *Corpus Linguistics: An Introduction*. Edinburgh: Edinburgh University Press, 2001.

Murphy, M. Lynne. *Lexical Meaning*. CTL. New York: Cambridge University Press, 2010.

———. *Semantic Relations and the Lexicon: Antonymy, Synonymy, and Other Paradigms*. Cambridge: Cambridge University Press, 2003.

Nida, Eugene A. *Componential Analysis of Meaning*. Approaches to Semiotics 57. The Hague: Mouton, 1975.

Nida, Eugene A., and Johannes P. Louw. *Lexical Semantics of the Greek New Testament: A Supplement to the Greek-English Lexicon of the New Testament Based on Semantic Domains*. Resources for Biblical Study 25. Atlanta: Scholars, 1992.

O'Donnell, Matthew Brook. *Corpus Linguistics and the Greek of the New Testament*. NTM 6. Sheffield: Sheffield Phoenix, 2005.

Porter, Stanley E. *Linguistic Analysis of the Greek New Testament: Studies in Tools, Methods, and Practice*. Grand Rapids: Baker Academic, 2015.

Prokopidis, Prokopis, et al. "A Suite of Natural Language Processing Tools for Greek." In *Selected Papers of the 10th ICGL*, edited by Z. Gavriilidou et al., 511–19. Komotini: Democritus University of Thrace, 2012.

Ravin, Yael. "Synonymy from a Computational Point of View." In *Frames, Fields, and Contrasts: New Essays in Semantic and Lexical Organization*, edited by Adrienne Lehrer and Eva Feder Kittay, 397–419. Hillsdale, NJ: Lawrence Erlbaum, 1992.

Riemer, Nick. "Lexical Decomposition." In *The Routledge Handbook of Semantics*, edited by Nick Riemer, 213–32. Routledge Handbooks in Linguistics. London: Routledge, 2016.

Ruhl, Charles. *On Monosemy: A Study in Linguistic Semantics*. SUNY Series in Linguistics. New York: SUNY Press, 1989.

Saeed, John I. *Semantics*. 4th ed. Introducing Linguistics 2. Malden, MA: Wiley Blackwell, 2016.

Silva, Moisés. *Biblical Words and Their Meaning: An Introduction to Lexical Semantics*. Grand Rapids: Zondervan, 1983.

———. Review of *Greek-English Lexicon of the New Testament Based on Semantic Domains*, by Johannes P. Louw and Eugene A. Nida. *WTJ* 51 (1989) 163–67.

Sinclair, John M. *Corpus, Concordance, Collocation*. Oxford: Oxford University Press, 1991.

Storjohann, Petra. "Sense Relations." In *The Routledge Handbook of Semantics*, edited by Nick Riemer, 248–65. Routledge Handbooks in Linguistics. London: Routledge, 2016.

Thompson, Geoff. *Introducing Functional Grammar*. 2nd ed. London: Arnold, 2004.

Wierzbicka, Anna. *Lexicography and Conceptual Analysis*. Ann Arbor, MI: Karoma, 1985.

Zhou, Jiayu, et al. "Learning Hierarchical Lexical Hyponymy." In *Developments in Natural Intelligence Research and Knowledge Engineering: Advancing Applications*, edited by Yingxu Wang, 205–19. Hershey, PA: IGI Global, 2012. http://services.igi-global.com/resolvedoi/resolve.aspx?doi=10.4018/978-1-4666-1743-8.

5

The Limits of Linguistics
Subjectivity, Metaphysics, and the Interpretive Enterprise

David J. Fuller

INTRODUCTION

THE FIRST MAJOR SECTION of the tripartite work that is Hans-Georg Gadamer's *Truth and Method* is entitled "The Question of Truth as It Emerges in the Experience of Art." It begins with a discussion of "the Problem of Method":[1] the fact that in the nineteenth century, the means by which the human sciences conducted their investigations and determined truth were based on the model of the natural sciences. Unfortunately, the observation of repeated patterns and causation is hardly helpful for the types of questions one is drawn to ask about literature and art. Adding further confusion was the simultaneous overwhelming obsession with the cultivation of the prized attributes of humanism (such as culture and taste) despite the fact that this was entirely without grounding in the supposedly authoritative scientific method.[2] In the ensuing segments, Gadamer subjects the ideal of the aesthetic realm as something disconnected from historical reality to a blistering critique,[3] leading him to ask the question

---

1. Gadamer, *Truth and Method*, 3.
2. Ibid., 8.
3. Ibid., 70–101. This viewpoint is traced from Kant through his successors. Note Gadamer's emphasis on self-understanding through art when he states, "Our experience of the aesthetic too is a mode of self-understanding. Self-understanding always occurs through understanding something other than the self, and includes the unity and integrity of the other. Since we meet the artwork in the world and encounter a world in the

of the human sciences' "mode of understanding in truth."[4] His proposal involves the concept of play (as something with an "essence" apart from the individual participants),[5] which has as its (and consequently art's) mode of being the concept of presentation, or performance, in which there are the elements of both repetition (the key illustration being season festivals)[6] and "contemporaneity."[7] After arguing that these properties are likewise applicable to literature,[8] he suggests that a solution based on historical investigation is inadequate. Although "understanding art always involves historical mediation,"[9] it must be admitted that "art is never simply past but is able to overcome temporal distance by virtue of its own meaningful presence."[10]

This brief summary of Gadamer's argument thus far is necessary to establish the context for his climactic dilemma, which is the undertaking of hermeneutics in light of historical mediation.[11] At this crossroads, one can compare the programmatic prescriptions of Schleiermacher and Hegel. Schleiermacher's approach can be termed "reconstruction," and it seeks to access the understanding of the work that arose in its original context by entering into that context as much as possible.[12] But here Gadamer provides a word of caution. Does this really capture the *meaning* of the work? Due

---

individual artwork, the work of art is not some alien universe into which we are magically transported for a time. Rather, we learn to understand ourselves in and through it, and this means that we sublate (*aufheben*) the discontinuity and atomism of isolated experiences in the continuity of our own existence" (83).

4. Ibid., 87.

5. Ibid., 103.

6. Ibid., 120–22.

7. Ibid., 123. Gadamer, defining this term, states, "In its presentation this particular thing that presents itself to us achieves full presence, however remote its origin may be." Thus, the temporal distance between the work's creation and the present day is both maintained and overcome: "The player, sculptor, or viewer is never simply swept away into a strange world of magic, of intoxication, of dream; rather, it is always his own world, and he comes to belong to it more fully by recognizing himself more profoundly in it. There remains a continuity of meaning which links the work of art with the existing world and from which even the alienated consciousness of a cultured society never quite detaches itself" (129).

8. Ibid., 153–57. Reading is understood as an act of presentation, in which only the act of understanding brings the meaning alive.

9. Ibid., 158.

10. Ibid.

11. Ibid.

12. See Schleiermacher, *Hermeneutics and Criticism*.

to the "historicity of our being," he sees this endeavor as "futile," fit only to produce a "derivative," "dead," meaning, not unlike taking a painting out of a museum and placing it back into the restored building it was originally taken from.[13] By way of contrast, Hegel's approach can be termed "integration." He sees such reconstructive efforts as mere "fruit torn from the tree," unable to allow a "living relationship" with the work.[14] Far more important is engagement with the "spirit of destiny," "the *interiorizing recollection (Erinnerung)* of the still *externalized* spirit manifest in them."[15] He relocates the problem of understanding to the plane of philosophy ("the historical self-penetration of spirit") as "absolute Mind," where the primary goal is *"thoughtful mediation with contemporary life."*[16] Needless to say, it is the approach of Hegel that Gadamer deems far superior.

Equally clear is the fact that, historically, the discipline of biblical studies has followed in the path set by Schleiermacher. Immense amounts of effort have been exerted towards the gathering of background data and parallel texts for the purpose of investigating authorial intent and original audience reception. For the most part, linguistic biblical interpretation has followed the research program of traditional historical criticism and operated with similar goals (see below). However, it has thus far showed relatively little interest in engaging with the philosophical questions raised by hermeneutics.[17]

The thesis of this study is simple. If the goals of linguistic biblical interpretation are commensurate with those of traditional historical

---

13. Gadamer, *Truth and Method*, 159.

14. Ibid., 160.

15. Quoted in ibid., 161. This is drawn from Hegel's illustration of a girl offering plucked fruits being more than Nature itself. See Hegel, *Phenomenology of Spirit*, 455–56. The context of this illustration is found in Hegel's section on "Revealed Religion," and more specifically, his description of "the condition of right or law . . . [where] the ethical world and the religion of that world are submerged and lost in the comic consciousness, and the Unhappy Consciousness is the knowledge of this *total* loss" (455). In this condition the expressions of art are robbed of all meaning and significance. Hegel summarizes this "integration" concept by stating, "the Spirit of the Fate that presents us with those works of art is more than the ethical life and the actual world of that nation, for it is the *inwardizing* in us of the Spirit which in them was still [only] *outwardly* manifested" (456).

16. Gadamer, *Truth and Method*, 161.

17. For a survey of different modern definitions of the word "hermeneutics," see Palmer, *Hermeneutics*, 33–45. The meaning used throughout this study would span his existential and cultural emphases. Thus, an appropriate working definition would be, "reflection on the nature and conditions of human understanding" (Marshall, "Philosophical Hermeneutics," 275).

criticism, and if the critiques raised about traditional historical criticism by philosophical hermeneutics and continental philosophy are valid, then those practicing linguistic biblical interpretation need to heed and address these issues in order for their discipline to continue to move forward.

LITERATURE REVIEW

Before commencing with the main content of this study, it is necessary to establish two foundational matters. Specifically, in order for this argument to move forward, the self-understanding of linguistic biblical interpretation will be articulated and shown to be in continuity with the goals of historical criticism. Next, a review will be conducted of viewpoints on the relationship between linguistics and hermeneutics, and the specific place of the subject's interest and prejudices in the process of linguistic analysis.

The Goals of Linguistic Biblical Interpretation (LBI)

While practitioners of LBI have not been hesitant to state that their labors will disclose textual meaning, discussion of the nature of this meaning has thus far eschewed consideration of what the operator brings to the equation. Porter's essay, "Greek Language and Linguistics," begins by referencing Bultmann's "Is Exegesis without Presuppositions Possible?" and notes that Bultmann answered the question negatively.[18] However, this becomes a point of departure for observing Bultmann's interest in grammatical investigation, and the opening question is not pursued.

Regarding categories of investigation, "Text-Linguistics or Discourse Analysis" is one of the three ways that Porter states modern linguistics can be applied to the Bible, and it is the most pertinent for the present study.[19] Porter further describes the contribution linguistics can make to biblical studies: "The promise of linguistics is not necessarily that new insights are to be gained . . . nor that it will overthrow all traditional opinions. . . . The promise of linguistics is that it can provide a proper interpretive founda-

---

18. Porter, "Greek Language," 7; Bultmann, *Existence and Faith*, 289. To be precise, Bultmann does state that one should seek to transcend their individual prejudices as much as possible (290) but proceeds to describe a mode of exegesis that assumes a living relationship between the exegete and the subject matter, expects existential encounter, and views understanding as continuously open, "because the meaning of the Scriptures discloses itself anew in every future" (295).

19. Porter, *Linguistic Analysis*, 85–91. The other two areas are "Morphology, Syntax, and Related Areas" and "Semantics and Lexicography."

tion for a text-based discipline—which, after all, is what biblical studies is supposed to be."[20] When discourse analysis is situated within the broader set of activities that comprise the task of exegesis, Porter places linguistic analysis at the level of discourse, as distinguished from context of situation and context of culture.[21] In his list of future possibilities for LBI, the discussion centers on issues of methodology rather than hermeneutics.[22] He addresses the relationship between discourse analysis and meaning by first noting that semantics (as an umbrella term for meaning) should not be understood in terms of translation, but that meaning should be viewed as "what authors attempt to do," and semantics should be understood as "the content stratum concerned with what we are trying to do with language."[23] More specifically, meaning is "what the text is 'about.'"[24]

Reed has touched on this issue in several places, most significantly in a monograph applying discourse analysis to the problem of the literary integrity of Philippians.[25] While it contains a section entitled "Discourse Analysis as New Testament Hermeneutic,"[26] this part merely describes the categories of field, tenor, and mode from Hallidayan functional grammar,[27] polemicizes against Schenk,[28] and states that his approach is based on a grammar of discourse. In an earlier essay, Reed addresses the relationship

---

20. Ibid., 92. Compare the similar statement made in Porter and Pitts, "New Testament Greek," 240–41: "Discourse analysis, however, is not intended to provide a mechanistic approach to the text that removes interpretation. Instead, its major contribution is its ability to provide New Testament interpreters with a formally grounded framework according to which they can discuss the data."

21. Porter, *Linguistic Analysis*, 98–111.

22. Ibid., 127–32. Three areas are identified: (1) The development of models (in which New Testament studies is noted as much more rigorous than many disciplines in the humanities); (2) application to specific topics in New Testament studies, such as linguistic integrity and the historical Jesus; and (3) integration with other methods.

23. Ibid., 140.

24. Ibid., 142. This is not to say that such a task is simple. Porter states, "Ultimately, we may need to say that what a text is about is expressed in highly complex relations between its various linguistic elements and at a high level of abstraction from its linguistic substance" (143).

25. Reed, *Discourse Analysis*.

26. Ibid., 403–6. It is also the title of the first part containing the introduction and methodology chapters.

27. Halliday and Matthiessen, *Introduction to Functional Grammar*.

28. Schenk, *Die Philipperbriefe*. Specifically, Reed charges that Schenk's multiple-source theory for Philippians is based on faulty linguistic reasoning.

between modern linguistics and historical criticism,[29] initially noting that many would be skeptical of such a connection,[30] but proceeding to argue for its ability to make significant contributions to the discussion about the methodology of source criticism.

For a relatively early example of LBI, Cotterell and Turner give some discussion of the kinds of "meaning" that LBI can be used to find. They differentiate authorial meaning, perceived meaning, and textual meaning,[31] and introduce the concepts of denotation and connotation.[32] They provide a two-stage definition of "hermeneutics," consisting of exegesis proper followed by "bringing to expression of the interpreter's understanding of the significance for his own world of the discourse meaning of the text."[33] Additionally, meaning is categorized as occurring at different levels of discourse, from the word to the whole discourse,[34] sense is distinguished from reference, and significance is said to depend on the continuities and discontinuities between the presuppositions of the speaker and the hearer.[35]

Significantly, while all of these sources rightly identified LBI as a valuable tool for determining discourse-level meaning and addressing the questions of traditional historical criticism, none of them considered the issue of the interpreter's role in processing the results, or his or her capacity to bias the analysis.[36]

Linguistics and Hermeneutics in Linguistics Proper and Elsewhere

It is now appropriate to turn to previous approaches to the question of the relationship between linguistics and hermeneutics. As a great deal of this work comes from the broader world of discourse analysis, the investigation below will start with an interchange that was published in a 2011 issue of

---

29. Reed, "Modern Linguistics," 36–62.

30. Ibid., 36.

31. Cotterell and Turner, *Linguistics and Biblical Interpretation*, 39–45. This is in the context of illustrating the difficulty of defining "meaning."

32. Ibid., 45–47.

33. Ibid., 72.

34. Ibid., 77–82.

35. Ibid., 94.

36. A caveat should be made that I am not accusing Porter of ignorance of philosophical hermeneutics, merely observing that the questions raised by philosophical hermeneutics have not been applied to the process(es) of LBI he advocates. See Porter and Robinson, *Hermeneutics*.

the journal *Discourse Studies*. The instigating article by Bell, along with the ensuing responses, provides a helpful sampling of different views on this issue and will be utilized to construct a taxonomy of ways that linguistics and hermeneutics can be positioned *vis-à-vis* each other.

Bell's article "Re-constructing Babel" is in many ways an ideal point of departure: it probes the question of what discourse analysis can really achieve, leverages Ricoeur to construct a model of interpretation that takes the reader's positioning and interests seriously, and even provides a sample reading of the story of Babel (Gen 11:1–9) to illustrate his points.[37] After suggesting that the title "Discourse Interpretation" is more accurate than "Discourse Analysis" (as most practitioners are in fact interested in the contents of their texts)[38] and providing his definition of hermeneutics as "the theory and practice of interpreting texts,"[39] he makes an observation that is crucial for the research gap under consideration in the present study: "A scan of textbooks, readers and other overview publications in discourse analysis over the past 30 years shows that hermeneutics is notably absent. It never figures in the contents of such works, and rarely in the indexes."[40]

Bell's concrete proposal is based on Ricoeur's "Hermeneutical Arc,"[41] Bell's adaption of which is the six-step "Interpretive Arc."[42] The first stage

---

37. Bell, "Re-constructing Babel," 519–68.

38. Ibid., 520. The main figures he considers to be representative of the Discourse Analysis field are the pioneer Zellig Harris (who was solely interested in structure) (Harris, "Discourse Analysis," 1–30) and the practitioners of Critical Discourse Analysis (Fairclough, *Language and Power*; van Dijk, *Society and Discourse*) (who had an overriding interest in issues of ideology).

39. Bell, "Re-constructing Babel," 524.

40. Ibid., 524. He substantiates this point with the following data: "For example, Van Dijk's useful early review of the origins of discourse analysis (1985) gives the fledgling field some pedigree in classical rhetoric, but makes no reference to hermeneutics. It is also undetectable in either edition of the excellent Jaworski and Coupland *Discourse Reader* (1999, 2006), or in Schiffrin et al.'s 2001 comprehensive *Handbook of Discourse Analysis*—not even among the chapters on 'Discourse across Disciplines,' or in Wodak and Chilton's strong collection (2005), which focuses on 'interdisciplinarity' in discourse. There are exceptions, but they are fleeting. The term appears in the glossary of Johnstone's introductory textbook (2008) but not obviously in the text. The high point of cross-disciplinary contact seems to be a half-page discussion of hermeneutics in Meyer's position paper (2001) in the Wodak and Meyer collection. Meyer characterizes CDA as having a 'mainly hermeneutic impetus' (2001: 16), which appears to be a recognition of its focus on the ultimate priority of meaning over form" (524).

41. See Ricoeur, *From Text to Action*, 130.

42. Bell, "Re-constructing Babel," 526.

is "Estrangement," which involves the recognition that the text, as a communicative act, has been detached from its author, original recipients, and original context; any subsequent reading necessarily means adapting to another context.[43] The second stage is "Pre-view," or the "state of knowledge or opinion in that moment just *before* we engage with a text,"[44] and the third stage is "Proto-understanding," or the initial, provisional impressions of the meaning of text prior to serious investigation.[45] Fourth is "Analysis," a step that Bell describes with both the theoretical concept of a dialectic between explanation and understanding (or in his words, "a circularity, between the guess and the procedures of validation")[46] and a demonstration of his hands-on exegesis of the Babel story.[47] The fifth stage is "Understanding," and it is here that the reader stands in front of the text, seeking the "gist" of the text, and seeking what the text intended to communicate. Significantly, for his example of the Babel story, this has the effect of unseating the traditional assumption that the scattering was a punishment for human pride, and instead locates the offence in humanity's refusal to spread throughout the earth.[48] The sixth and final stage is "Ownership," which takes as its starting point the principle that "Readers understand themselves and their situation differently through their encounter with a text,"[49] and involves the activity of "disowning through ideological critique."[50] In this light, the Babel account becomes a polemic against the centralizing and linguistically homogenizing efforts of empire.[51] Bell thus sees his model as combining the best insights of traditional Discourse Analysis and Critical Discourse Analysis, along with recognizing a meaningful place for the reader's perspective.

In the following sections, a typology of viewpoints on the relationship of linguistics and hermeneutics will be constructed. Each section will

---

43. Ibid., 527–29.
44. Ibid., 530–31.
45. Ibid., 531–33.
46. Ibid., 534.
47. Ibid., 533–42. Additionally, he notes that for Ricoeur, this stage was carried out with the twin opponents of absolute authorial intent and the objectivism of structuralism. His interpretive example includes the categories of sociocultural context, intertextual content, lexical analysis, word play and structure.
48. Ibid., 543–51.
49. Ibid., 552.
50. Ibid., 553.
51. Ibid., 554–58.

begin with a representative response to Bell's article,[52] followed by other works from that particular perspective. The three viewpoints are (1) the irrelevance of hermeneutics, (2) linguistics precedes hermeneutics, and (3) the interdependence of linguistics and hermeneutics.

The Irrelevance of Hermeneutics

Van Dijk, in his response to Bell, begins by noting that great progress has been made in the construction of mental models that accurately capture the process of receiving and comprehending communication.[53] This process goes far beyond the simple decoding of the lexicogrammar of a text to the reconstruction of intent and synthesis of general perspective.[54] For Van Dijk, the comprehensiveness and sophistication of recent cognitive research makes traditional philosophical hermeneutics simply unnecessary, and relevant only if they are adapted to fit these cognitive trends he champions.[55] Similarly, Wodak utilizes her response to detail the various means by which meaning, context, and significance can be carefully stratified and modelled, leading her to conclude that philosophical hermeneutics is simply unnecessary.[56]

Elsewhere, Rasmussen specifically rejects the trajectory of philosophical hermeneutics in favor of Luhmann's operative constructionism,[57] which is much more interested in methodology and describing the differences between the text and the interpreter in a controlled way, and meaning is revised as the "unity of the actual and the possible."[58] Finally, in the field of biblical studies, Kaiser briefly contrasts the traditional model of interpretation followed by application as suggested by Hirsch with the integrative

52. I have chosen to exclude the responses written by specialists in cognitive science.

53. Van Dijk, "Discourse Studies," 613.

54. Ibid., 614–17.

55. Ibid., 618. He states, "However, if hermeneutics claims to provide a theory and practice of actual discourse understanding by language users, it only has a future in contemporary Discourse Studies if it is based on the kinds of theoretical and empirical insights that have been developed during the last decades, for example, in the cognitive and social psychology of discourse processing, as well as in the sociology and anthropology of text and talk" (618).

56. Wodak, "Complex Texts," 623. She states, "I argue that much intuitive and non-transparent speculation in Hermeneutics might be transcended if more historical, cultural, linguistic and philological knowledges would be systematically and explicitly integrated into the analysis of text and discourse, in a retroductable manner" (623).

57. Luhmann, *Die Gesellschaft der Gesellschaft*.

58. Rasmussen, "Textual Interpretation," 7.

model of Gadamer and rejects the model of Gadamer as apparently being self-evidently wrong.[59]

Linguistics Precedes Hermeneutics

While none of the responses to Bell fit this category, Bell's essay itself could be said to be typical of this model. As articulated above, he essentially envisions a linear process of traditional analytical methods being performed, followed by reflection on contemporary significance. Similarly, Cotterell articulates a strict separation of original meaning and significance, with these being two methodologically distinct steps.[60] Louw addresses this question in the context of the dominance of the existential "New Hermeneutic," and begins by correctly noting that to ask the question of the meaning of a text necessitates transcending the mere words on the page.[61] He then notes that the presuppositions of the "New Hermeneutic" are highly fallacious when examined in light of sound linguistic theory (à la James Barr).[62] However, he notes that the laudable goal of the "New Hermeneutic" (i.e., language interpreting the reader and bringing him or her to a place of personal decision) can in fact be effectively carried out by modern linguistics, with linguistic analysis providing an objective summary of the large-scale structure and meaning of the text, thus clarifying the message and readying the interpreting for existential impact.[63]

---

59. Kaiser, "Inner Biblical Exegesis," 33–34. Kaiser further suggests studying innerbiblical exegesis as a model for how to perform application in a manner that is faithful to the original meaning of the text.

60. Cotterell, "Hermeneutics," 82. Interestingly, he cites and immediately rejects Ricoeur's suggestions that writing by nature is somewhat contextually autonomous. He is also very adamant that the interpreter should (and accordingly can) seek original meaning.

61. Louw, "Linguistics and Hermeneutics," 8.

62. Ibid., 9–11; Barr, *Semantics of Biblical Language*.

63. Louw, "Linguistics and Hermeneutics," 15–18. Some of Louw's phrasing is worth capturing here: "Modern linguistics is an indispensable means of directing and controlling one's analysis in order to make it effective in reaching out to our everyday existence.... [T]he method of modern linguistics .. starts from ... larger units like sentences—even pericopes! Moreover, these are incorporated in a structural analysis of the whole passage in which grammatical and historical data function as components of the total linguistic structure of which the semantic transformations serve as objective criteria in order to make the text communicate in such a way that it interprets its hearers.... Linguistics and hermeneutics join hands! ... [T]he linguistic structure thereof has become a language event ... the text shines on us, illuminating the sphere of our existence; the present is exposited with the help of the linguistic structure of the text, we

Two more sources can tentatively be included in this category. Teubert investigates the discipline of corpus linguistics in relation to diachronic concerns, such as the way in which a text necessarily is constructed in response to something previous, and will necessarily be understood in light of subsequent commentary.[64] His closing comments do not clarify the linear direction of his procedure or the exact place of the subject, but it is clear that he finds the concerns of philosophical hermeneutics relevant.[65] Finally, Rastier's model may be more accurately said to stratify linguistics and hermeneutics in a parallel configuration rather than a linear progression as in the sources above, but the overall tendency towards separation is similar.[66] Essential to his argument is the idea that text semiotics can bring philology and hermeneutics into dialogue by utilizing the categories of document, text, and work as the objects of investigation of philology, linguistics, and hermeneutics, respectively.

Two more important thinkers need to be included in this category. Thiselton deals with the issue of the relationship between hermeneutics and language by first highlighting the Antiochians, Luther, and the eighteenth-century biblical critics as being especially concerned with the importance of carefully studying language to understand the meaning of a passage.[67] However, he proceeds (using Sawyer's application of field semantics as his example)[68] to argue that this kind of linguistic work is only useful in creating distance between the text and the interpreter, and thus is only relevant for the first part of the hermeneutical endeavor,[69] a point he reinforces

---

are interpreted by a hermeneutics of language" (15–18).

64. Teubert, "*Parole*-linguistics," 57–88.

65. Ibid., 85. He states, "To facilitate such a comparison [between discourse-internal and discourse-external reality] is, as I see it, the prime task of *parole*-linguistics. This brand of linguistics may be less concerned with the regularities of co-occurrence or system-immanent oppositions than with the meaning of what has been and is being said in the discourse at large. This is a kind of linguistics founded on hermeneutics, a kind of linguistics that is interested more in the diachronic than in the synchronic dimension of the discourse" (85).

66. Rastier, "Text Semiotics," 99–122. As a whole, one of the starting problems of this essay is the challenge posed by digitization to the traditional practices of archiving and documentary evaluation. While introducing his highly specialized terminology is beyond the scope of the present study, it is noteworthy that he has an entire system for discussing the authorization and analysis of each of these three levels of written material.

67. Thiselton, *Two Horizons*, 115–17.

68. Sawyer, *Semantics in Biblical Research*.

69. Thiselton, *Two Horizons*, 117–20.

by an appeal to the authority of Ricoeur.[70] After positively endorsing the principles of synchronic study and clause-level as opposed to word-level meaning as found in Saussure and Barr,[71] he rejects the proposal that the resources of a particular language are determinate for one's thought-forms (as in the Sapir-Whorf hypothesis), and finally reiterates his contention that the role of linguistics is restricted to being an aid to exegesis proper (which occurs prior to hermeneutics) in the capacity of creating initial distance and enabling close textual observation.[72]

Finally, Van Hecke must be mentioned, if for no other reason than that the title of his monograph (*From Linguistics to Hermeneutics*) would seem to indicate that he shares the central concern of the present study.[73] He identifies two guiding questions: "the way in which the relation between the two disciplines has been understood by philosophical hermeneutics,"[74] and "which specific kind of linguistic analysis lends itself best to contributing to the hermeneutical process of interpretation."[75] In his investigation of the first question, he utilizes Ricoeur's distinction between "objective explication of the linguistic phenomena" and "comprehension of the intended meaning" as an interpretive grid for the history of philosophical hermeneutics.[76] Schleiermacher and Dilthey obviously valued the latter, though this understanding, paradoxically, is only reached through the device of the text.[77] Heidegger began with the question of "the mode of being of that being that exists only in understanding," while Gadamer emphasized the fusion of the horizons of the text and the reader; their combined influence led Ricoeur to inquire as to how one could maintain an "awareness of belonging" combined with a "refusal of distanciation," but nonetheless exercise a "critical instance."[78] The remainder of this section is spent in an exegesis of Ricoeur's understanding of texts as based on "distanciation" and

70. Ricoeur, *Conflict of Interpretations*, 62–78.
71. Thiselton, *Two Horizons*, 124–33; Saussure, *Course in General Linguistics*.
72. Thiselton, *Two Horizons*, 133–39.
73. Van Hecke, *From Linguistics to Hermeneutics*.
74. Ibid., 7.
75. Ibid., 8.
76. Ibid., 9.
77. Ibid., 9–11.
78. Ibid., 12–14. This is rephrased by Van Hecke as, "In other words: how is it possible to integrate an objective, linguistic analysis of the text in the hermeneutical process, which, ultimately, does not aim at an objective analysis but at an understanding which proposes a way of being?" (14).

"structure," followed by his dialectical movement between explanation and understanding.[79] After another section that describes a fusion of functional and cognitive linguistics (which need not concern the present study) he concludes his methodological discussion by noting that the linguistic investigation of Job 12–14 that is the concern of the rest of his monograph is merely a prolegomena to hermeneutics, and can only hope to provide the textual data from which hermeneutics would decide questions of meaning and significance.[80]

Interdependence of Linguistics and Hermeneutics

Other voices responding to Bell point out that if the claims about the positioning of the subject made by Heidegger and his ilk are correct, hermeneutics cannot merely be tacked on to the end of the traditional interpretive process. Working as a Ricoeur specialist, Pellauer argues that Bell's incorporation of hermeneutics has not gone nearly far enough.[81] Noting that any endeavor needs to have "an object of study, a method, and a goal or purpose,"[82] he states that Bell has only identified his method, and that his stated goal of understanding is both immensely ambiguous in light of the complexities of defining "understanding" (which could here mean anything from existential possibility to participation in tradition) and guilty of failing to take advantage of other work by Ricoeur on the subject (in particular, how he constructs the relationship between understanding and explanation). He further chastises Bell for neglecting a detailed description of the object, discourse, in that in Ricoeur's understanding the concept of discourse necessarily included the elements of genre and style; in any

---

79. Ibid., 14–21.

80. Ibid., 43. Specifically, he states, "In the following study, I propose an analysis of these linguistic processes as they are operative in the chapters 12 to 14 of the book of Job. My study does not, in the first place, seek to articulate an interpretation of the text that would be existentially meaningful for contemporary readers. Such an interpretation is strongly contextually determined; it, hence, takes the genius of someone or even of a community with a keen eye for the [sic] own context and a good insight into the meaning of texts to articulate those interpretations which are vital to the readers and to the text. My present purpose is more modest: to present a linguistic analysis that is relevant for this hermeneutical process" (43). After reading this humble admission, the title of the book seems misleading, as the hermeneutical exercise in the opening chapters was apparently all for naught.

81. Pellauer, "Some Comments," 583–87.

82. Ibid., 585.

case, changing one's understanding of discourse could radically alter their understanding of the hermeneutical task.[83]

Somewhat more provocatively, Pratt suggests the primary ingredient lacking in Bell is an exegesis of desire, or the articulation of what draws an interpreter to a text in the first place; in any case, this underlying (subconscious?) motivation will be far more personal than an interest in neutral understanding, and no method is immune to this kind of bias.[84] Furthermore, an interpreter always acts in a given political and communitarian context, one in which he or she is inevitably influenced by others.[85] To demonstrate this oversight and elasticity in Bell's reading, she suggests an alternate interpretation of the Tower of Babel account that is based on the experience of Amazonian peoples who deliberately keep the populations of their communities low in order to remain in balance with their limited plant and animal resources; this leads to a multitude of language groups in a relatively small area. She states:

> From the perspective of those who 'to live here must remain few in number', a deity who tells people to 'be fruitful and multiply and fill the earth' with people is a knave or a fool. Or perhaps an imperialist. From an indigenous, land-based perspective, empire is enacted not by the centripetal building of a city, but by centrifugal invasion and territorial expansion—the ambitious spreading Babel sets in motion.[86]

Regardless of the merits of this proposal as an exegesis of Gen 11:1–9, the fact remains that Pratt has demonstrated that Bell's method is not immune to having its conclusions reversed, and consequently must take the problem of the embeddedness of the subject more seriously.

Somewhat more translucently, Scott-Baumann suggests that Bell's proposal needs to be expanded by integrating more of Ricoeur's ethical concerns into the understanding side of the explanation/understanding dialectic,[87] as well as the imperative that an atmosphere of empathy must drive the entire process.[88] Elsewhere, Geeraerts has argued that cognitive

83. Ibid., 586–87.
84. Pratt, "Body," 590.
85. Ibid., 591.
86. Ibid.
87. Scott-Baumann, "Text as Action," 594.
88. Ibid., 595. She further leverages Ricoeur's thoughts on translation to note that interpretation depends on understanding the opposite of a word (596), and always

semantics, in its emphasis on diachronic, experiential, and psychological concerns, has significant connections to both pre- and post-structuralist semantics (as opposed to structuralist semantics). He additionally suggests that if one's personal history is significantly influential in how they process meaning, the obsession of linguists with objectivity may be misguided, and that linguists may need to take the questions of hermeneutics more seriously.[89]

The examination of the aims of LBI and different views on the relationship between linguistics and hermeneutics has demonstrated that although there has been relatively little investigation of this question, a considerable diversity of perspectives exists. A couple of preliminary comments may be made. Most understandings of orthodox Christian theology attest not only to a condition of "sin," resulting from the event of the fall, but also to intrinsic physical and mental limitations on humanity's capacity to perceive and make sense of the world around them. As a result, one would expect Christian practitioners of biblical studies to embrace, rather than reject, the study of the conditions and nature of interpretation.[90] The linear model of linguistics as preceding hermeneutics, while possessing a certain common-sense virtue, would also seem to involve a kind of hasty dismissal of the concerns of hermeneutics as well by excluding them entirely from the analytical process. However, the integration position is plagued by a certain ambiguity. The following section will investigate specific areas in which linguistics should heed hermeneutics.

PHILOSOPHICAL CONCERNS RELEVANT TO LBI

In this section, a prelude of sorts will first address the concerns of the ability to cross-dialogue the seemingly disparate worlds of abstract philosophy and concrete linguistic analysis. Following this, three major issues will be unpacked: Gadamer and the centrality of the guiding question, Heidegger's breakdown of the subject/object distinction, and Ricoeur's connection of subjectivity and meaning in Freud.

---

operates in a tension between order and disorder (ibid., 599).

89. Geeraerts, "Return of Hermeneutics," 257–82.

90. See Smith, *Fall of Interpretation*; Bartholomew, *Introducing Biblical Hermeneutics*, 326–29.

The Relevance of the Theoretical

An initial objection that must be addressed is the relevance of philosophical hermeneutics for concrete practice; phrased more colloquially, one might ask, "What difference does it make?" The perceived superiority of the "scientific" practices of linguistic investigation has led to at least one scholar's career being significantly marred by persecution from administrators and colleagues who believed his attempts to cross-pollinate the interests of linguistics and hermeneutics did not constitute meaningful academic work.[91] A preliminary response to this protestation would be to indicate that one is surely better off with an accurate idea of how understanding takes place, even if this does not lead to radically new results. As Gadamer states (in the context of examining Heidegger's ontological analysis of the fore-structure of understanding), "These consequences do not need to be such that a theory is applied to practice so that the latter is performed differently—i.e., in a way that is technically correct. They could also consist in correcting (and refining) the way in which constantly exercised understanding understands itself—a process that would benefit the art of understanding at most only indirectly."[92] Significantly, this statement is remarkably similar to a remark made by Porter in the context of the relatively slow adoption of linguistics in the field of biblical studies.[93]

This lack of immediate interpretive direction is illustrated in Westphal's contribution to a volume comparing different interpretive methodologies.[94] While the rest of the contributors include a sample application section, Westphal declines to do so, noting such an exercise would be outside the domain of hermeneutics proper.[95] However, in its place he offers

---

91. Anttila, "Return of Philology," 313–32. He relates that while giving an address while holding the Hermann Collitz Professorship at the LSA Linguistic Institute at Amherst in 1974, the audience had a very mixed reaction to his fusion of linguistics and hermeneutics (315). More seriously, he includes verbatim quotations of negative performance reports by his own chancellor while he taught at UCLA in the early 1990s; apparently his resistance to Chomskyan orthodoxy was inexcusable (325–28).

92. Gadamer, *Truth and Method*, 268.

93. Porter, "Linguistic Criticism," 199. Porter states, "There is a mixed response that is at the same time suspicious of new readings of texts on the basis of new methods and easily dismisses any method that does not put forward significant and new results that challenge the older ones. Traditional critics in this instance fail to realize that providing a surer foundation for a traditional exegetical position can still constitute a significant contribution" (199).

94. Westphal, "Philosophical/Theological View," 70–88.

95. See further discussion in Porter, "Biblical Hermeneutics," 33–34.

the observations that in any act of biblical interpretation plurality should be expected, the interpreter's guiding beliefs should be transparent, and both exegesis and application should be integrated.[96]

An instructive approach to this issue applied to the field of translation studies is provided by Chau.[97] After surveying the history of the field of translation studies and noting the predominance of an objective, scientific mindset that believes meaning can be accurately captured by the application of certain procedures, he suggests six guiding principles derived from hermeneutics.[98] In his concluding remarks, he notes the apparent lack of input hermeneutics would seem to have on the mechanics of how one performs translation. However, he qualifies this comment with some reflections on how insights garnered from hermeneutics can transform the attitude of the translator. Specifically, the translator should become humbler and less obsessed with the myth of a single perfect rendering of the source text.[99]

The Centrality of the Question

An important part of the substantial baggage brought into the interpretive event by the subject is the centrality of the instigating question: What inquiry is being brought before this text? Why is this text being engaged at all? This is not merely the choice of a research question and an arena

---

96. Westphal, "Philosophical/Theological View," 84. He also makes a suggestion more closely bound to the context of the edited volume (Porter and Stovell, eds., *Biblical Hermeneutics*) that philosophical hermeneutics would not be able to help decide how Matthew's Gospel utilized Hos 11:1.

97. Chau, "Hermeneutics and the Translator," 71–77.

98. Ibid., 73–76. These principles are: (1) "There is no truly 'objective' understanding"; (2) "'Prejudices' are unavoidable and can be constructive"; (3) "There is no final reading of any text"; (4) "The reader cannot but change the meaning of his [or her] text"; (5) "No translation can represent its source text fully"; and (6) "Understanding is not always explicable" (73–76).

99. Ibid., 76. Note some of the specific phrasing used in this section, as Chau summarizes his main points regarding this new awareness that hermeneutics will bring to a translator: "[he or she will be] fully aware of his [or her] existential limitation in his [or her] relation to the ST [source text], himself [or herself] being a finite being . . . he [or she] must 'lose himself [or herself]' in the communion before any valid interpretation comes about . . . he [or she] realizes the active creative role of the interpreter in shaping the meaning of a text, and therefore works harder to improve himself [or herself] as a partner . . . to participate in such 'self-forgetful communion'" (76).

in which to neutrally apply the results of a data set.[100] Rather, it is a set of concerns that functions to shape and guide every step of the interpretive process. As part of his discussion of the legitimate role of prejudices in making understanding possible, Gadamer states, "But the significance exists at the beginning of any such research as well as at the end: in choosing the theme to be investigated, awakening the desire to investigate, gaining a new problematic."[101] This awareness can assist in more carefully qualifying the type of objectivity that can be expected from LBI, and the ways it can be utilized.

At the outset of his specific discussion on the nature of the question, Gadamer notes that a question must necessarily have a "sense of direction," which orients one's perspective.[102] Furthermore, when one earnestly desires to learn (and not simply flaunt one's knowledge) this kind of questioning requires recognizing what one does not know. The posing of a question creates a "state of indeterminacy" that is nonetheless bound by certain presuppositions.[103] Knowledge is attained when one is able to concretely choose one answer and eliminate other possibilities as incorrect.[104] For Gadamer, this generative position of the question reveals the limitations of the concept of method, which is unable by itself to choose which questions to ask or cultivate the proper awareness of gaps in one's knowledge. This awareness is crucial, for questions can only arise when one possesses the requisite openness.[105] The process of dialogue allows meaning to be communicated between tradition and the present.[106]

If a text is understood as an answer to a question, this particular question possesses its own horizon, and investigating this necessitates going further afield than the contents of the text itself; this horizon "includes

---

100. Poynton, "Grammar, Language and the Social," 1–2. In her poststructuralist critique of Systemic Functional Linguistics, Poynton argues that linguistics needs to address the "questions of subject production through discursive positioning" (2).

101. Gadamer, *Truth and Method*, 283.

102. Ibid., 356.

103. Ibid., 357.

104. Ibid., 358–59. This point is not as banal as it may initially seem; Gadamer points to medieval dialectic as showing that weighing the merits of counterpoints is fundamental to knowledge itself

105. Ibid., 360.

106. Ibid., 361–62. Gadamer further appeals to the Platonic dialogues, letter writing, and Hegel's dialectic to ground the "primacy of dialogue."

other possible answers."[107] Thus, "the meaning of a sentence is relative to the question to which it is a reply, but that implies that its meaning necessarily exceeds what is said in it."[108] The meaning we seek is specifically text-based, not author-based due to the fact that the intentionality of the subject is often not determinative for historical occurrences, and that the written work will manifest its range of possible meanings in different settings.[109] This definition of meaning encompasses present significance as well, as the task of comprehending the question posed by the text necessarily involves dialogue between interpreter and text.[110] Significantly, there must be some overlap between the questions answered by the text and asked by the interpreter.[111] Understanding is only possible through the meanings disclosed through the questions one asks.[112] Only by denouncing the posture of a detached, objective position, can one be "open to the experience of history,"[113] and so experience the fusion of which Gadamer speaks.

---

107. Compare Poynton, "Grammar, Language and the Social," 9. Sympathetically addressing the limitations of Hallidayan field analysis, she states, "The analytic apparatus developed for delineating field is incapable of indicating the presence, much less accounting for the origins or effects, of competing discourses within texts. . . . In order to begin to delineate discourses, however, one needs to take account of what is *not*, what is absent within a particular discursive site, what the missing categories are with respect to which the categories present enter into oppositional relations" (9).

108. Gadamer, *Truth and Method*, 363.

109. Ibid., 365–66.

110. Ibid., 367. Here a dialectical relationship is established between the reconstruction of the question the text was answering and the question with which the text confronts the interpreter. Compare Poynton, "Grammar, Language and the Social," 14, who notes the need for a more sophisticated analysis of textual reception within SFL. She states, "The second aspect of the problem of the singularity of the text is the question of production/reception—specifically, the effective production orientation of systemic analysis . . . systemic analysis effectively focuses exclusively on textual production and has virtually nothing to say about reception . . . [systemics] produces singular readings . . . a concern for reception would soon put paid to naiveties about singular meanings. But a framework for analysis of text will not lead readily to a theorisation of reception, which of necessity involves understanding the positionality of readers, which in turn involves understanding how individuals are inserted into discourses in particular institutional sites" (367).

111. Gadamer, *Truth and Method*, 367. Here Gadamer invokes his term "fusion of horizons" and comments, "The text must be understood as an answer to a real question."

112. Ibid., 368. This excludes, then, questions that are irrelevant for the interpreter. He further contrasts the "question" with the concept of the "problem," which abstracts the issue and severs the relationship between it and the interpreter.

113. Ibid., 370.

What does this mean for LBI? It should be clear that the motivating question is present during every stage of the analysis process, that one is always caught in the dialogue among the questions they ask (from one's own context), the question the text answers, and the questions the text asks them. Most significant, however, is the definition of meaning that this implies: the meaning sought from the outset, and what inevitably obtains given the nature of the question-centric perceptual apparatus, is not only nuanced by the setting and prejudices of the interpreter, it necessarily exceeds the boundaries of the face value of the text itself. The implications of situating LBI within this more expansive definition of meaning should be clear. Not only can strict LBI only account for some of the original significance of the text, its operations and results should not be viewed as separate from the interests of the interpreter, and, indeed, are possible and desirable only because of those biases.

The Eclipse of the Sovereign Subject

As McLean observes, the phenomenology of Dilthey and Husserl led to the breakdown of the Enlightenment's distinction of subject and object, a distinction that most proponents of the historical-critical method likely find self-evident. McLean, however, states, "The so-called subject is never independent of the phenomena being perceived."[114] The gravity of the collapse of this distinction in the history of philosophy is emphasized by Bultmann. He begins by noting that what is thought to be "real" is generally thought to be relatable to a larger understanding of the totality of the world. He then states, "In both views [idealism and materialism], the picture of the world is conceived without reference to our own existence. We ourselves are observed as an object among other objects and are put in our proper place in the structure of this picture of the world which has been fabricated without reference to the question of our own existence."[115] However, he finds this common understanding to be grossly unsatisfying. Although it possesses the attractive quality of allowing humanity to escape the questions of its own existence, it places it falsely outside himself or herself.[116] In making this judgment, Bultmann is following Heidegger, who sought to investi-

---

114. McLean, *Biblical Interpretation*, 73. He continues, "Your consciousness of a thing is always a unity comprising the relation between yourself, as an observer, and the perceived thing, arising from your own phenomenological horizon" (73).
115. Bultmann, *Faith and Understanding*, 58.
116. Bultmann, *Faith and Understanding*, 59.

gate man's "being-in-the-world" at an ontological level prior to that of the subject-object distinction.[117]

At the outset of his explication of *Da-sein*, or the being which humans are,[118] Heidegger repeatedly makes it clear that the essence of *Da-sein* is bound up in its existence, but that this existence cannot be understood as objective presence, but rather "always-being-my-own-being," or possibility.[119] Presenting this being accurately is essential to understanding it. This existing, furthermore, is in constant relationship with "averageness," or "everyday indifference."[120] The "existential analytic" of *Da-sein*, then, comes before any psychological, biological, or anthropological explanation.[121] As the title of the second part of division one of *Being and Time* indicates, the fundamental constitution of *Da-sein* is "being-in-the-world."

The nature of this "being-in" is not spatial (or "next-to-each-other"), but means to "dwell" in a way that is "familiar."[122] This is essential to *Da-sein*; it does not exist apart from the world.[123] The statement that a person possesses an environment is accurate only to the extent that it is understood that this is due to the "being-in."[124] An important aspect of *Da-sein* is its "thrownness," which Heidegger defines as follows:

> We shall call this character of being of Da-sein which is veiled in its whence and whither, but in itself all the more openly disclosed, this "that it is," the *thrownness* of this being into its there; it is thrown in such a way that it is the there as being-in-the-world.

---

117. Thiselton, *Two Horizons*, 187–88. King, *Guide*, 67–68, notes that Heidegger's "ontological" interest is in clear contrast with the "Greek-Western" tradition that began with "things as mere substances," which led to endless questions of "cognition.... According to Heidegger, on the contrary, it is this 'subject-object relation' that demands a fundamental inquiry, so that its inner possibility can be brought to light. All problems of cognition lead back to the existential constitution of Da-sein as being-in-the-world from which they originally spring and on the basis of which alone they can be solved." See Heidegger, *Ontology*, 62–63.

118. Heidegger, *Being and Time*, 6.

119. Ibid., 39–40.

120. Ibid., 41.

121. Ibid., 42.

122. Ibid., 51.

123. Ibid., 53–54.

124. Ibid., 54. He states, "In its very possibility this 'having' has its foundation in the existential constitution of being-in" (54).

> The expression thrownness is meant to suggest the *facticity of its being delivered over*.[125]

Part of this "thrownness" is "entanglement," that *Da-sein* is "together with" the world.[126] Thrownness is also exposed by *Da-sein*'s constant "falling prey" to patterns of inauthentic being, such as idle talk [127] Such an ontological state comes before any concept of corruption.[128]

With this foundation laid, it is now possible to outline *Da-sein*'s activities of understanding and interpretation, and their implications for meaning. Heidegger defines understanding as the disclosedness of existing being-in-the-world in the for-sake-of-which. Because of the for-the-sake-of-which, understanding "is equiprimordially concerned with complete being-in-the-world."[129] Thus, understanding is not an action, but a state of existing. *Da-sein*'s fundamental nature of being-possible means that, "*Understanding is the existential being of the own most potentiality of being of Da-sein in such a way that this being discloses in itself what its very being is about.*"[130] Another important part of this understanding is that it fundamentally is a projecting of itself as potentials: "As projecting, understanding is the mode of being of Da-sein in which it *is* its possibilities as possibilities."[131]

Interpretation is based on understanding, as it is "the development of possibilities projected in understanding."[132] When something is interpreted, it has the configuration of something *as* something. Interpretation openly articulates the consequence of what is encountered within one's "totality of relevance."[133] This totality includes a conceptual framework

---

125. Ibid., 128.
126. Ibid., 164.
127. Ibid., 165, 167.
128. Ibid., 168. Heidegger states, "Falling prey is an ontological concept of motion. Ontically, we have not decided whether human being is 'drowned in sin,' in the *status corruptionis*, or whether he walks in the *status integritatis* or finds himself in an interim stage, the *status gratiae*. But faith and 'worldview,' when they state such and such a thing and when they speak about Da-sein as being-in-the-world, must come back to the existential structures set forth, provided that their statements at the same time claim to be *conceptually* comprehensible" (158).
129. Ibid., 134.
130. Ibid., 135. Italics in original.
131. Ibid., 136.
132. Ibid., 139.
133. Ibid., 140. The means by which *Da-sein* performs this interpretation is explicated

(fore-conception) with which to make sense of what is being interpreted. Heidegger's precise articulation of meaning is worth citing directly. It is, *"the upon which of the project in terms of which something becomes intelligible as something,"* and also the "formal, existential framework of the disclosedness belonging to understanding."[134] These observations lead one to draw the conclusion that interpretation is a circular process, as understanding is itself required for interpretation to take place. However, this circle is not to be viewed pejoratively as a detriment to understanding, but rather is to be defined as "the expression of the existential *fore-structure* of Da-sein itself."[135] Thus, through it, knowledge is truly possible as one continually revisits and revises their own fore-structure and experiences new significances.[136]

Reflection upon the above thoughts of Heidegger should result in a profound recalibration of the guiding concerns of LBI. The implications that one draws from one's analysis of a text should be viewed as illuminating the interpreter's own conceptual structure and existential possibilities, not just the text itself.[137] Reflection on the connections between the interpreter's own historical and temporal embeddedness and the text at hand should be encouraged rather than discouraged. The awareness that one's conceptual structures will be revealed through their choice of analytical methods and consequent results makes possible the better understanding of these structures, and accordingly interpretations that can be placed in dialogue with these structures.[138] This opens up the important question of why certain texts, and certain questions brought before them, are imbued with such significance. This significance affects all stages of the practice of LBI, and the results of LBI will be richer if they can be placed within this framework. As McLean states, "The point of interpretation is not to

---

in terms of the concepts of fore-having, fore-sight, and for-conception. For the purposes of the present study, only the last term will be considered.

134. Ibid., 142. Meaning thus properly belongs to *Da-sein*, not the things themselves.

135. Ibid., 143.

136. McLean, *Biblical Interpretation*, 117–18. Note this provocative statement from Heidegger, *Being and Time*, 143, regarding the "objectivity" of this approach: "Because in accordance with its existential meaning, understanding is the potentiality for being of Da-sein itself, the ontological presuppositions of historiographical knowledge transcend in principle the idea of rigor of the most exact sciences. Mathematics is not more exact than historiographical, but only narrower with regard to the scope of the existential foundations relevant to it."

137. Porter and Robinson, *Hermeneutics*, 69.

138. This perhaps could manifest itself in the analytical categories used to present the results of LBI.

progress toward greater objectivity but rather to catch a glimpse of the revelation of truth in one's own be(com)ing."[139]

Meaning and the Subject

A relatively underexplored consideration is the extent to which the nature of meaning is determined by one's understanding of the nature of the subject.[140] This is illustrated especially in the work of Ricoeur on the significance of the legacy of Freud. The point is not whether Freud, or Ricoeur's interpretation of Freud, presents an accurate portrayal of human nature. The point is that the chosen understanding of the subject matters, and there is no "neutral" or "self-evident" approach that is beyond suspicion. This point will emerge more clearly when Halliday is examined in this light

Ricoeur finds Heidegger's approach to be hasty in its immediate jump to the analysis, and instead opts to begin with language, guided by the principle that understanding symbols is understanding the self. Symbols are multivalent and allow humanity to express their relationship to their chosen ultimate concern.[141] He observes that every hermeneutic, from patristic allegory to modern psychoanalysis, has a higher plane of reference (or "semantic node") that exceeds the bare meaning of the text.[142] The rejection of the Cartesian autonomous consciousness raises the question of the connection between "signification and desire."[143] This desire can only be revealed through the act of interpretation itself. Ricoeur states, "It is behind itself that the *cogito* discovers, through the work of interpretation, something like an *archaeology of the subject*. Existence is glimpsed in this archaeology, but it remains entangled in the movement of deciphering to which it gives rise."[144] For Freud, dreams were illustrative of this concealment of desire, as

---

139. McLean, *Biblical Interpretation*, 118. See also Thiselton's thoughts on the implications of Heidegger for hermeneutics in *Two Horizons*, 187–97.

140. Thiselton, *Two Horizons*, 113–14.

141. Ricoeur, *Freud and Philosophy*, 7. He thus defines symbol as "the universal mediation of the mind between ourselves and the real" (10).

142. Ricoeur, *Conflict of Interpretations*, 11–12. He thus defines interpretation as "the work of thought which consists in deciphering the hidden meaning in the apparent meaning, in unfolding the levels of meaning implied in the literal meaning" (12).

143. Ibid., 20. Ricoeur also states, "Freud very clearly ignores and rejects any problematic of the primal or fundamental subject. We have repeatedly emphasized this flight from the question of the *I think, I am*" (*Freud and Philosophy*, 420).

144. Ibid., 21.

they raised the question of how desires could be put into speech.[145] For the subject, this is a movement of initial loss of recollection, followed by the utilization of linguistic signs to commandeer "effort to exist and desire to be."[146] All reflective thought thus carries this principle of double meaning, is "transcendental," and is based on "the conditions of the appropriation of our desire to be."[147]

Marx, Nietzsche, and Freud are significant for all rejecting the myth of consciousness in their own way.[148] For Freud, consciousness and the unconscious are essentially reversed, as the latter is not a negation of the former, but rather a zone of significant activity.[149] This has the further consequences of abandoning the traditional object as the mere accident of the direction of one's instinct and the relocation of the ego from "the subject of the Cogito . . . [to] the object of desire."[150] Their various views on the unconscious carry the implication that texts must be "deciphered" rather than taken at face value. The result of this "deciphering" is not only potentially more coherent than the base text; it possesses therapeutic value.[151] In this context, hermeneutics becomes "a demystification, a reduction of illusion."[152] The locus of meaning thus is transported away from an originating deliberate act of consciousness, to something that is much

---

145. Ricoeur, *Freud and Philosophy*, 5–6. He elsewhere states, "It may be that the possibility of moving from force to language, but also the impossibility of completely integrating force within language, lies in the positing or emergence of desire" (67). Dreams are illustrative of "regression," in which meaning is converted into force (91).

146. Ibid., 45–46.

147. Ibid., 48.

148. Ricoeur, *Conflict of Interpretations*, 148. He elsewhere states, "The reading of Freud is also the crisis of the philosophy of the subject" (161).

149. Ibid., 424.

150. Ibid., 425. Thus Freud also rejects the subject/object distinction in his own way.

151. Ibid., 150. Ricoeur states, "the method is justified by the fact that the discovered meaning not only satisfies the understanding through an intelligibility greater than the disorder of apparent consciousness but that it *liberates* the dreamer or the patient when he comes to recognize it or make it his own" (150). Ricoeur also notes that Marx, Freud, and Nietzsche essentially created "a mediate *science* of meaning, irreducible to the immediate *consciousness* of meaning" (*Freud and Philosophy*, 34). At the same time, this apparently damaged consciousness is still capable of mapping its own journey in the process of interpretation (34–35).

152. Ricoeur, *Freud and Philosophy*, 27. This is Ricoeur's summary of Freud. In the larger project of this book, Ricoeur adds to this a dialectical movement that is more constructive (59–64), but it is not relevant to the concerns of the present study.

less deliberate; acknowledging this is necessary for true understanding.[153] Further expanding on this process of interpretation, Ricoeur states, "Force relations are enunciated and dissimulated in meaning relations at the same time that meaning relations express and represent force relations."[154] This connection between force and meaning cannot be accounted for by a mechanical process, as these forces are image-based and are not easily reduced to a common language.[155] Some post-structuralist thinkers have explored further variations and implications of these concepts.[156]

With this foundation in place, it is possible to survey Halliday's understanding of the subject and observe its implications for textual meaning. He places a significant amount of emphasis on the role played by social environment, and the fact that the main determining factor in that environment that shapes humans is language.[157] Again, within the larger group of people that constitutes society, it is interchange with others through language that molds people. It is this embeddedness in society that Halliday sees as constituting the subject. He states, "we explain the nature of the individual as a derivation from and extension of his [or her] participation in the group. . . . Being a member of society means occupying a social role; and it is again by means of language that a 'person' becomes potentially the occupant of a social role."[158] Personality, as a larger category, emerges from a combination of different social roles.[159] This can be more clearly understood by being contrasted with views of language that instead emphasize individual psychology or begin with the individual.[160] As Halliday was appreciative of the language-heavy sociology of Bernstein, he is critical of viewpoints that

153. Ibid., 54–55. He states, "Can the dispossession of consciousness to the profit of another home of meaning be understood as an act of reflection, as the first gesture of reappropriation?" (55).

154. Ricoeur, *Conflict of Interpretations*, 167.

155. Ibid., 168–69. Ricoeur specifically isolates the linguistics of Saussure and Hjelmslev as being unhelpful for the interpretation of dreams.

156. McLean, "Exteriority of Biblical Meaning," 93–122. McLean helpfully summarizes how Deleuze and Guattari transformed Ricoeur's interpretation of Freud ("interiority of meaning") into an "exteriority of meaning" where texts only have meaning when brought into relation with other traditions, a concept they fruitfully applied to the literature of Kafka. See Deleuze and Guattari, *Anti-Oedipus*; Deleuze and Guattari, *Thousand Plateaus*; Deleuze and Guattari, *Kafka*.

157. Halliday, *Language as Social Semiotic*, 8–9.

158. Ibid., 14.

159. Ibid., 15.

160. Martin, *Interviews with M. A. K. Halliday*, 36.

place linguistics in a disciplinary isolation or that advocate the "autonomy of the subject."[161]

Unsurprisingly, this same emphasis on social roles assumed and projected by the subject has shown up in biblical scholarship utilizing the SFL paradigm. For example, one of the most significant results emerging from Toffelmire's analysis of Joel is the development of the power of the locusts, as they progress from being active and dominant to being increasingly acted upon.[162] Similarly, Martín-Asensio's study of Acts revealed that God was the most dominant character throughout.[163]

Just as Ricoeur demonstrated that Freud's understanding of the subject was determinative for the nature of interpretation, Halliday's understanding of the subject likewise has led to a mode of analysis that heavily emphasizes the discovery of social power. While this is not the place to discuss either understanding of the subject as such, it simply needs to be noted that these viewpoints are neither self-evident nor neutral; they are a deliberate foundational viewpoint that will be determinative for the focus and results of the analysis.

CONCLUSION

This study has made three constructive points. After an apologetic for the relevance of the theoretical in the hands-on discipline that is biblical studies, Gadamer was leveraged to argue that one's motivating question is so determinative for the nature of meaning that any "meaning" obtained necessarily exceeds the boundaries of the lexicogrammatical content of the text itself and is nuanced by the interpreter's own horizons. Second, Heidegger's ontology of being was resourced to make the point that any act of interpretation inevitably is a revealing of the interpreter's own existential possibilities. Finally, Ricoeur's interpretation of Freud demonstrated that

---

161. Ibid., 124. For further comparison of Halliday and Bernstein, see Hasan, "Semiotic Mediation," 130–56. Hasan further develops this concept of "semiotic mediation" in dialogue with Vygotsky throughout *Language, Society and Consciousness*. For more on Bernstein's understanding of how subjects are formed as the result of the ideology of social class being transmitted through language, see Bernstein, *Class, Codes and Control*, 4:13–62. He elsewhere displays a keen interest in the process of socialization, and how use of language as connected to social class is strongly determinative of educational success or failure in children. See Bernstein, *Class, Codes and Control*, 2:253–342; Bernstein, *Class, Codes and Control*, volume 1.

162. Toffelmire, "Orienting the Event," 303.

163. Martín-Asensio, *Transitivity-Based Foregrounding*, 171.

one's understanding of the nature of the subject is determinative for the nature of meaning one will discover in a text. These observations are not meant to be wholesale endorsements of every aspect of the thought of these thinkers, but rather to make the point that even the apparently objective and scientific process of analysis of modern functional linguistics is still not immune from the effects of one's underlying philosophical beliefs, specifically regarding the subject's constitution and relation to the world. These factors are philosophical decisions and must be decided within that arena. Linguistic biblical interpretation would greatly benefit from more attention to these factors, as they would play a significant role in clarifying what can be expected from the analysis of LBI, in terms of both extent and nature.

BIBLIOGRAPHY

Anttila, Raimo. "The Return of Philology to Linguistics." In *Thirty Years of Linguistic Evolution: Studies in Honour of Rene Dirven on the Occasion of His Sixtieth Birthday*, edited by Martin Putz, 313–32. Amsterdam: John Benjamins, 1992.

Barr, James. *The Semantics of Biblical Language*. Oxford: Oxford University Press, 1961.

Bartholomew, Craig G. *Introducing Biblical Hermeneutics: A Comprehensive Framework for Hearing God in Scripture*. Grand Rapids: Baker Academic, 2015.

Bell, Allan. "Re-constructing Babel: Discourse Analysis, Hermeneutics and the Interpretive Arc." *Discourse Studies* 13 (2011) 519–68.

Bernstein, Basil. *Class, Codes and Control*. Vol. 1, *Theoretical Studies Toward a Sociology of Language*. London: Routledge and Kegan Paul, 1971.

———. *Class, Codes and Control*. Vol. 2, *Applied Studies Towards a Sociology of Language*. London: Routledge and Kegan Paul, 1973.

———. *Class, Codes and Control*. Vol. 4, *The Structuring of Pedagogic Discourse*. London: Routledge, 1990.

Bultmann, Rudolf Karl. *Existence and Faith: Shorter Writings of Rudolf Bultmann*. Translated by Schubert M. Ogden. Living Age Books. New York: Meridian, 1968.

———. *Faith and Understanding*. Edited by Robert W. Funk. Translated by Louise Pettibone Smith. New York: Harper and Row, 1969.

Chau, Simon S. C. "Hermeneutics and the Translator: The Ontological Dimension of Translating." *Multilingua* 3 (1984) 71–77.

Cotterell, Peter. "Hermeneutics: Some Linguistic Considerations." *Evangel* 13 (1995) 78–83.

Cotterell, Peter, and Max Turner. *Linguistics and Biblical Interpretation*. Downers Grove, IL: InterVarsity, 1989.

Deleuze, Gilles, and Felix Guattari. *A Thousand Plateaus: Capitalism and Schizophrenia*. Translated by Brian Massumi. Minneapolis: University of Minnesota Press, 1987.

———. *Anti-Oedipus: Capitalism and Schizophrenia*. Translated by Robert Hurley et al. Minneapolis: University of Minnesota Press, 1983.

———. *Kafka: Toward a Minor Literature*. Translated by Dana Polan. Minneapolis: University of Minnesota Press, 1986.

Fairclough, Norman. *Language and Power*. London: Longman, 1989.

Gadamer, Hans-Georg. *Truth and Method*. Translated by Joel Weinsheimer and Donald G. Marshall. 2nd ed. London: Continuum, 2006.

Geeraerts, Dirk. "The Return of Hermeneutics to Lexical Semantics." In *Thirty Years of Linguistic Evolution: Studies in Honour of Rene Dirven on the Occasion of His Sixtieth Birthday*, edited by Martin Putz, 257–82. Amsterdam: John Benjamins, 1992.

Halliday, M. A. K. *Language as Social Semiotic: The Social Interpretation of Language and Meaning*. Baltimore: University Park Press, 1978.

———. *Halliday's Introduction to Functional Grammar*. Revised by Christian M. I. M. Matthiessen. 4th ed. London: Routledge, 2014.

Harris, Zellig S. "Discourse Analysis." *Language* 28 (1952) 1–30.

Hasan, Ruqaiya. *The Collected Works of Ruqaiya Hasan*. Vol. 1, *Language, Society and Consciousness*. Edited by Jonathan J. Webster. London: Equinox, 2005.

———. "Semiotic Mediation and Three Exotropic Theories: Vygotsky, Halliday and Bernstein." In *The Collected Works of Ruqaiya Hasan*. Vol. 1, *Language, Society and Consciousness*, edited by Jonathan J. Webster, 130–56. London: Equinox, 2005.

Hegel, G. W. F. *Phenomenology of Spirit*. Translated by A. V. Miller. Oxford: Oxford University Press, 1977.

Heidegger, Martin. *Being and Time*. Translated by John Stambaugh. Albany, NY: State University of New York Press, 1996.

———. *Ontology—The Hermeneutics of Facticity*. Translated by John Van Buren. Bloomington, IN: Indiana University Press, 1999.

Kaiser, Walter C. "Inner Biblical Exegesis as a Model for Bridging the 'Then' and 'Now' Gap: Hos 12:1–6." *JETS* 28 (1985) 33–46.

King, Magda. *A Guide to Heidegger's Being and Time*. Albany, NY: State University of New York Press, 2001.

Louw, J. P. "Linguistics and Hermeneutics." *Neot* 4 (1970) 8–18.

Luhmann, Niklas. *Die Gesellschaft der Gesellschaft*. Frankfurt am Main: Suhrkamp, 1997.

Marshall, Donald G. "Philosophical Hermeneutics." In *Dictionary of Biblical Criticism and Interpretation*, edited by Stanley E. Porter, 275–77. New York: Routledge, 2007.

Martin, J. R., ed. *Interviews with M. A. K. Halliday: Language Turned Back on Himself*. London: Bloomsbury, 2013.

Martín-Asensio, Gustavo. *Transitivity-Based Foregrounding in the Acts of the Apostles: A Functional-Grammatical Approach to the Lukan Perspective*. JSNTSup 202. SNTG 8. Sheffield: Sheffield Academic, 2000.

McLean, Bradley H. *Biblical Interpretation and Philosophical Hermeneutics*. Cambridge: Cambridge University Press, 2012.

———. "The Exteriority of Biblical Meaning and the Plentitude of Desire: An Exploration of Deleuze's Non-Metaphysical Hermeneutics of Kafka." *Neot* 43 (2009) 93–122.

Palmer, Richard E. *Hermeneutics: Interpretation Theory in Schleiermacher, Dilthey, Heidegger, and Gadamer*. Evanston, IL: Northwestern University Press, 1969.

Pellauer, David. "Some Comments on Allan Bell's Proposed Turn to Hermeneutics." *Discourse Studies* 13 (2011) 583–87.

Porter, Stanley E. "Biblical Hermeneutics and Theological Responsibility." In *The Future of Biblical Interpretation: Responsible Plurality in Biblical Hermeneutics*, edited by Stanley E. Porter and Matthew R. Malcolm, 29–50. Downers Grove, IL: IVP Academic, 2013.

———. "Greek Language and Linguistics." In *Studies in the Greek New Testament: Theory and Practice*, 7–20. New York: Peter Lang, 2006.

———. *Linguistic Analysis of the Greek New Testament: Studies in Tools, Methods, and Practice*. Grand Rapids: Baker Academic, 2015.

———. "Linguistic Criticism." In *Dictionary of Biblical Criticism and Interpretation*, edited by Stanley E. Porter, 199–202. New York: Routledge, 2007.

Porter, Stanley E., and Andrew W. Pitts. "New Testament Greek Language and Linguistics in Recent Research." *CurBR* 6 (2008) 214–55.

Porter, Stanley E., and Jason C. Robinson. *Hermeneutics: An Introduction to Interpretive Theory*. Grand Rapids: Eerdmans, 2011.

Porter, Stanley E., and Beth M. Stovell, eds. *Biblical Hermeneutics: Five Views*. Downers Grove, IL: InterVarsity, 2012.

Poynton, Cate. "Grammar, Language and the Social: Poststructuralism and Systemic-Functional Linguistics." *Social Semiotics* 3 (1993) 1–21.

Pratt, Mary Louis. "The Body in the Corpus." *Discourse Studies* 13 (2011) 583–92.

Rasmussen, Jens. "Textual Interpretation and Complexity—Radical Hermeneutics." Paper presented at the American Educational Research Conference, New Orleans, LA, April 3, 2002.

Rastier, François. "Text Semiotics: Between Philology and Hermeneutics—From the Document to the Work." *Semiotica* 192 (2012) 99–122.

Reed, Jeffrey T. *A Discourse Analysis of Philippians: Method and Rhetoric in the Debate Over Literary Integrity*. LNTS 136. Sheffield: Sheffield Academic, 1997.

———. "Modern Linguistics and Historical Criticism: Using the Former for Doing the Latter." In *Linguistics and the New Testament: Critical Junctures*, edited by Stanley E. Porter and D. A. Carson, 36–62. JSNTSup 168. SNTG 5. Sheffield: Sheffield Academic, 1999.

Ricoeur, Paul. *Freud and Philosophy*. New Haven, CT: Yale University Press, 1970.

———. *From Text to Action: Essays in Hermeneutics, II*. Translated by K. Blamey and J. B. Thompson. Evanston, IL: Northwestern University Press, 1991.

———. *The Conflict of Interpretations: Essays in Hermeneutics*. Evanston, IL: Northwestern University Press, 1974.

Saussure, Ferdinand de. *Course in General Linguistics*. Translated by Wade Baskin. Edited by Charles Bally et al. London: Fontana, 1959.

Sawyer, John F. A. *Semantics in Biblical Research: New Methods of Defining Hebrew Words for Salvation*. SBT 2.24. London: SCM, 1972.

Schenk, Wolfgang. *Die Philipperbriefe des Paulus: Kommentar*. Stuttgart: Kohlhammer, 1984.

Schleiermacher, Freidrich. *Hermeneutics and Criticism and Other Writings*. Translated by Andrew Bowie. Cambridge: Cambridge University Press, 1998.

Scott-Baumann, Alison. "Text as Action, Action as Text? Ricoeur, λογος and the Affirmative Search for Meaning in the 'Universe of Discourse.'" *Discourse Studies* 13 (2011) 593–600.

Smith, James K. A. *The Fall of Interpretation: Philosophical Foundations for a Creational Hermeneutic*. 2nd ed. Grand Rapids: Baker, 2012

Teubert, Wolfgang. "*Parole*-Linguistics and the Diachronic Dimension of the Discourse." In *Text, Discourse and Corpora: Theory and Analysis*, edited by Michael Hoey et al., 57–88. London: Continuum, 2007.

Thiselton, Anthony C. *The Two Horizons: New Testament Hermeneutics and Philosophical Description with Special Reference to Heidegger, Bultmann, Gadamer, and Wittgenstein*. Grand Rapids: Eerdmans, 1980.

Toffelmire, Colin M. "Orienting the Event: Register and the Day of YHWH in the Prophetic Book of Joel." PhD diss., McMaster Divinity College, 2014.

van Dijk, Teun A. "Discourse Studies and Hermeneutics." *Discourse Studies* 13 (2011) 609–21.

———. *Society and Discourse: How Social Contexts Influence Text and Talk*. Cambridge: Cambridge University Press, 2009.

Van Hecke, Pierre. *From Linguistics to Hermeneutics: A Functional and Cognitive Approach to Job 12–14*. SSN 55. Leiden: Brill, 2011.

Westphal, Merold. "The Philosophical/Theological View." In *Biblical Hermeneutics: Five Views*, edited by Stanley E. Porter and Beth M. Stovell, 70–88. Downers Grove, IL: InterVarsity, 2012.

Wodak, Ruth. "Complex Texts: Analysing, Understanding, Explaining and Interpreting Meanings." *Discourse Studies* 13 (2011) 623–33.

Part 2

Translation and Exegesis

6

Key Terms, the Lexicon, and How Languages Accommodate Translation

Scott Berthiaume

INTRODUCTION

TRANSLATION ATTEMPTS TO INTERPRET signs and meaning from one language to another while drawing on the rich lexical and grammatical inventories of each language and transferring a sense of the original language to the target language. At least that is the ideal, but the fog quickly sets in once the act of translation begins. The translator soon realizes that the language a text is being translated into consists of vocabulary and grammar that are changing, ever so slowly, according to the interests and needs of its speakers. Some linguistic forms such as words or phrases that recur and gain traction in the discourse become established lexical forms in the language. Other forms enter the language for a limited time or among a limited number of speakers, their usefulness to the wider language community being dubious at best. The translator has to reckon with the status of these forms in the target language and make a judgment as to how well known they are among its speakers.

In this paper, I investigate the notion of key terms in translation, which are topical foci that a speech community will use in discussion of diverse but important cultural themes or messages. This research began as personal observations while working on a Bible translation in the Northern Pame language, an Otomanguean language located in the eastern part of the state of San Luis Potosí, Mexico. The translators and I maintained a list of Northern Pame renderings of biblical key terms for important concepts such as "Holy Spirit" and "church." Over time I began to notice that some terms never gained traction beyond the five or so translators, while others were used by a wider population of speakers. The question I came to formulate was, "why do some terms incorporate into the wider use of a language, while others barely leave the text?"

My research in this paper investigates the notion of key terms by reviewing what has been said on this topic by biblical scholars and Bible translators and then by translation researchers in general. Considering the previous works of others on key terms, I will be able to frame my observations and subsequently apply them to a study of key terms in Northern Pame. The conclusions drawn from both the literature and my data sample suggest that key term incorporation into wider language use, among other things, is limited and somewhat resistant to modification.

WHAT ARE KEY TERMS?

Key terms have been used in the Bible translation enterprise for decades, but their general usage in the wider context of language studies is also well established in both concept and practice. For example, in a paper about translation theory, Anthony Pym mentions a failed attempt to create a key term when he recalls how one scholar tried to describe a translator's knowledge by coining the term *translatorial competence*.[1] The phrase included both the Chomskyan notion of tacit linguistic knowledge and a novel inflection of the word *translation*, resulting in what is, admittedly, a very usable phrase. However, the author eventually had to abandon his key term in favor of the more generic option, *expertise*, a term that had already filled the functional gap many years earlier. Though much less precise, it had been incorporated into the lexicon of the wider language and was the default choice for speakers in spite of its lack of semantic precision.

In Bible translation, it is common practice for translators to keep a database of key terms for concepts of a particular theological importance, and their importance cannot be overstated.[2] Common biblical key terms such as *disciple, kingdom of God, heaven, born again, beloved,* and *God-breathed* all found their way into an English translation through some sort of deliberate or accidental process, and have become the topics of discussion for all who reflect on their meanings. From a practical standpoint, a list of key terms can be a resource for translators as it serves to constrain the text to render-

---

1. Pym, "Redefining Translation Competence," 484.
2. See Barnwell et al., *Key Biblical Terms*.

ings previously decided. In a language where *kingdom of God* is a new idea, the translators decide on a form and make a record of it so that it can be applied to any future occurrences. Further, a key term list is often used by a reviewer (e.g., consultant) to check for translation errors and equivalence consistency. The counterpart of a key term list is a back translation, or a second translation from the target language to the language of wider communication, e.g., Greek to Navajo is translation, while Navajo to English is back translation.[3] Since the consultant rarely is able to speak the target language, a back translation serves as their primary interface to the translated text. With both a key term list and a back translation readily available, it is a straightforward process to check a translation for consistency.

Key Terms in Bible Translation

The vast majority of discussion about key terms in Bible translation revolves around the cultural and semantic baggage a particular term adds to or subtracts from the meaning in the target text as well as the term's semantic equivalence to the source text. One interesting example comes from Tippett who reports on the translation history of the Fijian Bible during the nineteenth century.[4] The first Fijian Christians came out of cannibalism, and as early missionaries contemplated translating the Scriptures into their language, they struggled with using Fijian vocabulary and its cannibalistic senses for biblical concepts. Tippett asks, "Can the gospel message of the Christian prayer either be meaningfully transmitted or relevant to the cultural felt needs in that context of situation when every word has come out of the paganism of the Contact period"?[5] For example, take the Fijian concept of *forgiveness*, which in its biblical sense had not been a part of Fijian culture, but, rather, their term more closely resembled the notion of *appeasement*. Tippett explains that the *appeasement* connoted the idea of a victorious chief preparing to deal with a conquered enemy while the enemy was begging for mercy. In order for the chief to *forgive* his opponent, some sort of sacrifice was required to satisfy the chief such as a plot of earth, his enemy's war club, and even his enemy's daughter's hand in marriage.[6] Although Fijian Christians and expatriate missionaries alike remained in disagreement for nearly a century on the acceptability of the term in the Bible,

---

3. Shuttleworth and Cowie, *Dictionary of Translation*, 15.
4. Tippett, "Ethnolinguistics and Bible Translation."
5. Ibid., 27.
6. Ibid., 22.

it was retained in Fijian translation and over time assumed the Christian meaning of *forgiveness* in concert with a maturing Fijian church and faith.

Another example comes from the Bible translation movement in India in the eighteenth and nineteenth centuries, during which time there were struggles about doctrinal beliefs that revolved around key terms. Hephzibah Israel describes the early years of the Bible in India as a time when there was an implicit message of "true" and "false" scriptures; because it was translatable, the Bible was sacred while the vernacular and untranslated Hindi sacred texts needed to be dispensed with as untrue and unreliable.[7] Israel states, "The question of how religious or technical terms ought to be translated from one language into another was a source of much controversy . . . the general thought among missionaries was that 'Christian thoughts cannot buy ready-made clothes in Hindi stores.'"[8] While some missionaries recommended using Hindi terms, they cautioned that that the precise meanings needed to be known.[9]

As translations became more abundant in local Indian languages, denominational lines began to be drawn over doctrinal issues. The United Bible Society responded by proposing a new Standard Version of the Bible in order to establish a base text for future translations and a new point of reference for the church. The Standard Version had neither exegetical notes nor interpretive commentary and was based on Sanskrit, the then assumed protolanguage for all Indian language varieties. It was from this base text that key terms were established, but even after this effort, which was intended to unite disparate factions of Christians, the situation became fraught with yet more disagreement. For one, speakers of Tamil correctly insisted that Sanskrit was not genetically related to southern Indian languages making the rendering of key terms in those languages an open question.[10] Also, some of the clerical leadership insisted that a Standard Version should not only unite Indian churches together, but as much as possible, it should use key terms that are part of the larger international Christian community. Israel mentions an Indian clergyman named Nehemiah Goreh who opined that Indians wanted to be connected with worldwide Protestantism. He preferred to use the term *Yesu Krist* a calque from the English *Jesus Christ*, as more desirable than the Hindi *yeshu* precisely because the

---

7. See Israel, "Translating the Bible," 174–90.
8. Ibid., 177.
9. Ibid.
10. Israel, "Translating the Bible," 183.

former allowed the Indian Christians to be the same, not different from the rest.[11]

Theological discussions around key terms are as much a present day affair as a past one. Kroneman gives an account of using key terms among the Uma people of Indonesia in the wider discussion of contextualization.[12] He insists that Scripture does not automatically change lives, but rather the Spirit does the work using a translation that is perceived as relevant, which necessitates an effort to combine missiology with contextualization. To Kroneman, forming discussion with key terms as the focal point creates a "dialogue between text and context."[13] He maintains that every person sees partial truth through their lenses of culture and worldview, but conversely, contextualization requires people to build a common understanding so that the truth of the individual will be climaxed by what he calls "supra cultural truth," which he defines as an eschatological category of "the end when all restoration occurs."[14] Key terms are a "window of opportunity" and a "venue for dialogue" where translators should be encouraged to study other cultural worldviews, evaluate values, needs, and problems, participate in worldview seminars with locals and outsiders, and create training materials such as simplified dictionaries, thematic Bible studies, short confessions, and sermons—all of which must incorporate key terms.[15]

Studies in Key Terms Outside of Bible Translation

Once a person or a committee forms a consensus about a key term and its usage, the term itself begins to be acquired by other speakers from within the target language. Under what circumstances and for what end the terms are incorporated into the lexicon are not questions we can easily answer here, but it does seem clear that some terms get more traction in wider language use than others.

Outside of Bible translation, there has also been some discussion about key terms. For example, Relevance theorists Wilson and Sperber

11. Ibid., 185.
12. Kroneman, "About Sin," 1.
13. Ibid., 12. It is important to mention that Kroneman makes a point to clarify that spiritual change is ultimately the work of the Holy Spirit, but that this can also be an excuse used by some translators to not contextualize a translation, thus making it highly uninterpretable.
14. Ibid., 14.
15. Ibid., 22.

make mention of this idea in their article, "Mapping between the Mental and the Public Lexicon," concerning the concept of *word stabilization*.[16] They maintain that word stabilization is never a straightforward process, but rather one that is relatively rare and slow, which involves coordination among many individuals over time in social and historical affairs. The authors estimate that less than a dozen new words would stabilize in a year in a given speech community that is more or less homogenous, and this includes homonyms of older words and excludes proper names. This is compared to the development of mental concepts, which can take root in an individual's mind more quickly and without a word necessarily attached to it.[17]

An interesting study by Skaffari entails the analysis of an allegorical text (c. 1200), which exemplifies a common phenomenon of that period—that of code switching between Latin and Middle English.[18] Latin, which was the language of the church, had already contributed a high amount of ecclesiastical vocabulary to Old English centuries earlier.[19] After the Norman conquest of 1066 and during what is known as the "long twelfth century," English went through a major shift due to the influence of the French among the governing aristocratic classes, while Old English and its rich inflectional system became fossilized resulting in the beginnings of Middle English.

At one time, Old English was one of many local European vernaculars spoken by local populations in what was largely an oral context, although Old English had made considerable advances in written language as well. There was a large body of literature, both verse and prose, that came out of the Anglo Saxon period right up to the eleventh century. After the conquest

---

16. Wilson and Sperber, *Meaning and Relevance*.

17. Ibid., 44–45.

18. Skaffari, "Code-Switching," 203–26.

19. Baugh, *History of the English Language*, 98. Baugh describes the entrance of Latin into Old English as coming in two waves over a four-hundred-year period (597–1000). The first wave would have come through the missionaries of the seventh century with vocabulary associated with church and monastery buildings. The second wave shows two time periods of vocabulary bursts. The first occurred before the period of Alfred the Great (871–899) and is well attested in the literature during his reign. Another burst of Latin vocabulary came during the Benedictine reform of the tenth and eleventh centuries beginning just 50 or so years after Alfred's ambitious literacy campaign ended in failure. Three great religious leaders with support by King Edgar led a monastic reform that culminated in the establishment of schools and invigorated the monasteries so that they were once again centers of literary activity.

of 1066, writers of English were much less ubiquitous, and French was the preferred language of government, while Latin was entrenched for writing and religious purposes.[20]

It is in this transitional linguistic context that the text "Vice and Virtues" was written. The manuscript is an allegorical dialogue between two participants, Soul and Reason, who are giving religious instruction about Christian virtues. The text is predominately in Middle English, while the key religious terms are in Latin, occurring in various forms such as a word, a phrase, or a sentence.[21] There are 315 instances of switches into Latin key terms. One example comes from the voice of Soul.

> Þurh ðessere senne ic unʒesali saule fel in to an oðer senne. ðe is icleped *propria voluntas*. þat is «auʒen wille." (*f. 5r*)
>
> Through this sin I, unhappy soul, fell into another sin, which is called *propria voluntas*, that is, self–will.

Embedded in the English is the Latin phrase *propria voluntas*, which the author then reiterates, or *supports*, in the vernacular form þat is auʒen wille, "that is, self–will." The author chooses to not simply use a vernacular translation of the key term, but to use the obviously less understandable term in Latin. Skaffari explains this phenomenon of *support* as a way "to authorize the teaching imparted by the author, by not changing the terms to English, but explaining them."[22] Skaffari further remarks, "Support facilitates understanding in case the reader or audience does not know the embedded language Latin well enough."[23] That is, the author of "Vice and Virtues" is as much cognizant of the potential acceptance or rejection of the terms as they are about the meaning they communicate. The best alternative seems to be to juxtapose the source language and the target language terms so that authorial *ethos* is preserved, but the meaning of the text is also not lost.

Another study that has a bearing on the topic of key terms in translation was done by Vera Savić and Ilijana Čutura, who analyze the strategies involved in the translation of *cultural words* in three separate texts, two of which are translations from Serbian to English, and the third, English to Serbian.[24] *Cultural words* are linguistic symbols that refer to culture units,

20. Skaffari, "Code-Switching," 205.
21. See Schendl and Wright, "Code-Switching," 23.
22. Skaffari, "Code-Switching," 214.
23. Ibid., 214–15.
24. Savić and Čutura, "Translation as Cultural Transposition," 125–49.

or what they define as "a collection of implicit knowledge shared by all members of a linguistic community."[25] An astute translator will be sensitive to cultural words and their referents as they move between the source and target language, looking for cues that the author might give in the source text itself as an explanation of the term. For example, the first translation in their analysis is an exposition on Serbian culture and cuisine where the author, Momo Kapor (1937–2010), goes to great lengths to demystify certain aspects of Serbian culture and manners, and to emphasize their interaction with other cultures.[26] In many instances, Kapor focuses on certain cultural words, providing a textual commentary on the meanings and nuances of particular Serbian words, words that clearly derive from another language. In the following translation, various food items are linked to their country of origins:

> The grill, for instance, comes from the Arab countries, while *ćevapčići* (a cylindrical-shaped piece of grilled meat) from Turkey, and further back from Persia. *Njeguška* smoked ham is a close relative of ham from Parma. . . . Ah, but what indescribable joy when my friends spread *kajmak* from *Čačak* on slices of New York bread![27]

In this excerpt from *A Guide to Serbian Mentality* Kapor overtly adds information in the text as a way to contextualize *Njeguška* by referring to its relationship to *Parma*. Compare this to the term *ćevapčići*, which contains the translator's parenthetical explanation as an aid to the reader. Later on, Kapor actually speaks to his translator in the text about a particular word, which he recognizes has zero equivalence from Serbian to English: "*inat*, something that is, of course, bound to make things harder on my translator. To assist him, I go to the Great Dictionary, where it explains. . . ."[28]

Savić and Čutura tie in their study of culture words to Venuti's dichotomy of *domestication* and *foreignization*. Domestication, as described by these authors, relates to keeping the source text invisible in the translation by using a strategy of diminishing the source's cultural elements and linguistic jargon in favor of interpreting those notions in a way that maximizes the

25. Ibid., 126.

26. Ibid., 130, quoting from Kapor, *Guide to Serbian Mentality*, 24, 25, 37, 43.

27. Kapor, *Guide to Serbian Mentality*, 25, quoted in Savić and Čutura, "Translation as Cultural Transposition," 130.

28. Kapor, *Guide to Serbian Mentality*, 25, quoted in Savić and Čutura, "Translation as Cultural Transposition," 132.

fluency and cultural cues of the target language. In Venuti's seminal work, *The Translator's Invisibility*, he refers to the notion of "fluency" in English language translation as an outgrowth of seventeenth century aristocratic England that has continued to be valued through social and cultural circles and has been associated with English speaking hegemony. Venuti insists that "transparency" is an illusion in the name of "fluency" and is really domestication, which "masks the manifold conditions of the translated text."[29] Regarding foreignization, Savić and Čutura emphasize the notion of highlighting cultural references of the source text even at the expense of fluency and adaptability for the translation. Venuti sees foreignization as a "strategic intervention in the state of world affairs."[30] He wants to unequivocally challenge ideological and political assumptions by writing, "my goal is not an essentializing of the foreign, but resistance against ethnocentrism and racism, cultural narcissism and imperialism, in the interest of geopolitical relations."[31] Foreignization is preferred to domestication because it seeks to restrain ethnocentrism—what Venuti refers to as the "violence of translation."[32]

What types of forms might indicate a translator's bias towards foreignization? These might include reflections of social and regional dialects, slang, obscenities, archaisms, neologisms, jargons, and even foreign borrowings.[33] By overtly preserving the foreignness of forms such as these, the translator begins to make him/herself visible, alerting the reader that they are indeed reading a translation.

Savić and Čutura provide a number of interesting examples that are pertinent to the topic of key term incorporation, some from a foreignization perspective, others more domesticating. First, there are orthographic means. For example, one translator prefers the foreign spelling of the word *tamboura* directly from the original Turkish rather than the Serbian *tambura*. This was done to reinforce the cultural nuances of Turkish culture existent even among Serbs. Another foreignizing approach can be seen by adding a glossary of terms to a translation, and likewise highlighting a term

29. Venuti, *Translator's Invisibility*, 43.

30. Ibid., 20.

31. Venuti, "Translation as Cultural Politics," 78.

32. Venuti also cites that whereas 2–3 percent of books published in the US and UK are translations, 25 percent of other countries' books are translations from English (ibid., 69).

33. Venuti, ed., *Translation Studies Reader*, 3.

with an appositive structure, such as "Chief Archivist (translation), the *Tefter Khefay* (source)."³⁴ In a translation of a poetry piece, they mention how a translator included about fifty notes to clarify references and allusions intended by the author, and they also included quotations, in both original (foreign) and translated form, with orthographic signals such as inverted commas as strategies to alert the reader that the translator was involved.³⁵ An interesting example of dynamic equivalence and domestication is found in the vernacular use of nicknames such as *ludi Švaba* (Serbian) being translated in the English with the colloquial form "Mad Fritz": "The Young Consul met all the notable figures in the market: Ibrahim Aga, the 'scalesman', Hamza the town-crier, and the bazaar fool Mad Fritz."³⁶

Proper names might also be domesticated as a way to preserve their etymological meaning in the target language, but at the expense of the original form such as the translated form "Reeling Hodja" for the source *Ljulj-hodža* as a way to contextualize the term to the readers (*hodža, hodja* "reeling"). In some cases, even deletion of a term can be a translation preference. The following example has to do with the culture word, *kahva,* an archaic Turkish form that refers to a coffee shop. The translator chose to delete this word in the target text (see bracketed form) leaving only the possessive as in the following: "As every year, the beys had begun to come out to talk together on the Sofa at Lutvo's [kahva]."³⁷

The role of the translation and the notion of equivalence becomes a two-level exercise where culture words are embedded in the source text. Savić and Čutura make this point explicit in their discussion of one Serbian-English translation that describes life in a multicultural area with references to four cultures in the local context (Orthodox, Catholic, Muslim, and Sephardic Jewish). As *culture words* are referenced in the text, they have certain meanings to the cultures in the text, while at the same time, they have a secondary meaning to the anticipated reader of the target language. In this sense, the aim of translation is not to teach the reader the source culture, but to emphasize the otherness and underlying cultural mixture that, although confusing at times, nonetheless maintains the intentionality of the author in revealing a complex, but important, situation.³⁸ Similarly,

---

34. Savić and Čutura, "Translations as Cultural Transposition," 136–37.
35. Ibid., 145.
36. Ibid., 137.
37. Ibid., 138, quoting from Andrić, *Days of the Consuls*, 395.
38. Savić and Čutura, "Translations as Cultural Transposition," 138.

they state, "The potentialities of these translations as cultural transpositions can be realised in reception, where translation achieves its communicative function."[39]

OBSERVATIONS

Key terms as a concept and practice are discussed in and outside the work of Bible translation, though they may be called different things and be considered important for varying reasons. Moving from my definition given in the section above for biblical key terms to a more general one that reflects the wider practice in the literature, the following definition is suggested: *a key term is a linguistic formalization for some topic about which people wish to converse.* Likewise, there are a number of preliminary observations we can make about key term usage:

1. They are focal points for discussion: Key terms are most commonly thought of as formalisms that represent a significant concept for a particular speech community. In Bible translation, this might include topics that unite (or divide) across denominational or ideological lines.

2. They signify the existence of some cultural unit: A term relates to a concept or an idea that is perceived to be intrinsically bounded to a culture. Texts often relate multicultural situations either overtly or covertly in forms used to convey certain responses from the reader. In translation, these terms and their connotations are seen as valuable to the target audience, though the rendering that best communicates that intention can vary considerably.

3. They point to an ideal past: A term in the form of an archaism or unknown loan word is often preferred, especially if the language of its origin maintains prestige in the target language. This is the case of Latin during the early Middle English period, and is also well illustrated in the multilingual source texts in Serbian.

4. They establish authorial *ethos*: Even when a term has a paucity of semantic content in the target language, this lack of meaning is offset by the amount of *ethos* it provides for the translator. As Skaffari points out, to translate key terms directly into Middle English would invite suspicion about the translator's credibility since Latin was the

---

39. Ibid., 146.

understood language of scholarship.[40] However, by using the Latin term together with Middle English support, the translator avoids the risk of challenging Christian doctrine.

5. They assume new meanings over time: Terms can originate with either too much or too little content at their creation, but over time the pragmatics of language can assuage many inaccuracies that their forms alone connote.

6. They are resistant to alteration: Once a key term has taken root in a speech community it becomes much more difficult for a new term to take its place. Regardless of the fact that a term can be challenged and alternates provided by anyone at any time, it is often resisted, and its incorporation into the wider language is quite dubious.

STUDY: KEY TERM INCORPORATION IN NORTHERN PAME

This study extends the literature base about key terms by examining key terms in a current Bible translation project. The language known as Northern Pame (classification: Otomanguean, Oto-Pamean, Pame) is spoken by approximately 3,000 people who live in small villages over approximately 50 square miles.[41] Below is a discussion of the assumptions and methodology applied to this study.

Assumptions

Although key terms may trace their origins to a particular person or group of experts and be the focal point for discussion of theological importance, their incorporation into the wider use of the language varies.[42] For the present study, I limit the path to three levels of incorporation: (L1) textual, (L2) speech community, and (L3) wider language, and below will exemplify each of these categories.

On the one hand, there are terms that were undoubtedly topics of discussion at one time, but by all accounts, their existence is bound to the text (L1), and their referents are highly constrained in the wider language.

---

40. Skaffari, "Code-Switching," 210.

41. Berthiaume, "Phonological Grammar"; Chemín Bässler, *Los Pames Septentrionales*; Soustelle, *La Familia Otomí-Pame*.

42. A notable exception is the Latin key terms incorporated into Old English, whose lexicon was vastly enriched with Latin terms with reference to religious and biblical concepts.

A L1 key term remains clearly related to the text even though it might be referenced in oral or written discourse. The term remains an object of conversation, but is not observed in use beyond its coinage in the text itself. Because of this, it is not surprising that a key term at the text level has a limited number of grammatical inflections, and it more than likely persists in the form it is known by in the text.

An example of a L1 English key biblical term is the literal rendering of the word θεόπνευστος as "breath" or "God-breathed" in English (2 Tim 3:16, NIV, ESV, BSB, BLB, ISV, NHEB, WEB, YLT). The first instance of this term comes from *Young's Literal Translation* (c. 1862). It is interesting that Robert Young describes his translation in his first edition preface as not to be in competition with the *"ordinary use* of the commonly received English Version (i.e., King James Version 1611) of the Holy Scriptures"; he appeared to be aware that his translation would be compared to the English Version, which he himself recognized as serving a purpose beyond the text itself, and being widely *used*.[43] A cursory search on the internet for Young's rendering suggests that "God-breathed" is not used outside of the Christian speech community (L3), and in fact, has little, if any, traction in discourse that is detached from a discussion of the text of 2 Tim 3:16.[44]

A few observations should illustrate why I assign the term "God-breathed" to a L1 category. First, consider the formal properties such as the use of a hyphen to indicate a newly formed compound adjective "God-breathed" and the limited grammatical inflections this term has. There are no alternatives such as a nominal "God-breathed-ness" instead of "inspiration," or a verbal form "God-breathes" instead of "inspires." The term remains grammatically static as an object of inquiry, but not free to be inflected in creative discourse. In terms of the public lexicon, "inspiration" was already widely used, despite the fact that notable scholars in different times have advocated for "God-breathed."[45]

43. Young, *Holy Bible*, ii.

44. Young maintains the distinction between the wider use of the English Bible and the literal translation of his New Testament to enable the student to access his key terms via the more commonly understood vocabulary of the Protestant faith. Thus, one will not find "God-breathed" as an entry, but predictably the common term "inspired." The key term and its Greek equivalent from the source are placed in italics on the space below the entry's heading (*Young's Analytical Concordance*).

45. The persistent use of "God-breathed" as an object of discussion for Bible translations remained the norm from the publication of the NIV (1973) to the present time. It is interesting to follow the narrative of this term used in the NIV. For example, the study note for 2 Tim 3:16 of the *NIV Study Bible* takes care to not use "inspired" but only

A L2 term is one that has moved beyond the text and is incorporated into wider language use at the dialectical level. These are the cases where we see key terms showing up in expressions through the arts, song, devotional material, and theological dialogue. We would expect that a term like "God-breathed" at one time did exist in some speech communities (and perhaps still does somewhere), but in the end, it lacked the stability to be incorporated for the long haul. Terms such as "redeemed," "daily bread," "light of the world," and "Word of God" are examples of current L2 key terms.

When a term is finally incorporated into the public lexicon, we observe a loosening of semantic precision in the context of creative discourse from within and without the original speech community. These terms may still be, and probably are, foci for discussion among clusters of speakers like Bible translators, but now the terms' topicality persists into new and original domains with echoes of their meanings popping up in interesting places.

Methodology

Looking further into the notion of key term incorporation into a language, this study utilizes a compare and contrast methodology of a set of Northern Pame New Testament key terms with a publication of Northern Pame monolingual journals and then catalogs their results in order to measure the degree of the incorporation of each into the wider use of the language. The results are tentative due to limitations of the text corpus size and medium, but nonetheless suggestive that what we know from the literature on key term incorporation is considerably accurate and predictive for translation studies in general.

The Northern Pame New Testament was first considered a translation need in the 1970s after a survey had been completed by SIL, and the results confirmed that there were two mutually unintelligible languages spoken within the Pame family, Northern and Central Pame.[46] The Northern Pame

---

"God-breathed" (Barker and Burdick, eds., *NIV Study Bible*). Moreover, in this instance the term is in italics suggesting that it is an object of discussion and distinct from a widely known term. Kenneth L. Barker produced a number of books to support and provide an apology for the NIV (see Barker, *Balance of the NIV*; Barker, *Accuracy of the NIV*; Barker, ed., *Making of a Contemporary Translation*). A review of the subject indices for these books reveals that "God-breathed" never was incorporated into the wider discussion about the version itself.

46. The Pame languages have been named in various ways depending on the time period and the language used in scholarly publications and likewise, due to internal

translation began in earnest in 2004 and saw a publication of the Gospel of Mark in 2007, and subsequent portions have been approved for publication by SIL including the Gospel of John, the Johannine Epistles, Revelation, the Gospel of Matthew, and 1–2 Thessalonians, with several other books nearing consultant approval.

The first translation committee was made up of three translators representing two sub-dialects of Northern Pame and myself as a linguistics consultant. Presently, the committee has five members, all of whom have participated in exegetical and translation training workshops. The translation itself undergoes the following stages: (1) exegetical discussion, (2) drafting from multiple Spanish source texts, (3) linguistic comparison to the Greek text, (4) revision, (5) community checking, (6) consultant review of the back translation and key terms, and (7) final editing and publication.

The translators for the Northern Pame New Testament use a variety of forms including near equivalents to Spanish, circumlocutions, calques, and loan words of Spanish origin. The key term database contains at present 131 entries, which are linked to the translation text through the software package Paratext 7.5 created by the United Bible Society.

A book was translated into Spanish called *Let Me Tell You What Happened to Me Today* from a collection of Northern Pame personal journals written from May 2008 to May 2010.[47] The 172,000-word book is almost entirely monoglot in Northern Pame with only some front matter and the back cover written in Spanish. There are four authors, two males and two females, with an age range at the time of writing from seventeen to fifty-six years. The two men are both Christians and served on the translation committee while also holding down jobs as a carpenter (Calixto Castillo, age fifty-six) and a farmer (Felix Baltazar, age fifty-five). Neither woman was

---

changes within the language family itself. Up until recently, three mutually unintelligible Pame languages existed (Northern, Central, and Southern Pame). Most, if not all, Pames and Pame scholars consider the Central variant to be the center of language use and cultural identity, and it is probably closest to the protolanguage. Southern Pame, known as Jiliapan Pame, was the least known by the wider Mexican population who considered it culturally and linguistically the same as Central Pame, and so it was, and still is, common to refer to the entire cluster as *Pame del sur*, "Southern Pame." Jiliapan Pame has since become extinct, so that what linguists call Central Pame is still known widely in Spanish as Southern Pame. Related to this is a cultural distinction made by anthropologists who separated Jiliapan Pame from the other two with the respective hemispherical terminology *meridional*, "southern" and *septentrional*, "northern." See Soustelle, *La Familia Otomí-Pame*; Chemín Bässler, *Los Pames Septentrionales*.

47. Baltazar Hernández et al., *Nakuɛnk' Nɛp Namitk Ntɛu'*.

on the translation committee at the time, although one has since joined as of 2014. The younger of the two (Eleuteria Castillo, age seventeen) was a non-Christian with no Christian family experience whatsoever, while the older one (Piedad Castillo, age thirty-two) was a new believer and was the daughter of Calixto Castillo.

Three of the four authors were experienced writers of Northern Pame at the time they began writing in 2008. The seventeen-year-old Eleuteria Castillo was highly literate in Spanish with only rudimentary experience writing Northern Pame. However, she proved to be a quick learner during a literacy workshop leading up to the journaling, and her quality quickly caught up to the other three authors after about four weeks of writing.

After the initial drafting was completed in May 2010, the authors spent the next year reading each other's work and correcting editorial and grammatical incidental errors. Care was taken to not change vocabulary or grammatical constructions where they did not inhibit the meaning of the entry, thus preserving to a good extent the style and register of each author. As the corrections were made, the entire manuscript was updated to reflect the changes. The year of 2012 through half of 2013 was dedicated to intelligibility testing in various Northern Pame communities through weekly reading groups. Most of the participants were functionally literate in Spanish and about half of them had at least two years of formal education that included focused reading in Northern Pame. The manuscript continued through the final stages of editing and typesetting until it was published as a book in 2014.

Results

The Northern Pame New Testament translation is housed in Paratext 7.5 and currently contains a key term list with 132 entries, four of which were at a status of enough uncertainty that I excluded them from this study ("holy," "lyre" or "harp," "to play a lyre or harp," "fellow-slave"). Level 1 terms—that is, terms bound exclusively to the translation text—were divided into two groups: (1) those with no attestation in the journals (fifty-one terms) and (2) those found in both the translation and the journals (sixty-four terms). Some of the unattested forms were "seal," "adultery," "wine press," and even words we might expect to be part of devotional material such as "savior," "almighty," "salvation," and even "spirit." The L1 attested forms might be near equivalents to the biblical source text, but with extra cultural baggage similar to the Fijian examples such as, "nation" (lit. "indigenous, native people"), "slave" (lit. "in bondage"), "pure" (lit. "washed"), and "abyss" (lit. "cave"). It is expected that over time and with a growing Christian speech community, these terms will assume more biblical overtones such as *Holy Ghost* in English. Where less literal approaches were taken, the great majority favored a dynamic equivalent and/or domesticating nature to translation. L1 terms of this sort include *ru' miayat Kristu*, "apostles" (lit. "the ones sent by Christ"), which is derived from a political term in Northern Pame to refer to ambassadors for a town mayor. Another example is *rudat 'liɛdat ru'nɛp de biu' npu'*, "people/things of the world," where the word for "world" is framed to convey a meaning similar to the Greek word κόσμος "world." In this case, the Pame word for "world" by itself can only refer to a physical object, much like the Greek word γῆς, but a repair is easily achieved by making it an attribute of people.

I identified ten L2 forms that are key terms appearing in the journals and used with Christian or biblical referents, yet not directly associated with some biblical verse. Two of the words were used in a formal equivalent way in the translation and now appear within the Christian community; these are the words for "forgive" and "sibling." Both terms, of course, were productive in the wider use of Northern Pame long before a translation. In its central meaning, the term "forgive" refers to unfulfilled contracts or promises such as "forgiving a debt," but now *Dius pa na'juatp* "God will forgive him (it)" is understood to refer to some offense towards God. The phrase *bu' nda ju'u njĕu' Hugo*, "my brother (lit. sibling) named Hugo," echoes the familiar Christian title for the family members of the faith, not a kinship term with which it is normally associated.

Five of the L2 terms reveal a more domesticating strategy, which are "demon," "daddy," "disciple," "hell," and "heaven." Likewise, there are nascent signs of foreignization for three L2 terms, which are a calque of Spanish (*verbo de Dios*) in Northern Pame *rañ'jiĕp Dius*, "word of God," and two loans referring to leaders taken from the Spanish words *rey*, "king," and *señur*, "Lord."

Finally, two terms, *dius*, "god" and *bibiayp Dius*, "angel" are used in the wider Northern Pame language and would be classified as L3. The following passage illustrates some of these forms at work in a journal entry:

> Niñ'ã' datèu' kiau nanã̀ nda pelikula ke pik la'uĩ nda 'lɛ ke nip lakuajay' de Dius y era ranuye 'lɛye ke ban'duàye run biu' moto y san'ta ùjuy gatsũ'y gatũ. Bìjiy bu'xiñ'ing ni datsi'y dajua'al biu' ñ'kiè'n'kiuè y ùjuy bu' aa'u, u la'kuĩts biu' kanè, pur ke nip mãng

njuã'ãl biu' pɨk mã̀ tsi', bɨ̀jɨy u da'mã'ã̀ bu' na'u ke da'uajãu de biu' ñ'jiẽ̀p Dius y bu' nda 'lɛ ke njẽu' Lazaro, u gatũ̀ y gu'nẽ̀dat ru' bibiaybat Dius y datsi' ast biu' kantàu' Dius y nkjuande bu''njẽu' bu' rey Herodes u daljau' biu' ka'pi'int. Nã̀'ãñ bu' rey Herodes u gatũ̀ y danjãung ru' gutsje'dat y nɨ̀jɨ̀y biu' kiau nanũ̀ chiñi niñ'ã̀' ganu'.[48]

This evening I saw a film that showed a man who didn't believe in *God*, and there were two men riding a motorcycle, and one of them fell and died. Then the *devil* took him and he went to *hell*, and there he was standing at the entrance, but he didn't want to enter where he was leading him, and all of a sudden he remembered and spoke the *word of God*. There was also a man named Lazarus who died and the *angels* came to him and took him before God. There was also a man named *King Herod* who was a drunk. Later on, *King Herod* died and was eaten by worms, and these were the things I watched during that time.

Northern Pame has only a few deity terms, all of which have their origin in the natural world such as "sun," "moon," "thunder," etc. The term *dius*, "god" (Spanish *dios*), must have entered the language during the post-Spanish conquest period of the sixteenth and seventeenth centuries, for which there is ample evidence of Pames interacting with Catholic monasteries and nearby *haciendas*. For all intents and purposes today, *dius* is used widely in Northern Pame. For example, the term for "thank you," *dius sajẽ'ẽuk'* (lit. "God thanks you") is used productively throughout both Northern and Central Pame. Likewise, *xiñ'ing*, "devil" (lit. "demon"), is a traditional word that has been dynamically used to refer to the biblical "devil" or, alternately, a particular "demon" in the New Testament, but with an interesting twist. Pamean languages are sensitive to the notion of animateness, and this is marked in their morphology in a number of ways. The term "demon" is regularly marked as "animate-non human" reflected in the definite article *biu'*.[49] In the journals, "devil" is referred to with the definite article *bu'* denoting "animate-human." This makes sense from a functional point of view because this sort of marking would be forced by verbal constructions that are usually required by human arguments such as verbs of speaking. The term for "hell" (lit. "source of fire") has the idea of a collection of "flames" and reveals a domesticating feature. On the other hand, "word of God" is a calque directly from Spanish; the construction *biu' ñ'jiẽ̀p Dius* is marked. The term

---

48. Cruz in Baltazar Hernández et al., *Nakuɛnk' Nɛp Namitk Ntɛu'*, 208–9.
49. Baltaz'r Hernández et al., *Diccionario Xi'iuy (Pame Norte)*, 21.

for "angels" (lit. "helpers of God") is a well-known phrase throughout the language area that has Catholic suggestions of angelic statues holding up the Christ child in a Catholic church. In fact, the translator has discussed an alternative term that means something like "announcers for God," but the term has never been accepted by even the Christian speech community, let alone the entire language group. The term *rey* is exclusively used with biblical figures at the exclusion of several authority titles available in Northern Pame (e.g., "governor," "leader," "chief"). This makes sense in that the idea of *kingship* where power is contained within one person is generally frowned upon, and there is no evidence to suggest that Pame culture valued a developed authoritarian hierarchy.

CONCLUSION

Whereas Bible translators' mention of key terms refers to a step in a larger process of revision towards publishing Scripture, translation studies in other domains may refer to them as *culture terms*, *key words*, or *key phrases*. We see cases where these terms have organically grown into formal expressions of topics that only later obtained a term that speakers would refer to in an objective way. At the same time, such terms may be created, or prescribed, and used as discussion points, where the terms themselves are just beginning to gain traction among a committee. In reality, both the organic and the prescribed often coexist to contribute to a complex language lexical inventory and an even more complex translation endeavor. The terms that are used in a wider language context have the advantage of being well known and greased for translation work. However, factors such as semantic fossilization and language shift can have some deleterious effects causing such terms to maintain just a shadow of their original or precise meaning. On the other hand, prescribed terms can be much more precise and, as such, excellent topic choices both within and outside a speech community. Their incorporation into the wider language, however, remains a question to be played out over years of use and practice by the speakers themselves.

BIBLIOGRAPHY

Andrić, Ico. *Days of the Consuls*. Translated by Celia Hawkesworth. Belgrade: Dereta, 2003.

Baltazar Hernández, Felix, et al. *Nakuenk' Nep Namit'k Nteu': Giriuyat Xi'iuyat Kjuent Ru' Ganu'bat*. San Luis Potosí, Mexico: Instituto Lingüistico de Veranom, A.C., Universidad Autónoma de San Luis Potosí, 2014.

———. *Diccionario Xi'iuy (Pame Norte): De Los Municipios De Tamasopo, Rayón, San Luis Potosí*. San Luis Potosí, México: IIH, 2007.

Barker, Kenneth L. *The Accuracy of the NIV*. Grand Rapids: Baker, 1996.

———. *The Balance of the NIV: What Makes a Good Translation*. Grand Rapids: Baker, 2000.

Barker, Kenneth L., ed. *The NIV: The Making of a Contemporary Translation*. London: Hodder and Stoughton, 1986.

Barker, Kenneth L., and Donald W. Burdick, eds. *The NIV Study Bible: New International Version*. Grand Rapids: Zondervan, 1985.

Barnwell, Katharine, et al. *Key Biblical Terms in the New Testament: An Aid for Bible Translators*. Dallas: SIL, 2009.

Baugh, Albert C. *A History of the English Language*. 2nd ed. New York: Appleton-Century-Crofts, 1957.

Berthiaume, Scott Charles. "A Phonological Grammar of Northern Pame." PhD diss., University of Texas at Arlington, 2004.

Chemín Bässler, Heidi. *Los Pames Septentrionales de San Luis Potosí*. México: INI, 1984.

Israel, Hephzibah. "Translating the Bible in Nineteenth-Century India: Protestant Missionary Translation and the Standard Tamil Version." In *Critical Readings in Translation Studies*, edited by Mona Baker, 174–90. London: Routledge, 2010.

Kapor, Mamo. *A Guide to Serbian Mentality*. Translated by John Ružica et al. Belgrade: Dereta, 2006.

Kroneman, Dick. "About Sin, Faith and Spiritual Warfare: An Exploration into the Relation between Translation, Contextualization, and the Study of Worldview." Paper presented at the Bible Translation Conference 2009, Dallas, October 16–20, 2009.

Pym, Anthony. "Redefining Translation Competence in an Electronic Age. In Defence of a Minimalist Approach." *Meta: Translators' Journal* 48 (2003) 481–97.

Savić, Vera, and Ilijana Čutura. "Translation as Cultural Transposition." *The Journal of Linguistic and Intercultural Education* 4 (2011) 125–49.

Schendl, Herbert, and Laura Wright. "Code-Switching in Early English: Historical Background and Methodological and Theoretical Issues." In *Code-Switching in Early English*, edited by Herbert Schendl and Laura Wright, 15–46. Topics in English Linguistics 76. Berlin: de Gruyter, 2011.

Shuttleworth, Mark, and Moira Cowie. *Dictionary of Translation Studies*. Manchester: St. Jerome, 1997.

Skaffari, Janne. "Code-Switching and Vernacular Support: An Early Middle English Case Study." *Multilingua* 35 (2016) 203–26.

Soustelle, Jacques. *La Familia Otomí-Pame Del México Central*. Mexico City: Fondo De Cultura Economica USA, 1993.

Tippett, A. R. "Ethnolinguistics and Bible Translation: A Diachronic Case Study: Fiji." Paper presented at the Anthropology Consultants' and Advisors' Seminar, Dallas, TX, March 1986.

Venuti, Lawrence. "Translation and Cultural Politics: Régimes of Domestication in English." In *Critical Readings in Translation Studies*, edited by Mona Baker, 65–80. London: Routledge, 2010.

———. *The Translation Studies Reader*. 2nd ed. London: Routledge, 2004.

———. *The Translator's Invisibility: A History of Translation*. London: Routledge, 1995.

Wilson, Deirdre, and Dan Sperber. *Meaning and Relevance*. 2nd ed. Cambridge: Cambridge University Press, 2012.

Young, Robert. *The Holy Bible Consisting of the Old and New Covenants: Translated according to the Letter and Idioms of the Original Languages*. Edinburgh: G. A. Young, 1898.

———. *Young's Analytical Concordance to the Bible: Containing About 311,000 References Subdivided under the Hebrew and Greek Originals with the Literal Meaning and Pronunciation of Each: Based Upon the King James Version*. Nashville: Nelson, 1982.

7

The Human One?
A Controversial CEB Translation Choice[1]

Cynthia Long Westfall

INTRODUCTION

THE ENGLISH TRANSLATION OF the idiom ὁ υἱὸς τοῦ ἀνθρώπου in the New Testament is often a problem for Bible translators who do not ascribe to a strict formal equivalence theory of translation. There is also a related translation problem for rendering the singular and plural of בֶּן־אָדָם in the Old Testament, and the Aramaic בַּר אֱנָשׁ, which is in Daniel and is generally acknowledged as the language that Jesus actually used in most registers.[2] The choice of the editors of the Common English Bible (CEB) to translate Greek, Aramaic, and English phrases as either "The Human One" or "the human being" has been a point of controversy.[3] This paper will discuss the semantics of the idiom in the New Testament and its relationship to the corresponding idioms in Hebrew and Aramaic in the Old

---

1. The content of this paper has been published as "The Human One: A Controversial CEB Translation Choice," *Open Theology* 2 (2016) 895–906.

2. The majority of scholarship has assumed that Jesus spoke Aramaic, but given the linguistic composition of Palestine as a multilingual society, it is possible or probable that Jesus engaged in code-switching in which there was a correspondence between register and language selection. See Ong, *Multilingual Jesus*. Register is described in Halliday and Hasan, *Language, Context and Text*, 29, as "a variety of language, corresponding to a variety of situation." See also Peterson, "Multilingualism," 109–48 for a discussion of the interaction between multilingualism and register variation.

3. Most of the discussion and criticism has occurred online on discussion lists and blogs.

Testament. It will then evaluate the semantics of the English phrases "The Human One" and "the human being" in contrast with the formal equivalent phrase "The Son of Man." Finally, it will evaluate this translation choice both in the context of the purpose of the translation and in the light of modern translation theory.

WORD STUDY IN THE SOURCE TEXT

The Phrase ὁ υἱὸς τοῦ ἀνθρώπου in the Greek New Testament

In the Gospels, this phrase is Jesus's favorite way of referring to himself (only in John 12:34 is this term used by somebody else citing him). It is used in the New Testament 86 times. It is used 69 times in the Synoptics, and twelve times in John. However, it is not used in the early church confessions, and it is used only four times in the rest of the New Testament. Three of the four times occur in narratives and the fourth is a citation of the Old Testament. In Acts 7:56, Stephen refers to a vision of Jesus as he died, which would be understood in the context of the Synoptic tradition. Two are in Revelation where visions of Jesus described as ὅμοιον υἱὸν ἀνθρώπου allude to Dan 7:13 (1:13; 14:14).[4] The fourth occurrence is in the citation of Ps 8:4–6 in Heb 2:6–8.[5] These patterns suggest a high collocation of the idiom with genre (narrative) in its use by the early church.

Many, if not all, of Jesus's self-references were likely spoken in Aramaic. In Aramaic, the term is an idiom meaning "human being."[6] Bock claims that in certain texts, "There is no need to invoke Dan 7 in order to make sense of the usage in these passages. Nor should such a background be assumed. Indeed, in such idiomatic uses Jesus simply presents himself as a human with certain rights and authority."[7] In all three Synoptic Gospels, Jesus constrains the idiom with layers of references to his suffering, but he also gives the idiom a special kind of authority, with messianic and

---

4. Daniel 2:4—7:28 is written in Aramaic. The Aramaic phrase ⬜⬜⬜⬜ ⬜⬜ means "human being" and is not a title.

5. Paul uses the plural of the idiom once in Eph 3:5: "this mystery was not made known to humankind" (NRSV).

6. See Casey, *Solution*, 67, 80; Casey, "Son of Man Problem," 11–12. However, Casey's conclusion that Jesus "considered himself less unique than Christian scholarship on the whole supposes" does not follow in the way he is depicted by the Gospel writers, because the role it plays in the Synoptic strategy culminates in him emphasizing his unique role at the trial before the Sanhedrin.

7. Bock, "Son of Man," 895. See also the direct association between "the son of man" and "humans" (ἀνθρώποις) in Matt 9:6, 8.

apocalyptic associations.[8] However, he controls the flow of information that defines the idiom.

According to the Gospel accounts, Jesus's use of the idiom through the majority of his ministry was not transparent to his listeners. They realized that he was giving it significance (this would be clear from the contexts and the grammatical markedness resulting from the consistent addition of two articles), but they could not figure out for sure what he meant when he applied the idiom to himself. John describes the confusion of the crowds after his triumphal entry and shortly before the upper room discourse. The crowd says, "We have heard from the law that the Messiah remains forever. How can you say that the *son of man* must be lifted up? Who is this *son of man*?" (John 12:34 NRSV). His language was still ambivalent enough to keep the crowds confused. Similarly, in the Synoptic tradition, Jesus asks his disciples "Who do people say that *the son of man* is?" and the disciples associate the term with various prophets (John the Baptist, Elijah, and Jeremiah), which would be consistent with the association of the term both generally to refer to a "human being" and specifically to refer to a prophet as in Ezekiel (Matt 16:13–14).[9] But when he asked, "Who do *you* say that I am?" Peter answered, "You are the Messiah, the Son of the living God" (Matt 16:15–16). This suggests that Jesus was exploiting the meaning of the idiom in the linguistic system as well as the biblical tradition and giving the idiom new meaning when applied to himself. Also in the Synoptics, he first associates the idiom with Dan 7 privately with the disciples in the Olivet Discourse (Matt 24:1–51//Mark 13:1–37//Luke 21:5–36), which is after the Triumphal Entry.

It was in his trial before the Sanhedrin that Jesus for the first time publicly associated the idiom with Dan 7.[10] In Matt 26:63–64 (Mark 14:62//

---

8. See Porter's three categories in which he organizes the information that occurs with the Son of Man sayings in the Synoptics (*Sacred Tradition*, 58–62).

9. It is interesting to note that in the Synoptic parallels in Mark 8:27–29 and Luke 9:18–20, Jesus asks, "Who do people [the crowds] say I am," rather than using the idiom "the son of man."

10. It is possible that Jesus was speaking Greek during the trial. According to Ong, code-switching occurs in multilinguistic cultures in predictable patterns, and trials would be conducted in the *lingua franca*, which would have been Greek (*Multilingual Jesus*, 282, 247–48, 297–98). Consider, then, Casey's suggestion that when the generic Aramaic idiom is in Greek, it sounds like a title to a reader who is not acquainted with Aramaic, and therefore, "This shift of meaning has taken place with the transmission of the saying from Aramaic to Greek. The Aramaic idiom has been lost" (Casey, "Son of Man Problem," 150). However, if Ong is correct, then Jesus would have translated the

Luke 22:69), "the high priest said to him, 'I put you under oath before the living God, tell us if you are the Messiah, the Son of God.' Jesus said to him, 'You have said so. But I tell you, From now on you will see *the son of man* seated at the right hand of Power and coming on the clouds of heaven'" (NRSV). That was the point at which they charged him with blasphemy— when he finally made a clear connection of the idiom with a passage that would point to a possibly angelic or divine association. I agree with Porter that Jesus drew from the sacred tradition in Dan 7 and the Second Temple writings in 1 Enoch in the associations he made with the idiom.[11] However, the idiom is clearly utilized in discourse staging in all four of the Gospels. The idiom was not recognizable to the crowd or the authorities as a messianic title because of its function as a common idiom in both Aramaic and the language of the Old Testament.[12] If the leaders had recognized it as a messianic title that must be associated with Dan 7, they would have killed him sooner, so it is part of the "Messianic Secret" pattern.[13] To understand the flow of the story, we need to translate it in such a way that it semantically reflects the idiom and allows the reader to follow Jesus as he progressively constrains it. The translation of the term in the narratives must be distinguished from what Jesus actually meant when he used the term or its significance in constructing a biblical theology.

The CEB translation of the idiom as "the human being" in the citation of Ps 8:4 in Heb 2:6 maintains the meaning of the idiom in the context of the Psalm, in which the referent is understood to be humans who are the objects of God's regard and who have a role in fulfilling the creation mandate.[14] It has been argued that the idiom was a technical term and

---

idiom to Greek in certain contexts, and the evidence would indicate that he added the articles, since they occur in every instance of the idiom in the Gospels but one.

11. Porter, *Sacred Tradition*, 76–77.

12. Contra Casey, who argues that Jesus meant the idiom to be generic and his usage reflected the stock idiom, but to do so he only accepts twelve sayings as authentic and attributes the rest to the early church tradition ("Son of Man Problem," 152).

13. This is an allusion to the Markan motif in which Jesus commanded his followers to be silent about his identity and mission. The Gospels indicate that explicit messianic (or apocalyptic) connections with the idiom resulted in a charge of blasphemy and directly led to his death. Wrede published his classic work *The Messianic Secret* in 1901. His thesis was that Jesus's suppression of demonic confessions of Christ's identity was not historical, but rather an addition by Mark. The role the idiom plays in the narratives suggests that it was a survival strategy in a politically dangerous environment.

14. A number of translations make the same choice. Though the NRSV translates the other occurrences of the idiom in the New Testament as "the Son of Man," in the Old

a messianic title in the early church, so it should be understood as messianic in this citation. However, there are two objections to this argument. First, for a Jewish Christian audience (or Jews within a mixed group), the idiom, particularly in a citation of the Old Testament, would have the same ambiguity as it had for Jesus's audience in the Gospels.[15] Second, the rhetoric and the line of argument in the passage require it to be understood as "the human being." The point of the citation in 2:6–8a is that the human destiny is to be crowned and rule everything. The author then states in 2:8b–9 that we do not see humanity fulfilling the human destiny, but we do see that Jesus has fulfilled the human destiny *because* of his identification with humanity in his incarnation (lower than the angels) and death. That is to say, much like the patterns in the Gospels, the Hebrews author cleverly takes the stock idiom and then gives it an explicit messianic meaning—but the rhetoric is missed if we translate it as a messianic title in 2:6, and the introduction of the theme of his identification with humanity is lost.[16] In the following passage in 2:10–18, the author shows that Jesus's identification with humanity qualified him to be a merciful and faithful high priest. So translating the idiom as the titular "Son of Man" in Heb 2:6 actually detracts from the author's elegant Christological argument and the use of rhetoric where he introduces the name and person of Jesus in contrast with the human condition.

The Old Testament as a Source

In discussing the theory of translation, Pym asks why we limit ourselves as translators to one source in our theory. "Surely each source can be traced back to a number of previous sources?"[17] Anyone acquainted with

---

Testament, the Hebrew idiom is translated as "mortal," and here "mortal" is also used. See also Heb 2:6 in the TNIV and the NLT, which render the idiom "mere mortals." The NJB renders the idiom "child of Adam." The CEB did not prefer "mortal" because it accentuates the human characteristic of death, which is not reflected in the Hebrew or Aramaic idiom, and would not transfer well to Jesus's use of the idiom, though Jesus's use of the idiom is clearly connected with the Old Testament and pseudepigrapha.

15. If Hebrews was written to a Jewish Christian audience, the stock idiom could still be in use by the community or at least the recipients could have had a background in Aramaic. Furthermore, since it is a citation of the Old Testament, the original meaning and the Old Testament idiom would have been influential. It is notable that Paul never used this as a Christological title in his epistles, which may suggest that he thought that the idiom would be misunderstood by a Gentile audience.

16. See also Blomberg, "But We See Jesus."

17. Pym, *Exploring Translation Theories*, 2.

any discussion of this phrase knows that the answer to this must be "yes," and our understanding and discussion of the phrase has been completely dominated by its use in the Old Testament and the pseudepigrapha. This invokes theories of intertextuality and the broad discussion of the use of the Old Testament in the New Testament. In the Old Testament, בֶּן־אָדָם occurs 107 times in the singular (but it also occurs in the plural) as an idiom to designate a human being, particularly in the poetry books and Ezekiel. It is used to contrast humanity with God in Num 23:19. Psalm 8:4 speaks of the status of humanity and the creation mandate in contrast with God and the angels, while a parallel passage in Ps 144:3 speaks of the transitory nature of humanity.

The idiom occurs 93 times in Ezekiel, which is the most marked use of the idiom in a single text in the Old Testament; it is God's form of direct address to the prophet, emphasizing his humanity. Caragounis suggests that his role is one of representative, intercessor, and substitute for the people, so the idiom identifies him and his role with them.[18] This is an important distinction because some assume that the reference to humanity emphasizes weakness and a low status. That is certainly not the case in Ps 8:4, nor in the contrast between humans and animals, so it should not be assumed in the case of Ezekiel.

Daniel's vision in Dan 7:13 is that of a human-like figure in a supernatural context: "one like a *son of man* coming with the clouds of heaven" who is given glory, authority, and power and is worshipped. However, the idiom means human-like regardless of the status of the referent—and in this passage the idiom is in Aramaic, in which the stock idiom is well-established. In Dan 8:17, Daniel is directly addressed by God with the idiom. The evidence from the Old Testament suggests that the idiom in Hebrew is also a stock idiom. It was translated as υἱὸς ἀνθρώπου in the LXX or with the vocative in Ezekiel and Dan 8:17, so that the occurrence of the idiom in Greek would not have been strange to most Jews. The idiom also occurs in 1 Enoch and refers to a "son of man" who is described in a similar way as the one in Daniel, but it is significantly expanded to a preexistent chosen messiah who judges and has the face of an angel (e.g., 1 En. 46:1–4; 48:2–11). Similarly, the semantic contribution of "son of man" indicates that this individual resembles a human, which is consistent with the use of the idiom.[19]

---

18. Caragounis, *Son of Man*, 60.

19. The dating of the Similitudes of Enoch (1 En. 37–71) has been debated for the

In the case of the application of the idiom and its Old Testament associations to Jesus, I suggest that making the semantic information of his humanity clear through translation is theologically important, and even crucial. The figures in Daniel and 1 Enoch were *humanlike*. However, when Jesus alluded to the phrase in its apocalyptic contexts, he significantly omitted the qualifier that indicated he was "like" a human, from which one infers that the figures in Daniel and 1 Enoch are not human. Jesus edited the phrase in a way that indicated he was fully human—which is what the idiom means.

Larger Linguistic Context: The Idiom of υἱὸς τοῦ [X]

The construction υἱὸς ἀνθρώπου is part of an even more common idiom where "son of" can occur with a variety of nouns to indicate that a person is characterized by a quality associated with the noun: "one who has the character of [x]." It is clearly a metaphorical extension of a genetic relationship such as υἱοὶ Ισραηλ. The extension to non-genetic relationships include οἱ υἱοὶ τοῦ θεοῦ and οἱ υἱοὶ τῶν προφητῶν, which are quite common. Mark 3:17 is an interesting case, where Jesus calls James the son of Zebedee and his brother John Boanerges, which John translates from Aramaic as υἱοὶ βροντῆς (the Sons of Thunder). However, he expects the reader to understand the idiom. The idiom occurs in Hebrew, Aramaic, and the Greek of the LXX and the New Testament.[20]

The Question of Gender

Gender issues have been a concern in the discussion because the masculine singular "son" is omitted and the masculine singular "man" is changed to

---

past two hundred years. While the majority will date the Similitudes at the "turn of the era," so that Christian tradition was able to utilize them as a source, others suggest that the Christian tradition is the source for the Similitudes. See Ehro, "Historical-Allusional Dating," 493–511.

20. Paul rarely uses the singular idiom. He refers to Jesus as the Son of God only four times (Rom 1:4; 2 Cor 1:19; Gal 2:20; Eph 4:13). He also uses the singular idiom with destruction (2 Thess 2:3), and in Gal 4:30, Paul cites Gen 21:10: "son of the bondwomen," and adds "son of the free woman," but then uses τέκνα to apply the passage to the readers. Paul collocates the plural of υἱός with a genitive for God (four times: Rom 8:14, 19; 9:26; Gal 3:26), Israel (three times: Rom 9:27; 2 Cor 3:7, 13), disobedience (three times: Eph 2:2; 5:6; Col 3:6), Abraham (one time: Gal 3:7), light (one time: Eph 5:5), and day (one time: Eph 5:5). However, he clearly prefers to use the neuter τέκνα with the genitive for the same concepts when referring to the readers.

the gender inclusive term "human," so that the choice appears to support an ideological agenda. One relevant question is whether the male gender or the quality of masculinity is an uncancellable quality of the υἱός idiom in either the plural or the singular. That is, would an accurate translation of the semantics of the idiom require a masculine reference or references in the target language?

The masculine plural in the Greek, as in Hebrew, Latin, and many modern languages, must be used to refer to groups that include males and females. So the rule of thumb would be that idioms in the Greek New Testament that occur with the plural of υἱός would include women unless the context indicated otherwise. The most common example in the Greek New Testament would be υἱοὶ θεοῦ (Matt 5:9), rendered "children of God" by the NRSV which occurs first in the canon in the beatitudes in Matt 5:9: "Blessed are the peacemakers, for they will be called children of God" (Matt 5:9). More importantly, Rom 8:14 states: "All who are led by the Spirit of God are children of God" (Rom 8:14 NRSV). Women can make peace and can be led by the Spirit of God. See also Luke 20:34: οἱ υἱοὶ τοῦ αἰῶνος τούτου, "the sons of this age," rendered as "those who belong to this age" (NRSV), which would include women.

Is the idiom gender specific when it occurs in the singular form? A good test case would be the phrase in Luke 10:6: ἐὰν ἐκεῖ ᾖ υἱὸς εἰρήνης in the context of the pericope where Jesus sends out the seventy-two: "Whatever house you enter, first say, 'Peace be to this house!' And if a *son of peace* is there, your peace will rest upon him. But if not, it will return to you" (Luke 10:5–6 ESV).[21] This demonstrates the function of the masculine singular as the default or unmarked gender that is less specific by definition and can be used in a generic way for both genders—anyone who is characterized by peace will have the messenger's peace rest on them. Therefore, the masculine should not be considered an essential part or an uncancellable quality of the semantics of the υἱός idioms. Since the referent of the idiom is male in the case of Jesus, the gender is constrained and semantically

21. Note the translation in the TNIV for 10:6: If the head of the house loves peace (Luke 10:6 TNIV), which is an addition of information in contrast with the NIV: "someone who promotes peace." This is an example of the practice of "explication" in which additional information is added to the text. The addition in the TNIV is not necessarily gender exclusive, since a woman could be the head of a house (though the default understanding of the head of the house would be male), but it is questionable whether the Gospel's offer of peace would be withdrawn from all family members if the head of the house did not qualify.

unambivalent, so that maintaining the masculine gender over-emphasizes or overloads the reference to gender in a way that is inconsistent with the semantics of the source text.

On the other hand, an insistence on using the word "man" to translate ἄνθρωπος, which is semantically gender inclusive, is beginning to assume the aspect of an ideologically-driven agenda, particularly in light of the current discussion on gender and translation. It is true that sometimes ἄνθρωπος can best be translated into natural English idiom as "man" when it has a masculine referent as is the practice in the CEB: "A man [ἄνθρωπος] was there whose right hand was withered" (Luke 6:6 CEB). However, if the quality of humanity is in view, it should be rendered as "human" unless it is unnatural in English: "There is one God and one mediator between God and humanity [ἀνθρώπων], the human [ἄνθρωπος] Christ Jesus" (1 Tim. 2:5 CEB).[22] The CEB brings out the inclusive language of the semantics of the Greek text in this theologically crucial passage so that the target audience may understand its universal application in a way that is comparable to the source audience.[23]

---

22. Contrast the CEB rendering with that of the ESV: "For there is one God, and there is one mediator between God and men, the man Christ Jesus" (1 Tim 2:5 ESV). Grudem and Poythress insist that passages such as this would not be misunderstood (Poythress and Grudem, *Bible Controversy*, 223–32). However, the ESV renders both ἀνήρ and ἄνθρωπος as "man." They helped compose and follow the Colorado Springs Guidelines that argue that "man" is a precise translation of ἀνήρ (308; cf. 321–33). Counter arguments aside, this practice fails to acknowledge that the author's choice of ἄνθρωπος instead of ἀνήρ has meaning and theological significance. In addition, the target audience must use implicature to determine whether "man" is precise or generic in this theologically crucial passage. It is far more accurate (and equivalent) to use the resources in the English language to make the distinction, particularly since there is a distinction in Greek. Furthermore, I suggest a field test which the reader could use to determine whether this use of "man" is confusing or ambiguous: ask both adults and children to interpret the gender references and infer the context in the following phrase: "There is one mediator between the management and the men: the man John Smith." I predict that the interpretations would at least entertain a gender exclusive interpretation, and I can promise that this language would not be allowed in a legal document or contract if it were meant to apply to women. If that is the case, why would we allow it in a passage from which readers will construct their theology?

23. Note that according to LSJ, the CEB translation could be considered formally equivalent, since the meaning of the plural of ἄνθρωπος includes "humanity." However, technically, the change from a plural to a singular is an implication that the lexicographers have already made for the translators.

MEANING AND ETYMOLOGY OF THE TARGET IDIOM

The Etymology of "Human"

All through the discussion above, it was stated that related idioms in Hebrew and Aramaic that are translated as υἱὸς ἀνθρώπου all semantically refer to a human. The English word "human" has an extremely close correspondence to the Hebrew word אָדָם in its etymology.[24] While Barr argued that we should not base the meaning of a word on its etymology, in this case it is illuminating for those interested in equivalence and because the etymology is apparent in the composition of the word.[25] It was first used in the fifteenth century, and comes from Old French humain or Latin humanus, which mean "of man" or "belonging to a man." Etymologists directly compare it with the Hebrew אָדָם "man," which comes from אֲדָמָה "ground." It therefore communicates the semantic information of the idiom fairly well, and actually shares some corresponding associations. However, ἄνθρωπος alone can be translated as "human." The use of extra words mark the phrase, including two articles that occur in all but one of Jesus's citations. Therefore, instead of replacing four words in the Gospel with two words ('the Human'), 'the Human One' was preferred. However, it may be argued that 'the Human Being' renders the idiom in more natural English.[26] Some have expressed concern that the intertextual links with Dan 7 and 1 Enoch will not be clear with this gloss. However, the idiom in Dan 7 is translated the same way in the CEB. Those who are interested in the textual ties with 1 Enoch will generally learn of them and access them through study notes, teaching, or other sources. A valid concern is that the symmetrical tie between the Son of God and the Son of Man is lost, which elegantly reflects the divinity and humanity of Jesus. That is a loss, but observation in the church and the classroom suggests that most of the readers of the English Bible do not make that connection.

---

24. See online: http://www.etymonline.com/index.php?term=human for the etymological entry for "Human (adj.)."

25. See Barr's influential work, *Semantics of Biblical Language*, 107–58.

26. The addition of the articles in ὁ υἱὸς τοῦ ἀνθρώπου in the Gospel occurrences made it more emphatic, but it did not particularize the idiom as it would in English.

Linguistics and the Bible

The Meaning of "The Son of Man" in English

The traditional way of translating ὁ υἱὸς τοῦ ἀνθρώπου as "son of man" is what is known in translation theory as a "false friend" which involves "lexical, phraseological and syntactic forms that look similar but have different functions in different languages."[27] It not only fails to communicate the semantics of the idiom but it may communicate undesirable information. Three areas of concern include the specific criticisms of the CEB's translation choice, interpretations of the idiom by lay people in the church and predictions of how a reader without a church background might read the phrase.

A large number of criticisms of the CEB insist that "the son of man" is a reference to the divinity of Christ. This group understands it as a Christological title and it is assumed that Christology is concerned with Jesus's divinity. In a phone call I was recently told that a man stood up in church and called the CEB Satanic because it called Christ "the Human One." This reflects an unfortunate gnostic tendency in the evangelical community in which the divinity of Christ significantly overshadows his humanity, and it would seem to require attention and correction. However, the context of this criticism was a debate on the leadership of women in the church, so that it was linked to gender issues and "muting the masculinity of Christ."

In the classroom and the church, when I have asked lay people who read the Bible or even students going into ministry what "the son of man" means, they often cannot come up with a coherent answer at all other than that it is a title. Some may suggest that it is messianic, but they have no idea why. It has some traction in the culture as an exclusively apocalyptic reference because it has appeared in popular apocalyptic literature, so that it may carry undesirable intertextual ties to other popular contexts.[28]

An even more serious concern is what "the Son of Man" might mean to someone who has neither a background in the Bible nor any relationship with the church. To a naïve reader, Jesus can be claiming over and over again that he is the son of a man. One can easily ignore the lack of an indefinite article as a strange feature of a foreign text. Without a background a reference to Jesus as "the Son of Man" appears to contradict the virgin

---

27. Pym, *Exploring Translation Theories*, 14.

28. Google searches can be a great help to translators both in testing one's notion about contemporary "natural English" and in discovering associations. A Google image search on "the Son of Man" yields disturbing imagery. A number of traditional biblical terms have been "hijacked" in art, in literature, and for commercial purposes.

birth. This is a very real concern given the purpose and target audience of the CEB.

"The son of man" is a false friend in translation in English and probably in any modern language because it is semantically empty if the reader does not share the background information with the translator or the source text. It is particularly deceptive because the meaning lies in the whole phrase (idiom) and its intertextual ties, but the individual words are easily recognizable and will have very high recognition in a readability test, but the semantic whole is significantly different from the sum of its semantic parts.

THE PURPOSE AND GUIDELINES OF THE CEB

The CEB was committed to principles that served a particular target audience, and which were sensitive to changes in the cultural context that affect language. These changes include a cultural preference for plain language, an emerging worship reformation in text and music, and the equal power of image and text.[29] While the publisher (Abingdon) determined the CEB's purpose, it was first suggested in a consultation committee.

Target Audience

There was a double goal for the translation. It was to be missional in that it should be understandable to people with no church background with a maximum seventh grade reading level. Within those parameters, it was to be suitable to use in congregational worship, in that it was translated so that it could easily be read out loud.

Readability

The translators of the CEB were encouraged to insure readability in a number of ways. They were directed to use shorter sentences, use default English word order and fewer passive verbs. They were encouraged to measure the readability of the text as they worked.[30] Each translator had a consulting reader whose purpose was to insure accuracy and readability. The editors used contractions for appropriate genres such as letters. In practice, the

---

29. "Our New Bible Style Guide," 2.

30. The translators were encouraged to use the readability tool in Microsoft Word, but the publisher measured readability with the Dale-Chall method, which measures both vocabulary and syntax (particularly sentence length).

editors aimed at a fifth grade reading level if possible. Each book had two translators, then it was read out loud by a small group of lay people who gave their observations on the readability, and then it was edited.

Explicit Guidelines

The following guidelines summarize the purposes of the CEB:[31]

- Clear (plain) English vocabulary
- Seventh grade reading level
- Accurate English grammar
- Natural English syntax
- Evocative, imagistic language (in contrast to precise, wooden, and systematic rhetoric)
- Effective in oral recitation in a worship or educational setting

A Purpose-Driven Choice

If the translators were going to be true to the purpose of the CEB, it would have to impact the translations of idioms: specifically, we were not able to retain the traditional "literalistic" word for word rendering of ὁ υἱὸς τοῦ ἀνθρώπου as "the Son of Man." Even though each individual word passes a readability test at the primary level, the phrase "the Son of Man" is incomprehensible for a seventh grade reading level. The target audience's use of implicature will invariably lead the reader to the wrong interpretation. "The Son of Man" is neither clear English nor natural syntax. While the CEB is written to appeal to the ear and to be used in oral worship in a church setting, the editors intentionally avoided traditional language that only occurs in a church register, or what we like to call "biblish." Similar considerations also led to the use of contractions in narrative dialogue and letters and any other non-formal genres.[32]

I remember that when I participated in an online Bible translation group, we were asked to list the resources that we found the most helpful. I

---

31. These guidelines are an accurate overview of the considerations that were first articulated in 2007 (cf. "Our New Bible Style Guide") and reflected in the "Style Guide for Translators, Editors and Proofreaders."

32. A contractions chart was distributed to the translators, editors, and proofreaders, which was adapted from material provided to teachers of English as a Second Language (ESL).

was the only one to list a thesaurus. I was sensitized to how the King James vocabulary was deeply ingrained in most English translations, so that many of us assume an equivalent correspondence between the languages of the source text and archaic, theological, or uncommon terminology. I tried to approach the vocabulary selection as a translator would in translating to a language or dialect in the emerging world—you translate into the language in use. I was constantly asking myself, "How do we really say that?" I would search for phrases on Google to see which syntax or wording expressed the Greek semantic context in the most common, current English. Given the guidelines and missional purpose of the CEB, the traditional and formal equivalent translation of ὁ υἱὸς τοῦ ἀνθρώπου was neither advisable nor necessary.

EVALUATION OF THE CEB ACCORDING TO TRANSLATION THEORY

The remaining question to answer is how the CEB would be evaluated in the light of modern translation theories. The evaluation will include the detection of the translation theories that were practiced by the CEB in the light of recent theories, and at least a partial discussion about its success in terms of theory. The theories include formal equivalence, dynamic equivalence, the Skopos theory of translation, and the descriptive approach to translation.

According to Pym, formal equivalence is close to what "many translators, clients and translation users believe about translation."[33] Formal equivalence assumes that there is "equal value" between what is said in a source-text and what is said in a target text, which may be applied to any linguistic level, so that it is assumed that the target text should be as close as possible to the source text on every level. Formal equivalence translators strive for a straightforward word-for-word correspondence and attempt to mimic the form of the source language in such a way that the text could be back-translated. The CEB translators were not encouraged to mimic the form of the source language as a great effort was made to shorten sentences for readability. As far as vocabulary choice, few critics would recognize how close the CEB actually comes to formal equivalence on a comparative scale because many assume that only the archaic and theological words in their favourite translation are the words that have an equal value to the words

---

33. Pym, *Exploring Translation Theories*, 6.

in the source text.[34] While probably none of the CEB editors believe that words can be translated from one language to another with equal value,[35] in practice, much of the efforts in translation attempted to stay as close to the source text as possible. However, the vocabulary choice in the target language was supposed to be freshly drawn from contemporary English in use, rather than resources and translation helps that reinforce KJV vocabulary such as Metzger's *Lexical Aids* or Kubo's *Reader's Greek-English Lexicon*, which are used by Greek students in translation exercises. Contemporary English words have more semantic correspondence to the Greek terms for the target audience than seventeenth century words have.

The translation approach of the CEB is indebted to Nida's theory of dynamic equivalence and functional equivalence, which recognizes that there are different forms of equivalence and nuances the concept of "natural equivalence." While formal equivalence mimics the form of the source language, dynamic equivalence activates the same or similar cultural function: "Translating consists in reproducing in the receptor language the closest natural equivalence of the source-language message."[36] However, the concept of "dynamic" has come to be misunderstood and associated with some extremes such as translating "the Lamb of God" in John 1:29 as "the Pig of God" or "the Seal of God" when the target group has no knowledge of sheep. These are examples of provocative types of choices that the CEB wanted to avoid. Therefore, the term "functional equivalence," which was also suggested by Nida, was adopted to attempt to limit contextualization and to communicate that limitation, or what some have described as a balance between formal equivalence and dynamic equivalence. The choice of "the Human One" or "the human being" as a translation of ὁ υἱὸς τοῦ ἀνθρώπου is a good example of maintaining that balance.

A more recent translation theory, developed primarily by German theorists, claims that the idea of equivalence is illusionary in the practice

---

34. The publishers state that their approach is located between formal and dynamic equivalence.

35. As Louw and Nida assert in the introduction of their lexicon on semantic domains that was primarily designed for translators, "The most serious mistake which people make in dealing with the meanings of Greek terms is to presume some kind of one-to-one correspondence in meaning" (*Greek-English Lexicon*, xiv). Furthermore, there is a complementary principle on synonyms in the same language: "The first principle of semantic analysis of lexical items is that there are 'no synonyms,' in the sense that no two lexical items ever have completely the same meanings in all of the contexts in which they might occur" (xvi).

36. Nida and Taber, *Theory and Practice of Translation*, 12.

of translation in general, as shown in the translation process involved in producing game shows in different languages and cultures. According to Skopos theory, every translation serves a purpose (or the Skopos).[37] A text may be translated different ways to accomplish different purposes and functions.[38] The closer the purpose of the target text is to the source text, the closer the equivalence would be. The publisher or the client determines the goals, so that the translator needs information about the purpose of the translation, which determines the principles of translation. As described above, the CEB indeed had specific purposes that were determined by the publisher. It may be argued, and has been argued, that the purposes and function of the translators of the CEB would not be explicitly the same as the function and purpose of the original authors of the biblical texts. However, that is true for virtually every translation of the Bible, including the KJV—one may consult the forward or preface of any translation to verify how the purposes of various translations would differ from how one understands the various purposes of the original authors. Perhaps the primary question should be whether the purpose and function of the CEB is complementary to the purpose and function of the collection and transmission of the canon to subsequent generations and ultimately to the spread of the gospel. Furthermore, the missional purpose of the CEB is not at cross-purposes with, for example, Paul's goals in writing his epistles. "The Human One" translates ὁ υἱὸς τοῦ ἀνθρώπου in such a way that the idiom would not be misinterpreted by the target audience. That is fully consistent with the widely accepted practice of Bible translation into new languages in unreached regions.

The final translation theory with which we will evaluate the CEB is description theory, which is an academic approach practiced separately from the training institutions on translation. This approach studies translation rather than prescribing what it should be. Among other things, theorists detect common standard practices of translation that can be comparable to a "client's" job description. The client would be the target reader, and it is suggested that in addition to stated goals, there are cultural norms or reader expectations that may be unstated. Chestermann suggests that the study of

---

37. Hans Vermeer is the primary founder of Skopos theory. For a description, see Nord, *Translating as a Purposeful Activity*, 27–31.

38. In Skopos translation, the target-side purpose is dominant, so that the source text is "dethroned" and the translation is not "source-bound."

norms will help to predict the relative success of one strategy or another.[39] In the case of the CEB, the goal of functional accuracy and the missional goal of readability for a reader without a church background might have undermined the Bible's success with the public that actually purchases Bibles. Though the CEB was translated to be read out loud, it does not sound "liturgical" to those who are used to words that echo the KJV vocabulary ("biblish")—that is, the churched public expects the Bible to have an Elizabethan accent.[40] In the case of ὁ υἱὸς τοῦ ἀνθρώπου, much of the public that purchases and reads Bibles does not necessarily know what the idiom means. Therefore, the CEB's semantically/functionally accurate rendering appears to violate whatever "sacred" or spiritual meaning that a reader has projected into the idiom (as in the case of those who assume that it directly refers to Jesus's divinity). So this raises questions of whether the intentional "norm-breaking" of the CEB would violate any hope of a good reception. However, the CEB was released in an award-winning children's version (*Deep Blue Kid's Bible*) that has experienced considerable popularity.

Therefore, while the CEB may be placed between formal equivalence and dynamic equivalence as it claims, its attributes are not apparent to many readers because of its choice of simple contemporary vocabulary over more theological words that are considered the "norm" for biblical language. While it is clear that the language of the CEB is different from other translations because of its purposes/goals, it needs to be recognized that every English translation has its own sets of purposes and goals that are not exactly the same as those of the original authors of the books of the Bible. In fact, many popular assumptions about formal equivalence translations fail to adequately understand the nuances of the actual practice of translation. The choices of "the Human One" and "the human being" as translations of ὁ υἱὸς τοῦ ἀνθρώπου are appropriate and semantically accurate choices within the theory and purposes of biblical translation as it

---

39. See Chesterman, "Empirical Status," 9–19.

40. Some theorists and Bible translators suggest that a translation should retain a foreign character to communicate to the reader that the context of situation, including the culture, was far different from the readers'. Sometimes this is a defense of tortured syntax that is unreadable for lower reading levels, but more often it is a defense of archaic vocabulary. However, this would clearly not be a defense of accuracy in choice of words, but rather a functional equivalent choice that evokes a far different culture (i.e., Shakespearean) rather than the biblical context of situation. Furthermore, it rather retains a *familiar* church register (not a foreign one) at the expense of a clearer meaning in contemporary idiom.

has been practiced world-wide, but we also have here examples of "norm-breaking" of the religious register that the reading public expects for the English Bible.

CONCLUSION

It has been shown that the CEB translation of ὁ υἱὸς τοῦ ἀνθρώπου as "the Human One" or "the human being" is the accurate meaning of the stock idiom both in the Aramaic of Jesus's day and in the Hebrew and Aramaic language in the Old Testament. The idiom plays a part in the plots of all four of the Gospels in which Jesus confuses the crowds and Jewish leaders about his claims. His repeated references to himself as "the Human One" or "the Human Being" baffle the public until his trial before the Sanhedrin when he finally associates the idiom with Dan 7:13 and possibly 1 Enoch. Therefore, a translation that allows the narrative and the plot to be understandable is to be preferred. For those who are not taught the actual meaning of the idiom, the traditional literalistic word-for-word translation of ὁ υἱὸς τοῦ ἀνθρώπου as "the Son of Man" is either meaningless or misleading both in terms of Christology and for following the narrative of the Gospels. The purpose of the CEB is to use clear English vocabulary that is understood at a seventh grade level by those who have no church background. Therefore, a clear and accurate translation of the sense of the Aramaic and Hebrew idiom was virtually a necessary choice for semantic accuracy, and reflects the CEB's translation theory. It is also a missional choice to render the Word of God in a way that is understood in the target audience's language in current use. However, the majority of the public that purchases Bibles has religious and theological commitments and tends to expect or even demand specific theological vocabulary and technical terms that are part of a specialized religious register, even though they are misunderstood. The CEB engages in "norm-breaking" by attempting to choose vocabulary from registers that are currently in use in the English language in comparable contexts as those that are represented in the source text.

BIBLIOGRAPHY

Abingdon Press. "Our New Bible: Style Guide for Translators, Editors, and Proofreaders." Editorial meeting material. October-November 2007.

———. "Common English Bible: Style Guide for Translators, Editors and Proofreaders." November 2008 (distributed 10/31/2008).

Blomberg, Craig. "'But We See Jesus': The Relationship between the Son of Man in Hebrews 2:6 and Verse 9 and the Implications for English Translations." In *A Cloud*

of Witnesses: The Theology of Hebrews in Its Ancient Contexts, edited by Richard Bauckham et al., 88–99. London: T. & T. Clark, 2008.
Bock, D. L. "Son of Man." In *Dictionary of Jesus and the Gospels*, edited by Joel B. Green, 894–900. 2nd ed. Downers Grove, IL: IVP Academic, 2013.
Caragounis, Chrys C. *The Son of Man: Vision and Interpretation*. Tübingen: Mohr Siebeck, 1986.
Casey, Maurice. *The Solution to the 'Son of Man' Problem*. London: T. & T. Clark, 2007.
———. "The Son of Man Problem." *ZNW* 67 (1976) 147–54.
Chesterman, A. "The Empirical Status of Prescriptivism." *Folio Translatologica* 6 (1999) 9–19.
Erho, Ted M. "Historical-Allusional Dating and the Similitudes of Enoch." *JBL* 130 (2011) 493–511.
Halliday, M. A. K., and Ruqaiya Hasan. *Language, Context, and Text: Aspects of Language in a Social-Semiotic Perspective*. Geelong: Deakin University Press, 1985.
"Human (adj.)." Online Etymology Dictionary. Accessed July 4, 2016. http://www.etymonline.com/index.php?term=human.
Kubo, Sakae. *A Reader's Greek-English Lexicon of the New Testament*. Zondervan Greek Reference. Grand Rapids: Zondervan, 1975.
Louw, Johannes P., and Eugene A. Nida. *Greek-English Lexicon of the New Testament Based on Semantic Domains*. 2 vols. New York: United Bible Societies, 1988.
Metzger, Bruce M. *Lexical Aids for Students of New Testament Greek*. 3rd ed. Grand Rapids: Baker Academic, 1996.
Nida, Eugene A., and Charles R. Taber. *The Theory and Practice of Translation: With Special Reference to Bible Translating (Helps for Bible Translators)*. Leiden: Brill, 2003.
Nord, Christiane. *Translating as a Purposeful Activity: Functional Approaches Explained*. New York: Routledge, 2014.
Ong, Hughson T. *The Multilingual Jesus and the Sociolinguistic World of the New Testament*. LBS 12. Leiden: Brill, 2016.
Peterson, John Michael. "Multilingualism, Multilectalism and Register Variation in Linguistic Theory—Extending the Diasystematic Approach." In *Explorations of the Syntax-Semantics Interface*, edited by Jens Fleischhauer et al., 109–48. Studies in Language and Cognition 3. Düsseldorf: Düsseldorf University Press.
Porter, Stanley E. *Sacred Tradition in the New Testament: Tracing Old Testament Themes in the Gospels and Epistles*. Grand Rapids: Baker Academic, 2016.
Poythress, Vern S., and Wayne A. Grudem. *The Gender-Neutral Bible Controversy: Muting the Masculinity of God's Words*. Nashville: Broadman and Holman, 2000.
Pym, Anthony. *Exploring Translation Theories*. London: Routledge, 2010.
Wrede, William. *The Messianic Secret in the Gospels*. Translated by J. C. G. Greig. Cambridge: James Clarke, 1971.

8

What is the Relationship between Exegesis and Our Views of Greek, or Vice Versa?

Stanley E. Porter

INTRODUCTION

IN THIS PAPER, I work from several definitional assumptions. The first is that *exegesis* is the word that we use for the process of explicating a text, in our case a biblical text and more particularly the ancient Greek New Testament. Exegesis is a particular and ideally definable application of one of the many types of biblical interpretation[1] that falls within the larger category of biblical hermeneutics or general principles of biblical understanding.[2] Whereas questions of exegesis inevitably encounter differing methods and theories, and these may well play a part within a robust definition of exegesis, I am assuming that there is enough latitude within the conception of exegesis that it will allow various methods and theories while retaining its fundamental orientation within New Testament studies. The second assumption is that, since we are explicating a text that was written nearly two thousand years ago in an ancient language, the analysis of the language in

---

1. There are many volumes that use the word "interpretation" in their titles. They are excluded from consideration, even though some of their content overlaps with my discussion below. I examine books that explicitly use the word "exegesis," with two exceptions: Porter, ed., *Handbook*, which treats Greek language (in a linguistically informed way, incidentally) but does not present an exegetical method, and Larkin, *Greek Is Great Gain*, which is less a book on exegesis than one on exposition.

2. Hermeneutics books are also explicitly excluded, even though, especially in the field of biblical studies, the terms "interpretation" and "hermeneutics" often overlap in usage.

which that text was written must figure in some estimable way into this process that is called exegesis. In other words, examination of the Greek of the New Testament must constitute a definable component within the exegetical process, regardless of what other elements comprise the process. The third assumption is that, if these two previous assumptions hold, there must be a relationship between the approach that we take to the Greek of the New Testament and the results of our exegesis, since our examination and study of the Greek language is a part of that exegesis.

In light of these three assumptions, in this paper, I wish to perform two tasks. The first is to examine a number of either recent or reasonably well-known books on exegesis of the New Testament (available in English, either written in that language or translated into it). I do this so as to examine what role they give to the study of the Greek language. The second task is to examine what the implications are for exegesis of these views of Greek in light of major current theories, both traditional and linguistic, of how to approach language. This seems like a reasonably straightforward exercise, involving two clear steps. The first is simply descriptive-analytical—that is, what is the role of examination of the Greek language in a variety of treatments of New Testament exegesis—and the other is interpretive—that is, what are the implications of these views in light of several contemporary alternatives. I realize, however, that my two assumptions may well influence, if not skew, the results of my findings. However, I have tried to formulate assumptions that I believe should command widespread, if not universal, assent among biblical scholars and students alike.

APPROACHES TO EXEGESIS IN NEW TESTAMENT STUDIES

There are no doubt many other treatments of exegesis within the field of New Testament studies, but I have simply identified eight of them that have been ready to hand. From what I can see, they are written by mainstream, evangelical, and Roman Catholic scholars, represent a range of theological positions, both European and North American approaches, and hence should give, if not an exhaustive, at least a representative view of approaches to exegesis, in particular how study of Greek enters into New Testament exegesis. I will examine these eight treatments of exegesis in roughly chronological order from oldest to most recently written. (I will also attempt to resist the temptation to be diverted into a variety of other interesting and intriguing topics raised by these various volumes on exegesis.)

Werner G. Kümmel (1967)

Kümmel begins with a short but intriguing discussion of exegesis, in which he both retains the notion of determining authorial intention and problematizes the task of exegesis as being subject to the questions that are asked of the text. Kümmel then turns to textual criticism, noting that the student is to begin with the Nestle-Aland Greek New Testament—with suitable caveats that the text is what he calls an "average text" and is not to be equated with the original Greek text.[3] The next section—and the one with which I am most concerned—addresses linguistic resources. He calls "*linguistic understanding*" the "second indispensable step in recovering the original meaning of the text."[4] However, Kümmel identifies linguistic understanding with "a correct translation of the text."[5] Despite this, Kümmel's presentation is fairly nuanced, recognizing the "*various possible meanings* of the ambiguous words" and "the *grammatical possibilities* in the constructions involved."[6] This is within the context that the Greek of the New Testament is no longer classical Greek, and so various changes in the language may have occurred. To aid the student, Kümmel recommends two lexicons (LSJ and BAG) and two Greek grammars (BDF, and the German edition edited by Friedrich Rehkopf, and C. F. D. Moule's *Idiom Book*). With these two sets of tools one should be able to "work out a provisional translation, which must, of course, be confirmed by the appropriate exegetical considerations" (which he does not list, apart from checking translations).[7] Kümmel then goes on to matters of introduction, the task of exegesis, exegetical resources (other than those already listed, such as *TDNT*), and then two examples of exegesis (Rom 5:1–11; Matt 12:22–37).[8]

This is a very brief, but surprisingly helpful (considering when it was written), introduction to exegesis, in which language study is placed early in the process (even if it is mistakenly equated with translation). A limited number of traditional grammars are offered as examples, BDF reflecting a

3. Kaiser and Kümmel, *Exegetical Method*, 45.
4. Ibid., 46.
5. Ibid., 46.
6. Ibid., 46.
7. Ibid., 47.
8. A very similar approach is taken in Schnelle, *Einführung*. Schnelle recognizes the place of the Greek New Testament, concentrates upon translation, offers only one short paragraph on Greek grammar (recommending Blass/Debrunner and Radermacher, along with a beginning grammar), and, near the end of the volume discusses linguistics in less than two pages.

comparative grammar of New Testament Greek with classical Greek and Moule offering a traditional handbook. The German perspective of the work is present, and the grammars cited reflect the state of play at the time the book was written.

Hans Conzelmann and Andreas Lindemann (1975)

Conzelmann and Lindemann's book uses the word "exegesis" in its English title but is better considered to be a handbook (or workbook) to study of the New Testament as its German title indicates (*Arbeitsbuch*). As a result, there is plenty of material that resembles the content found in other books on the New Testament, such as New Testament introductions. However, in part one, on methodology, Conzelmann and Lindemann assert that exegesis, which they equate with interpretation, "constitutes the most important task of the study of the NT."[9] They emphasize the similarity biblical exegesis has to other areas of ancient study, while also noting its theological dimension. After a survey of tools for study, their first major topic is language. Their bibliography, as one might expect in a German work of the time, includes all traditional grammars, such as Fredrich Blass/Albert Debrunner, Moule, James Hope Moulton/W. F. Howard, and Ludwig Radermacher, as well as Eduard Norden.[10] Hence their approach is to emphasize differences between classical or Attic Greek and the Greek of the New Testament, an exercise in comparative philology. This includes discussion of Semitisms.

In a work of this date, one might have expected some reference to the work of James Barr, but instead the traditional and comparative grammatical paradigm is firmly in place to the point of perhaps being skewed toward issues of Semitic influence. However, Greek occupies a place of unquestioned significance in the exegetical process.

John H. Hayes and Carl R. Holladay (1982)

Hayes and Holladay approach exegesis from the perspective of communication theory, in particular the semantic triad of C. K. Ogden and I. A. Richards.[11] Nevertheless, they recognize many of the problems encountered in exegesis, such as reader distance, differences in language, cultural

---

9. Conzelmann and Lindemann, *Interpreting*, 1.

10. Ibid., 14.

11. Hayes and Holladay, *Biblical Exegesis*, 22–24, reflecting Ogden and Richards, *Meaning of Meaning*.

distance, and historical gap, among several others, along with recognizing problems peculiar to the Bible. After a discussion of textual criticism, and then historical criticism, they offer a chapter on grammatical criticism. Even though they recognize that meaning is conveyed by organized groups of words, they nevertheless start with discussion of tools that tend to focus upon the word, such as Bible dictionaries and encyclopedias, wordbooks and lexicons, and especially concordances. Hayes and Holladay show awareness of the kinds of lexical fallacies identified by James Barr, but offer no further discussion than to list several of these problems with studying individual words. When it comes to syntax, they suggest that sentence diagramming may be useful. The chapter concludes (as do the others) with an extensive bibliography heavy on lexical works, concordances, and wordbooks. The bibliography of Greek grammars includes BDF, Moule, A. T. Robertson, and Daniel Wallace, as well as a number of the other traditional grammars (besides numerous beginning grammars), with only one of them reflecting a clear modern linguistic approach (R. W. Funk). There are also listings of lexicons, concordances, interlinears, and a short section on semantics and linguistics with works by such authors as Barr, G. B. Caird, Arthur Gibson, Johannes Louw, Eugene A. Nida, and Charles Taber. This list is shorter than the one provided in the previous edition (second edition of 1987).

There are flashes of insight into the role of Greek language in Hayes and Holladay. They are aware of various semantic theories, especially the work of Barr, but in fact make no reference to any specific Greek grammar or approach to grammatical study. They are better at identifying the possible abuses than they are outlining a constructive program.

Gordon D. Fee (1983)

When Fee wrote the first edition of his guide to exegesis, he already assumed that "exegesis requires a minimal knowledge of Greek."[12] He does note, in the second edition of 1993, that he still does insist that his students learn the Greek alphabet—we are relieved to hear.[13] Knowledge of Greek clearly does not figure prominently in Fee's approach to exegesis. As is reflected in other works by Fee, he takes a genre-based approach, beginning with context and background and ending with application. Included in the

12. Fee, *New Testament Exegesis*, xv, in the "Preface to the First Edition."
13. Ibid., xvii, citing the "Preface to the Second Edition." He makes no reference in the preface to the third edition regarding knowledge of Greek, with the implication that the situation is as it was from the first and second editions. See ibid., xi–xii.

process is both structural and grammatical analysis. In structural analysis, Fee suggests that "it is helpful to rearrange the Greek into the standard English order," with the exceptions of preserving chiasms and adverb clauses.[14] Treatment of grammar itself follows the principles of traditional grammar. Fee not only examines Greek using these categories but recommends such works (e.g., Blass/Debrunner, Moulton/Howard/Nigel Turner, Robertson, among others).[15] Grammatical study becomes a process in naming the various elements, such as problematic words and clauses, and determining the cases, the *Aktionsart*, voice, and mood of verbs (with Fee noting not to "overexegete"),[16] the meanings of conjunctions, the sense of prepositions, the relationships of participles and infinitives, and what requires further discussion. There is also a separate chapter on analyzing words, which, again, requires identification of words needing further study and their range of meanings. A concordance is recommended for this chore.

This volume, first published just before a turning point in Greek studies, nevertheless disrupts the entire enterprise by attempting to make Greek unnecessary. Nevertheless, the Greek that is advocated falls into the category of traditional grammar.

Werner Stenger (1987)

Despite its origins in German academia, Stenger's exposition of exegesis requires knowledge of no language "other than English." The preface proudly declares that "[n]o Greek is used—as in the book's German predecessor."[17] Nevertheless, the New Testament is to be read like any other book, and to be heard in its original context. Stenger tends to associate exegesis with determining "the text's linguistic form" and its historical circumstances.[18] This limits historical-critical exegesis to what the text meant. However, those who are limited to using translations are themselves using interpretations. Those translations that favor the original language tend to represent formal equivalence and those that favor the target language tend to be dynamic

---

14. Ibid., 42.

15. Ibid., 74–75.

16. Ibid., 76; cf. 75–78. Fee is very inconsistent in the examples he chooses, sometimes underemphasizing phenomena of importance (e.g., various imperative forms) and sometimes overemphasizing others (e.g., a conjunction). He unfortunately equates *Aktionsart* with tense.

17. Stott in the "Preface" to Stenger, *New Testament Exegesis*, xiii.

18. Stenger, *New Testament Exegesis*, 3.

or functional equivalence. Stenger includes a chapter on textual criticism before turning to exegetical method. He begins with defining a text as being "cohesive and structured" and "relatively self-contained and intending a specific effect"[19]—which he exemplifies with analysis of a three-word construction into its segments. From these segments he claims to be able to determine arrangement and relationships, from which he determines intention. Stenger calls dividing a text into its segments form criticism (a type of synchrony), as opposed to various diachronic approaches such as tradition criticism, source criticism, redaction criticism, and genre criticism.

This is by far the quirkiest book on exegesis that I have investigated. Not only does it depart from Germanic exegesis at various points (e.g., its definition of form criticism and its explicit lack of use of Greek), but it shows an odd mix of linguistic knowledge and traditional historical criticism. Stenger seems to be wanting to press the boundaries of German historical criticism but cannot fully launch his attempt.

Michael J. Gorman (2001)

Gorman describes three methodological approaches to exegesis: synchronic (i.e., literary and rhetorical analysis, linguistic analysis, and social-scientific criticism, although it is unclear that he follows any of these synchronic approaches, instead opting for theological interpretation), diachronic (i.e., historical-critical method), and (in a poor choice of terms) existential (i.e., canonical criticism, theological exegesis, missional hermeneutic, spiritual reading, embodiment, advocacy and liberationist exegesis, and ideological criticism), according to his appendix on methods.[20] Then the author outlines seven steps in his exegetical approach that follow from a primarily synchronic approach. None of the steps explicitly involves the use of Greek. In fact, the author develops his entire method without requiring any use of the biblical languages. His only discussion of Greek grammar is a section on "resources" that lists Blass/Debrunner and Wallace's traditional grammars.[21] However, Gorman does say that "you should obviously do as much of your exegetical work as possible with the Hebrew or Greek text,"[22] even though he never says what it means to do exegesis using Greek or Hebrew apart possibly from preparing a translation. He instead recognizes that

19. Ibid., 23, 24.
20. Gorman, *Elements*, 234–40.
21. Ibid., 213.
22. Ibid., 38.

even an interlinear might demand too much or overextend the exegete, so he advocates for avoiding interlinears and using translations instead, if the exegete does not have competence in the original languages. More telling is Gorman's statement that not "everyone has the luxury of mastering ancient languages before doing exegesis."[23] From Gorman's perspective, rather than Greek being essential to exegesis, it is now a dispensable luxury.

In the twenty-first century, the use of Greek has become an optional, in fact unnecessary, luxury in the exegetical process. There is an implicit assumption that Greek grammar is traditional grammar, and that it is dispensable within the exegetical process.

Richard J. Erickson (2005)

Not only has Erickson taken the fear out of exegesis, to play on his sub-title, but he has taken Greek entirely out of it. Greek is not even listed in his index and occupies no significant place in his exegetical method. Erickson's book was written in response to Fee's "thoroughness" in his approach.[24] Nevertheless, Erickson does intend in his book "to lay a groundwork for the exegesis of the *Greek* New Testament"—even if all of the examples are also given in English.[25] He thus has an early section on the importance of the biblical languages, the languages in which the Bible was written. He recognizes that we have a large number of Bible translations but also that one who wishes to be an expert in, for example, a literature other than English must not rely simply on English translations but must master the original language and use it in exegesis. He recognizes that there are pressures of time and disparaging comments made about learning Greek (especially by those who never have), but he insists upon it anyway.[26] Grammatical analysis occupies a place in his overview of biblical exegesis. His approach to exegesis takes a discourse analytical approach. He begins with the structure of texts including its coherence and the elements that indicate its structure, followed by a chapter on syntax and discourse analysis. Erickson here provides some comments on the elements of grammar and some examples of how texts are connected together beyond the clause. Ironically, the only Greek grammar that he cites in his annotated bibliography, Wallace, is antithetical to discourse analysis.

23. Ibid., 39.
24. Erickson, *Beginner's Guide*, 13.
25. Ibid., 15.
26. Ibid., 21–22.

Erickson provides a theoretically robust defense of Greek, but without actually showing how Greek plays a significant role in exegesis. His appeal to discourse analysis is timely and useful, although his understanding of Greek grammar fails to support this approach in any substantive way.

Craig L. Blomberg and Jennifer Foutz Markley (2010)

This volume by Blomberg and Markley is arguably the oddest of the exegesis books that I have surveyed. The order of the chapters makes this clear, especially in relation to how Greek is treated. The chapters proceed in this order: textual criticism, translation and translations, historical-cultural context, literary context, word studies, grammar, and then interpretive problems, outlining, theology, and application. Only a moment of consideration will show the illogicality of this approach. One is expected to be able to formulate findings regarding the state and condition of the text, but not weigh grammatical matters until near the end of the exegetical process. Translation is the first substantive interpretive step in exegesis, and apparently can be done satisfactorily without appeal to word studies or grammar. Of course, one cannot avoid matters of Greek in translation, unless one is simply adopting a particular translation. Nor can one ignore Greek grammar in literary analysis as well. This makes it particularly odd that matters of Greek only appear in later chapters. I will not comment here on the chapter on word studies, except to note that it is a mixed bag of attempts at linguistic assertions while at the same time retaining traditional diachronic study. More important is to note the chapter on grammar. The reason for its late appearance is perhaps found in the justification for the chapter appearing so late in the book. The reason offered is that there "may be intricacies of grammar that help us fine-tune our understanding of the text."[27] These intricacies are several; they can give insights into clausal connections and various individual grammatical forms such as the meanings of verbs, the meanings of particular cases, the use of the article, etc. Most of the chapter is devoted to the very task of refining or correcting various translations or well-known interpretations, using a wide variety of grammatical works without apparent differentiation between traditional grammars and more recent linguistic works.

The inclusion of an entire major chapter on Greek grammar is welcome, although its purpose and placement raise questions about the actual role of Greek within the exegetical model of Blomberg and Markley. Their

---

27. Blomberg and Markley, *Handbook*, 143.

use of traditional grammars side by side with linguistic works, while it shows a broad knowledge of the secondary literature, does not indicate a knowledge of their differences or distinctives.

Summary

As is reflected by this survey of major works on exegesis published since the 1960s to the present, there has been a significant transformation in the place of Greek within exegetical method. There are several observations to make. The first is that fifty years ago there was the assumption that exegesis was grounded in knowledge and use of ancient Greek. There was not the necessity of establishing the importance of Greek or debating its usefulness, since Greek as a necessary component of the exegetical process was assumed from the outset as one of the abilities that was brought to the task of exegesis. The second is that Greek has lost its place of significance within the exegetical process. The transformation appears to have been a relatively subtle yet progressive one from a position of priority to one in which entire exegetical methods are constructed in which Greek occupies no necessary place—even if the expositions of exegesis wish or try to maintain a place for Greek as a concession to the history of exegesis. Even Blomberg and Markley's treatment, which devotes an entire chapter to Greek, by placing it as one of the last substantive chapters of the exegetical method, indicates its demotion. The third observation is that translation has clearly taken the place of Greek within the exegetical process, to the point that at least one of the authors identifies the learning and knowledge of Greek as a luxury, rather than as a necessity. The fourth and final observation to make is that, apart from the last treatment by Blomberg and Markley, all of the treatments of exegesis approach Greek from the standpoint of traditional grammar. For some, such as the early works, this is understandable, as they were written before the significance of modern linguistics was felt in Greek language study of the New Testament (that is, around 1961 with publication of Barr's *Semantics of Biblical Language*). However, for the only work that makes reference to the wider range of Greek grammars available, Blomberg and Markley, there is no differentiation or apparent recognition of the difference between a traditional and a linguistically informed grammar. The result is that they treat all of them in the same way, citing them without differentiation. They do not realize that traditional grammars have a different linguistic orientation than do modern linguistically informed grammars.

The implications for exegesis of these different views of grammar is what I wish to discuss in the next section of this paper.

MODELS OF GREEK GRAMMAR AND THEIR IMPLICATIONS FOR EXEGESIS

Virtually all of the treatments of exegesis noted above, when they invoke Greek grammar as part of the exegetical process, refer to grammars that were written within the traditional grammatical framework. Only one of the works cited above makes reference to works produced from a modern linguistic framework reflecting the kinds of interests brought to the fore by Ferdinand Saussure and the Prague Linguistics Circle—but even this exegesis book does not appear to recognize such a linguistic distinction but cites the various grammars indiscriminately. In this section of the paper, I wish to discuss the differences between traditional grammar and a modern linguistic approach, and within this modern linguistic approach the differences between two linguistic schools of thought that have emerged on the scene.

Traditional Grammar

Traditional grammar is often associated with classical philology.[28] Classical philology is traditionally concerned with the establishment and reading (note in light of our discussion above that this is often interpreted to mean nothing more than to provide a translation) of the texts of the ancient world, with the result that these literary masterpieces were preserved in reliable editions for scholarly use (much as the UBSGNT or NA is preserved for those in New Testament studies). When these ancient texts were studied, they were often studied in relation to comparative philology. Comparative philology was the product of Enlightenment expansion of knowledge regarding language. In the early nineteenth century, expansion of knowledge led to recognition that languages of the world enjoyed common origins. This led to the development of means of classifying languages on the basis of their family relations. The Indo-European family, among several others (which have continued to be re-examined in more recent thought), encompassed a wide range of language that spanned from the Indian subconti-

---

28. See Porter, "Studying Ancient Languages," 162–66, citing Crystal, *What Is Linguistics?* 9–24; Lyons, *Introduction*, 4–38. I note also that modern linguistics is not the ability to translate, something emphasized by several of the exegetical methods above. See Porter, "Studying Ancient Languages," 166–67.

nent to western Europe and beyond. A combination of classical philology and comparative philology has driven much of the study of the Greek of the New Testament, especially as traditional grammar was utilized.

Traditional grammar is characterized by, as with classical philology, giving priority to written over spoken language, especially as seen in the best representative writing of a culture. As a result of the accidents of preservation, the literary remains of a language are not necessarily reflective of the representative range of uses of language within a language community. Particular kinds of texts were often preserved for various reasons, whether these were political, economic, social, or otherwise. The categories of traditional grammar often reflect a highly regularized form of the language. This often reflects not only linguistic terminology based in Latin—because of its position as the language of western scholarship and a perception of it as a suitable language for emulation—but Greek philosophical thought regarding language from the fifth century BC, which was the origin of the debate over nature and convention. The result is a rule-based account of language that attempts to account for regularity but finds anomalies difficult to characterize within its view of language, to say nothing of its difficulties with such phenomena as regional or dialectal variation, register variation, and stylistic variation—all features of language use. Traditional grammar also tends to emphasize description of a language in the language of the students studying that language. The result has been the domination of German and more recently English of the scholarship on language, and the tendency to conceive of other languages in terms of the categories of German or English. Some problems of the ancient languages are thereby overlooked because they are not translated into problems in the metalanguage, or unnecessary problems are created by means of the metalanguage and its characteristics. Related to the previous feature is that traditional grammar tends to impose logical standards upon language that are foreign to natural languages, such as rules regarding infinitives or prepositions in English (and in Greek issues regarding negation, among others). If languages fail to attain to particular perceived or imposed logical standards, value judgments are often made regarding the nature and even quality of the language involved, labeling such language as in some way vulgar, corrupt, or otherwise inferior (Semitic perhaps?). The labeling systems used with languages often reflect such a perspective. Traditional grammar has also often been subject to the imposition of other areas of interest upon the study of language. These include views of anthropology, sociology, politics, economics, rhetoric, theology, and others. Finally, traditional grammar is usually characterized by a non-systematic or more atomistic approach to language. A given language is not seen as a system so much as a set of discrete and separate entities, each of which can be examined apart from its relationship with other components of the language.

It is not hard to see that many, if not most, of the standard Greek grammars that are used in the study of New Testament Greek reflect traditional grammar, often with other features of comparative and classical philology. The classic example is the grammar by Blass and Debrunner, still widely cited as a standard reference tool in New Testament studies. The first edition of this grammar was published in 1896 by Blass, a classical philologian, and it was revised in subsequent editions by Debrunner, a comparative philologian. The grammar continues to be published in German in much the same form, retaining essentially the same paragraph numbering system of the first edition. The basis for examination of the Greek of the New Testament is in relation to its deviations from classical or Attic Greek, with the resulting judgments being made about the quality of the Greek, and explanations being offered in relation to such justifying factors as Semitisms and Septuagintalisms. Moulton's *Prolegomena* is similar in nature. Moulton incorporated into his grammar many of the categories from the recent work in comparative philology pioneered by such scholars as Karl Brugmann and Berthold Delbrück, whose multi-volume studies of comparative philology remain landmarks of this period in linguistic study. Moulton, however, to his credit, was determined to turn the tables upon classical philology (in which he was trained, along with comparative philology, at Cambridge) by establishing the individual character of koine Greek, especially as it was more profitably compared to the language found in the documentary papyri of Egypt. These documentary papyri represented not the literary remains of the Greco-Roman world but the common writing of the period. Robertson's massive grammar follows in this tradition, with the noted feature not only of its thoroughness in exemplification but its compendious nature in relation to comparative philology (and to the detriment of his introduction of new ideas into the discussion). I could continue by discussing other grammars as well.

A major problem, however, is that many of the Greek grammars that continue to be produced are written within the traditional grammatical framework. A good example of this is Wallace's grammar.[29] Even though

---

29. See Porter, "So What Have We Learned," 13–14, from which this section is taken.

Wallace claims to be informed by linguistics, his *Greek Grammar* is probably better described as an attempt to salvage traditional grammar through a selected few principles formulated to sound linguistic.[30] Several of his principles regarding his approach have linguistic potential, such as his reference to "semantic situation," "unaffected vs. affected meaning," and "synchronic priority,"[31] but even these raise questions. For example, why does Wallace feel compelled to use the labels he does when there are suitable terms from the broader field of linguistics? I fear that it is because he means something different by them. For example, his notion of semantics is extensive and inclusive, to the point that he cannot use the typical semantic vs. pragmatics distinction. He recognizes the tension, but it appears that he wishes to categorize and discuss pragmatics but arrive at semantic conclusions. However, on a number of other issues, he appears very unlinguistic, such as what seems to be confusion over the notion of structure in language. His notion of "structural priority" seems to be confined to individual structures,[32] rather than the structure of language (or even of a given language), a notion that seems absent from his approach. Most disconcerting is his statement regarding "the cryptic nature of language."[33] The matter is not nearly as cryptic as he contends, except that he has unnecessarily restricted himself to a minimal notion of context, wants to deal predominantly with what he variously calls "morpho-syntactic uses/element(s)/categories/features/structure(s)/construction,"[34] and arrives at semantics through forms (what he apparently labels a type of word grammar).[35] In relation to traditional grammar, Wallace rejects the notion of being systematic, clearly calls into question descriptivism by advocating a form of prescriptivism (as well as

---

30. Wallace, *Greek Grammar*, esp. 1–11. His definition of syntax is also to be questioned (e.g., p. xv). The one linguistic theory that Wallace seems to acknowledge but clearly disagrees with is Noam Chomsky's transformational grammar, based upon the work of Ian Robinson (*New Grammarians' Funeral*), whose work is interesting but cannot be said to speak for the field of linguistics in its reaction to Chomsky (e.g., Robinson's statement that linguistic fashions come and go, with the implication that Chomsky's will soon go!). Wallace seems to draw upon the work of Matthews (*Syntax*), but I am not convinced that he has always understood Matthews (e.g., p. xv n. 14 and n. 15), and more than that, what syntax is.

31. Wallace, *Greek Grammar*, 2–5.

32. Ibid., 5–7.

33. Ibid., 7–9.

34. These various terms are found (inter alia?) in ibid., x, xii, xiii, xiv, xvi, 5, 6, 10, 11.

35. Ibid., xvi. His treatment does not have the other characteristics of a word grammar, such as dependency syntax (see below).

mistaking the notion of what it means to be ungrammatical), and does not address the issue of spoken vs. written language apart possibly from recognizing the need for sufficient data. Further, he does not address problems related to the priority of spoken language, he only tacitly acknowledges problems regarding the corpus, he apparently makes a plea for regularization (and this is exemplified in his work), his actual descriptions are often in terms of English (e.g., the use of English-based sentence diagramming, description of the genitive in relation to English "of").[36] he seems to adopt a logical view of language (hence his discussion of "ontological" meaning in relation to other types of meaning),[37] he emphasizes the importance of theology in his overall discussion, and there is the definite tendency toward atomization (and categorization—note the 33 uses of the genitive).[38] Hence he summarizes his approach as a type of (unstable) hybrid that continues to endorse traditional grammar.[39]

The implications of the use of traditional grammars in exegesis are several—besides the obvious one that I will mention below that they are not reflective of or even attempting to avail themselves of subsequent linguistic thought and insight. The first is that use of a traditional grammar invokes a set of questionable presuppositions regarding the Greek language, including the Greek of the New Testament, with value judgments often attached. Much of the confusion over the nature of the Greek of the New Testament, and with it problems or supposed problems regarding its vulgar or Semitic or Septuagintal nature, are grounded in a traditional grammatical framework that has been unable to understand or appreciate register, stylistic, or dialectical variation of various types. A second implication is that there have been a number of issues that have been foisted upon Greek while neglecting others that are of importance. Questions regarding the Greek tense system (regardless of what one thinks of the indicative) are more reflective of the metalanguages used to study Greek than of Greek itself, as are questions regarding typological word order. A third implication is that the efforts at labeling individual categories has resulted in what verges upon a prescriptive approach to grammar. The categories of, for example,

---

36. Ibid., 73–74, 86, 83, 118.

37. Ibid., 2 n. 8.

38. Ibid., 72. Wallace notes at the beginning that he has developed categories, "some of which have never been in print before" (ibid., xii). This is believable but often regrettable that some of them made it into print.

39. Ibid., 7 n. 32; cf. 5 n. 20.

the genitive, continue to multiply, even if understanding of the semantics of the genitive case do not grow equivalently. Rarely is the case system seen to be an integrated system within the structure of the Greek language.

We are at a place in Greek grammatical study where we must finally lay to rest the traditional grammars that have so long dominated our field and turn to linguistically informed grammars.

Linguistically Informed Greek Study

Having defined traditional grammar, and seen that the tendency is to continue to promote traditional grammar as what is meant by the use of Greek grammatical study in exegesis—where it is used at all—I now wish to lay out some of the agreed assumptions regarding a linguistically informed approach to Greek grammar. Despite the acknowledged diversity within linguistics—something to be recognized and even welcomed—there are enough common features to identify that distinguish a modern linguistic approach from traditional grammar, including comparative and classical philology. These features include the observation that modern linguistics is empirical, explicit, systematic in method, concerned with language structure, synchronic over diachronic, and descriptive. It is not primarily concerned with the history of language or of a language, is not focused upon origins such as etymologies, and especially not the ability to translate. Each of these areas begs for further elucidation but indicates that traditional grammar and modern linguistics have noticeable and substantial differences—especially as seen in how language is treated within exegetical works. Having said that we must use linguistically informed grammars, however, I realize that such language is not precise enough for our discussion, because there are at least two major schools of thought regarding what linguistically informed grammar means. I spend more time on the first, cognitive-functional linguistics, because it is perhaps less well known to many but has some serious shortcomings that must be exposed, and less on the second, Systemic Functional Linguistics, because it is better known in New Testament studies and has already proven itself as a productive approach to the text.

Cognitive-Functional Linguistics

There has been an intriguing interest in cognitive-functional linguistics within New Testament studies in recent years. This is in some ways surprising, as the approach of one of its major advocates has been on the scene since at least 1992. Some of the reasons are probably that his approach is in some ways highly eclectic, requiring no high degree of specialist knowledge within the field of linguistics; his most widely used work on the subject is written in an accessible way that appeals to a wide range of audience; his work has been strongly advocated by a few others who have dedicated themselves to it; and advocates of it have unfortunately heralded it as an exclusive approach to analysis of Greek. Stephen Levinsohn has come to be seen as the figurehead for this particular movement in Greek language study, followed by his acolyte Steven Runge. Most of what I say about Levinsohn also applies to Runge, who essentially adopts Levinsohn's linguistic framework.

Levinsohn characterizes his approach as eclectic and functional. For him, functional means, citing Robert Dooley, "an attempt to discover and describe what linguistic structures are used for: the functions they serve, the factors that condition their use."[40] He distinguishes function from structure, as "an attempt to describe linguistic structure ... essentially for its own sake."[41] The "one basic principle" of his functionalism that he cites is "choice implies meaning," with the idea that where no choice exists nothing is to be distinguished or examined.[42] I will return to the notion of function in Levinsohn's framework. I here simply wish to note that the term functionalism encompasses wide and diverse approaches to language, probably only unified by the fact that they are not formalist or Chomskyan. The other tenet of Levinsohn's approach is that it is eclectic. He defines this eclecticism as "making use of the insights of different linguists and different linguistic theories to the extent that I feel they are helpful," even if this means drawing conclusions that "are the exact opposite" of those of the scholar being used, such as Talmy Givón.[43] This methodological statement, such as it is, is problematic. Levinsohn cites no other figure or methodological approach, and the one that he does cite is used to state that he at times draws the opposite conclusions. However, Levinsohn does identify three areas of presumed focus of his volume: the value of discourse analysis, markedness, and semantic meaning and pragmatic effects. A very similar introduction

---

40. Levinsohn, *Discourse Features*, vii, citing Dooley, "Functional Approaches," 1.

41. Levinsohn, *Discourse Features*, citing Dooley, "Functional Approaches," 1.

42. Levinsohn, *Discourse Features*, viii. Levinsohn does not cite any of the abundant literature on the notion of choice and its relationship to meaning.

43. Ibid., vii. He cites two works by Givón, *Topic Continuity* and his two volume *Syntax: A Functional-Typological Introduction*.

to his own approach is given by Runge, who often paraphrases or cites similar concepts as Levinsohn. Runge defines his "function-based approach" (he also defines it as cross-linguistic) in terms very similar to those used by Levinsohn and Dooley. Runge sets his work within a discourse framework and has three major presuppositions: choice implies meaning, a differentiation of semantics from pragmatics, and a theory of markedness expanded to prominence (the principles are the same as Levinsohn's, even if the ordering is different).[44]

Returning to Levinsohn's work, we can examine more carefully his theoretical foundations (I will not do the same for Runge, who, as noted above, appears to be highly dependent upon Levinsohn). Within the area of discourse analysis, he appeals to Knud Lambrecht's work on "information structure." Within the area of markedness he cites my work. Concerning semantics and pragmatics, he cites the work of Vladimir Zegarac on relevance theory. Thus, besides himself, Levinsohn refers to five other linguists: Dooley, Givón, Lambrecht, Porter, and Zegarac. I will return to Dooley, but Givón is one of the leaders of the functional/typological linguists of North America (but who also has cognitive tendencies),[45] Lambrecht has taken a noble notion of information structure (which originated with Halliday, inspired by the Prague linguists)[46] and cognitivized it in terms of mental representations, and Zegarac is a relevance theorist using this cognitive theory (Levinsohn only cites Porter to criticize him). Some of the common threads in this at-first-appearance disparate group are brought together in the work that Dooley and Levinsohn were writing at the same time as Levinsohn was writing his revised version of his *Discourse Features*. Dooley and Levinsohn's work is described on its back cover as a "functional and cognitive approach." This approach is confirmed in a number of ways. These include: a number of the fundamental linguists cited in their work, such as the leading cognitive scientist Philip Johnson-Laird, who have cognitive orientations (some of whom are noted above); the use of the cognitive category of mental representations as fundamental for understanding most of the chapters and their content, including coherence, thematic groupings,

---

44. One of the major shortcomings of Runge's work (*Discourse Grammar*) is that it is very limited in its scope, confining itself to a small, select number of discourse features mostly concerned with the textual function (the organizational elements of texts). They include forward-pointing devices, information structuring devices, and thematic highlighting devices.

45. See Givón, "Grammar of Referential Coherence," 5–55.

46. Halliday, "Notes."

activation and referential status of words and phrases, discourse-pragmatic structuring of sentences, kinds of information in sentences, semantic relations, conversation, and organization (half of the chapters of the volume), and a variety of terms such as point of departure, activation, cognitive status, chunking, coherence, and processing. This helps to explain a number of the features not only of Levinsohn's work but also of Runge's. Runge throughout his volume utilizes language and concepts that are cognitively conceived, besides drawing upon many of those noted above in Dooley and Levinsohn. For example, Runge invokes frames, adopted from cognitive linguistics, including two chapters on framing;[47] makes fundamental reliance upon the "processing hierarchy" that links levels of explanation;[48] and has explicit concern for cognitive views of information structure, which constitutes one of the three divisions of his book, among others.

The explicit cognitive-functional framework of Dooley and Levinsohn, along with all of the other features that I have noted, indicates that both Levinsohn's and Runge's works have a greater cognitive dimension to them than they perhaps wish to admit. I am not saying that they are not eclectic—they are, possibly to a fault, as it is difficult to grasp exactly what model they are following (since Runge seems mostly simply to follow Levinsohn, who is imprecise at this point)—but that there is a strong cognitive component. The Dooley and Levinsohn book addresses many of the same linguistic categories as are exemplified in Levinsohn's and Runge's books addressed to Greek, which seems to indicate that their treatment, even with its eclectic features, is essentially cognitively conceived and cognitively executed.

There are several implications if I am correct at this point. The first is that we probably must revisit how we view these works within a general understanding of the study of Greek. The field of cognitive linguistics has emerged as a reaction to Chomskyan formalism (and for good reason), while retaining many of the elements that are concerned with the human brain as information processor. There are implications of this view linguistically and exegetically, but also philosophically and biologically—as well as possibly theologically.[49] The second implication is that we probably

---

47. Runge, *Discourse Grammar*, 207–42, 243–68.

48. Ibid., 131–32, 291–92. I note that the language of "processing" is very much the language of cognitive linguistics, where the metaphor of the human brain as computer is exploited.

49. Regarding the theological question, I wish merely to note here that there are some who argue that some kind of cognitively oriented view of language is a more theologically defensible view than a functional one. The argument apparently is that innate

must also revisit what is meant by the notion of being cognitive-functional. Dooley and Levinsohn, along with Runge, define functional in a particular way that is amenable to a variety of linguistic models. However, I wonder whether their definition is not more amenable to the more limited cognitive perspective. The functions that the linguistic structures serve appear to be functions that are more or less directly related to various types of cognitive processing. For example, Levinsohn uses the term "point of departure" from the outset. "Point of departure" is defined as linking the subsequent material to something "accessible in the hearer's mental representation."[50] Runge does not choose to use the term "point of departure," but instead uses the term "frame of reference" to mean the same thing (it is known as "topicalization" within information structure), to the point of citing Levinsohn's definition.[51] If this is the case, then their approach is not functional in the same sense as I believe many functionalists maintain, but it has the implication of being confined to the function within the cognitive framework or mental representation of the language user. This is not the place to address this perspective in detail. However, I wish merely to note here that there are numerous inherent problems in accepting a cognitive view of language, especially when attempting to describe an ancient language without native users.

On the basis of the above discussion, one might well argue that both fundamental principles of cognitive linguistics—the Generalization Commitment and the Cognitive Commitment—seem to be at odds with the kind of description needed for an ancient language such as Greek. The Generalization Commitment demands fuzzy boundaries, in which there are many family resemblances among categories and polysemy characterizes human language.[52] I think that we will have a hard time convincing other exegetes that the kinds of assumptions of precise distinctions that we think are fundamentally important in examining the meaning of a text are in fact not essential to the linguistic perspective. In fact, both Levinsohn

---

language ability, even to the point of some kind of universal grammar (in some forms of the argument), is what it means for the human to be made in the image of God. I would argue that Gen 1 contradicts this and exemplifies a functional view of language in which God creates through the use of language, and the human performs similar functions in the naming of the animals.

50. Levinsohn, *Discourse Features*, 8, referring to another of his earlier works.
51. Runge, *Discourse Grammar*, 190 n. 29.
52. See Evans and Green, *Cognitive Linguistics*, 28–40, referring to Lakoff, "Invariance Hypothesis," 39–74 for this and the following "commitments."

and Runge in their descriptions go beyond the kinds of overriding principles endorsed by cognitive linguistics and attempt precise formulations, including precise formulations concerning individual words, such as conjunctions. The Cognitive Commitment to utilizing the latest in cognitive research may itself be unobjectionable in theory, but is hard to know how to utilize in practice.[53] We may agree that there is no separate language module in the human brain, but it is more difficult to use in exegesis the notion of symbolic structures associated with cognitive processing. Again, neither Levinsohn nor Runge seems to do so, and when they do their categories are less useful than those that are more formally based. The nature of linguistic description, and with it the ability to label particular cognitive functions, must be reconceptualized as a result (notwithstanding cross-linguistic typologizing) if we are to take a cognitive approach. I do not believe that all of these factors have been duly considered by Levinsohn and Runge. As a result, even though there has been some penetration of such cognitive-functional models into Greek exegesis, and even if they would provide a substantial advance over traditional grammar, I do not believe that they offer a satisfactory resolution to the contemporary exegetical situation. The implications of such an approach outweigh the benefits.

Systemic Functional Linguistics

There are many other possible approaches to Greek that might be used within an exegetical framework. As noted in the first section of this paper, the demands of exegesis have been surprisingly small with regard to Greek, even to the point of not demanding its knowledge at all. Recognition of the exegetical interpretive situation would seem to demand closer attention to the demands made of the study of ancient Greek. Some of the presuppositions of exegesis are that the language of the ancient text is used for determinable communicative purposes within particular situational contexts. The situational contexts may result in variations in language on the basis of the field of discourse, the participants involved, their varying relationships, and the varying media and modes available for communication. We may not know the specific historical factors involved in this exegetical context, but we need a form of language analysis that will make it possible to describe and then discuss these various factors. The ability to be able to describe the various "meanings" instantiated in a text in many ways constitutes an exegetical method that is sensitive to the appropriate linguistic

---

53. See Evans and Green, *Cognitive Linguistics*, 40–44.

factors—as well as providing meaningful links to other important factors within a full-bodied approach to exegesis.

This is not necessarily the place to argue for Systemic Functional Linguistics (SFL) as a suitable approach to Greek grammar for exegetical purposes. That has been done elsewhere in abundance and continues to be done in a variety of work that addresses major interpretive and exegetical issues in the Greek of the New Testament.[54] I wish here merely to point out that an approach like SFL (at least as it has been used in the study of the New Testament)[55] addresses the major concerns raised above regarding the role that study of Greek should play in exegesis. The first concern is authorial vs. interpreter meaning. One of the problems of the cognitive approach is that it becomes unclear whether we are dealing with the cognition of the author or of the interpreter. This is especially true in a cross-linguistic framework where generalization is prioritized over specificity in treating a language. SFL, however, attempts to depict the language system of the language user, and hence is compatible with views of authorial meaning (even if we recognize the complexity of this concept). The second concern is recognition of language potential. Traditional grammar, as well as the cognitive approach outlined above, tends to equate what the user can mean with what the user does mean. The recognition of language potential, and with it the capacity for various linguistic means of expression, is part of the semantic potential of the language, realized in the lexicogrammar. This meaning potential can be expressed in the form of systemic networks. The third concern is context. Even those exegetical models that do not fully integrate or appreciate the use of Greek usually wish to find a place for a notion of context. SFL incorporates a robust notion of context as one of the major strata of abstraction, with a definable relationship to the language. The fourth concern is features of Greek. A major problem with cognitive linguistics, as well as cross-linguistic typology, is that it generalizes language usage to the point of not representing any given language. SFL, as a descriptive approach to language, has the capacity to base its descriptions upon Greek. This has not always been done, but is increasingly being done in SFL

---

54. A few representative works include Reed, *Discourse Analysis*, esp. 16–122; and Porter, *Letter to the Romans*. For individual essays, see the various volumes of the journal *Biblical and Ancient Greek Linguistics*.

55. Contra Runge, *Discourse Grammar*, 202–4 on how SFL is unsuited to handling some phenomena (such as focus) because it was developed on English. The English origins of SFL are true, but Runge fails to note various developments of SFL in Greek study that address these issues.

work. This allows Greek criteria to be used to speak of verbal aspect, focus, or any number of other features, without necessarily being constrained by either cognitive or other language categories. The fifth concern is discourse features. Several of the exegetical treatments begin with recognition of discourse features, which tends to put their discourse analysis at odds with Greek grammar. Such a disjunction can be overcome by a SFL approach that integrates discourse considerations into the semantic framework, especially as seen in something like register analysis. The sixth concern is language variation. There is a tension within traditional grammar, as well as cognitive linguistics, over language variation and how this relates to various notions of standard languages and cognitive adequacy. SFL recognizes the importance of language variation, whether this is variation according to user or use. The latter, variation according to use, is captured in register analysis as a recognition of how situational context affects language.

CONCLUSION

This paper has been concerned to examine the role of Greek in New Testament exegesis. I must confess that, when I began this study, I did not expect to find the results that I did. The fact that so many exegetical methods are content not to put knowledge of Greek at the heart of their exegetical process has noteworthy and significant consequences. These include the failure to appreciate the contribution that Greek makes to exegesis and lack of awareness of developments in Greek study that should be incorporated into the exegetical task. However, once we investigate the Greek approaches available, we also see that there is a range of possibilities. Of those exegetical treatments that do mention Greek language study, most of them are content to endorse traditional grammars. However, traditional grammars share a number of assumptions that are worth questioning and in fact have been so questioned. There seem to be two ways forward being indicated in Greek language study. One of them is cognitive-functional and the other is systemic-functional. I have tried to show that the cognitive-functional approach is less concerned with the functions of language than the function of cognition, and hence provides a less satisfactory orientation to Greek language study. More in keeping with the requirements of New Testament exegesis is a systemic-functional approach that is concerned with a truly functional approach to language.

BIBLIOGRAPHY

Barr, James. *The Semantics of Biblical Language*. Oxford: Oxford University Press, 1961.

Blomberg, Craig L., with Jennifer Foutz Markley. *A Handbook of New Testament Exegesis*. Grand Rapids: Baker Academic, 2010.

Conzelmann, Hans, and Andreas Lindemann. *Interpreting the New Testament: An Introduction to the Principles and Methods of N. T. Exegesis*. Translated by Siegfried S. Schatzmann. 1975. Peabody, MA: Hendrickson, 1988.

Crystal, David. *What Is Linguistics?* 3rd ed. London: Edward Arnold, 1974.

Dooley, Robert A. "Functional Approaches to Grammar: Implications for SIL Training." Unpublished manuscript, 1989.

Dooley, Robert A., and Stephen H. Levinsohn. *Analyzing Discourse: A Manual of Basic Concepts*. Dallas, SIL International, 2001.

Erickson, Richard J. *A Beginner's Guide to New Testament Exegesis: Taking the Fear out of Critical Method*. Downers Grove, IL: InterVarsity, 2005.

Evans, Vyvyan, and Melanie Green. *Cognitive Linguistics: An Introduction*. Edinburgh: Edinburgh University Press, 2006.

Fee, Gordon D. *New Testament Exegesis: A Handbook for Students and Pastors*. 1993. 3rd ed. Louisville: Westminster John Knox, 2002.

Givón, Talmy. "The Grammar of Referential Coherence as Mental Processing Instructions." *Linguistics* 30 (1992) 5–55.

———. *Syntax: A Functional-Typological Introduction*. 2 vols. Amsterdam: Benjamins, 1984–1990.

———. *Topic Continuity in Discourse*. Philadelphia: Benjamins, 1983.

Gorman, Michael J. *Elements of Biblical Exegesis: A Basic Guide for Students and Ministers*. 2001. Rev. ed. Peabody, MA: Hendrickson, 2009.

Halliday, M. A. K. "Notes on Transitivity and Theme in English, Part II." *Journal of Linguistics* 3 (1967) 199–244.

Hayes, John H., and Carl R. Holladay. *Biblical Exegesis: A Beginner's Handbook*. 1982. 3rd ed. Louisville: Westminster John Knox, 2007.

Johnson-Laird, Philip N. *Mental Models*. Cambridge, MA: Harvard University Press, 1983.

Kaiser, Otto, and Werner G. Kümmel. *Exegetical Method: A Student Handbook*. Translated by E. V. N. Goetschius and M. J. O'Connell. 1967. Rev. ed. New York: Seabury, 1981.

Lakoff, George. "The Invariance Hypothesis: Is Abstract Reason Based on Image-schemas?" *Cognitive Linguistics* 1 (1990) 39–74.

Lambrecht, Knud. *Information Structure and Sentence Form: Topic, Focus, and the Mental Representation of Discourse Referents*. Cambridge: Cambridge University Press, 1994.

Larkin, William J. *Greek Is Great Gain: A Method for Exegesis and Exposition*. Eugene, OR: Wipf & Stock, 2008.

Levinsohn, Stephen H. *Discourse Features of New Testament Greek: A Coursebook on the Information Structure of New Testament Greek*. 2nd ed. Dallas: SIL International, 2000.

Lyons, John. *Introduction to Theoretical Linguistics*. Cambridge: Cambridge University Press, 1968.

Matthews, P. *Syntax*. Cambridge: Cambridge University Press, 1983.

Moule, C. F. D. *Idiom Book of New Testament Greek*. Rev. ed. Cambridge: Cambridge University Press, 1959.

Ogden, C. K., and I. A. Richards. *The Meaning of Meaning: A Study of the Influence of Language upon Thought and of the Science of Symbolism*. London: Routledge and Kegan Paul, 1923.

Porter, Stanley E. *Idioms of the Greek New Testament*. 2nd ed. BGL 2. Sheffield: Sheffield Academic, 1994.

———. *The Letter to the Romans: A Linguistic and Literary Commentary*. NTM 37. Sheffield: Sheffield Phoenix, 2016.

———. "So What Have We Learned in the Last Thirty Years of Greek Linguistic Study?" In *Getting into the Text: New Testament Essays in Honor of David Alan Black*, edited by Daniel L. Akin and Thomas W. Hudgins, 9–38. Eugene, OR: Pickwick, 2017.

———. "Studying Ancient Languages from a Modern Linguistic Perspective: Essential Terms and Terminology." *FN* 2 (1989) 147–72.

Porter, Stanley E., ed. *Handbook to Exegesis of the New Testament*. Leiden: Brill, 1997.

Reed, Jeffrey T. *A Discourse Analysis of Philippians: Method and Rhetoric in the Debate over Literary Integrity*. LNTS 136. Sheffield: Sheffield Academic, 1997.

Robinson, Ian. *The New Grammarians' Funeral: A Critique of Noam Chomsky's Linguistics*. Cambridge: Cambridge University Press, 1975.

Runge, Steven E. *Discourse Grammar of the Greek New Testament: A Practical Introduction for Teaching and Exegesis*. Peabody, MA: Hendrickson, 2010.

Schnelle, Udo. *Einführung in die neutestamentliche Exegese*. 1983. 5th ed. Göttingen: Vandenhoeck & Ruprecht, 2000.

Stenger, Werner. *Introduction to New Testament Exegesis*. Edited and translated by Douglas W. Stott. 1987. Grand Rapids: Eerdmans, 1993.

Wallace, Daniel B. *Greek Grammar Beyond the Basics: An Exegetical Syntax of the New Testament*. Grand Rapids: Zondervan, 1996.

Zegarac, Vladimir. "Relevance Theory and the Meaning of the English Progressive." *University College London Working Papers in Linguistics* 1 (1989) 19–31.

9

The Benefits of Being an "Outsider"
Mark 4:12 as an Epexegetic Ἵνα Clause

Mark Proctor

Stanley E. Porter's landmark dissertation on Koine Greek's verbal network describes Mark 4:12 as "one of the most problematic verses of the entire NT"[1]—and for good reason. Most English Bibles present this verse as disclosing the motivation behind Jesus's public use of parabolic speech, and so accordingly gloss its opening conjunction with the words "in order that" or "so that."[2] As a direct consequence of rendering ἵνα this way, Mark's text would appear to claim that Jesus delivers his tantalizing stories not to enlighten the public about life in God's Kingdom, but to engage them instead with intentionally ambiguous speech, impenetrably opaque metaphor, and purposefully evasive language. While the Twelve as kingdom "insiders" have direct access to its mystery, those outside their inner sanctum encounter Jesus's parables instead as "riddles" he crafts in an effort to preclude their widespread public understanding.[3] Under the influence of this approach to the Greek text of Mark 4:12, William Wrede more

---

1. Porter, *Verbal Aspect*, 325. Tolbert concurs: "Verses 10–12 have probably elicited more scholarly debate than any two [sic] similar verses in all of the New Testament. The problem is that the verses suggest that Jesus is teaching in parables *so that* 'those outside' will not understand what he is saying" (*Sowing the Gospel*, 160, emphasis hers).

2. See the ASV, CEB, ESV, (N)KJV, NASB, NET, (T)NIV, NJB, NLT, and (N)RSV. A notable exception is the God's Word to the Nations version (GWN), which by not representing ἵνα in translation seems to adopt a perspective on the verse's content that is amenable to this paper's argument.

3. Rhoads et al., *Mark as Story*, 57. They accordingly gloss Mark's use of the noun παραβολή as "riddle."

than a century ago sought to include the Second Gospel's parables under the aegis of Mark's messianic secret motif: "Jesus is veiling himself from the people by his teaching.... He speaks in parables and only in parables (v. 33) to the crowd, intentionally offering them everything in this and no other form—because it is an essential feature of this form to be incomprehensible: it permits the audience to perceive something, to be sure, but in such a way that they do not grasp its significance."[4] For those not within Jesus's circle of associates, everything comes in obscure and indiscernible riddles, "*so that they* may indeed look, but not perceive, and may indeed listen, but not understand; *so that* they may not turn again and be forgiven" (NRSV, emphasis added).[5] On this reading of Mark 4:12 Jesus's short stories do more to obfuscate kingdom truth than illuminate it, and for this reason the parables seem geared to keep outsiders guessing about the precise

---

4. Wrede, *Messianic Secret*, 56–57. Wrede moves on to equate the word παραβολή with "riddle" in Mark, and suggests Jesus's stories contain "secret teaching" appropriate only for the disciples (57, 60). While some rightly scrutinize Wrede's decision to read Mark 4:12 as a mechanism for the messianic secret (since the parables generally do not concern Jesus's personal Christological identity), his more fundamental conviction about the function of this ἵνα clause has become a scholarly commonplace. Commentators who read Mark 4:12 as a purpose clause include the likes of M. Eugene Boring, Adela Yarbro Collins, C. E. B. Cranfield, R. Alan Culpepper, Robert H. Gundry, Joel Marcus, and Vincent Taylor. Parable scholars such as Craig L. Blomberg, Madeleine Boucher, John Dominic Crossan, C. H. Dodd, John R. Donahue, Charles W. Hedrick, Arland J. Hultgren, Joachim Jeremias, and Klyne Snodgrass also find this understanding of Mark 4:12 convincing. Indeed, this strategy for reading Mark 4:11–12 dates at least as far back as Origen: "Jesus covered up the deeper mysteries of the faith in veiled speech to those who were not yet ready to receive his teaching in straightforward terms. The Lord wanted to prevent the unready from being too speedily converted and only cosmetically healed" (*Princ.* 3.1).

5. Larry W. Hurtado attempts to mitigate Mark 4:12's harshness by suggesting the verse points not to the motivation informing Jesus's parabolic speech but to its divinely predetermined result: "The parables are described as producing no insight because that is their prophetically foreseen *result*. Stating the *result* of the parables in this ironic fashion suggests that the lack of response by the crowds is not something in which to take satisfaction, but is sad and lamentable, and reflects frustration, not joy" (*Mark*, 74 emphasis added). Unfortunately for Hurtado, however, his approach to Mark 4:12 allows the parables to continue functioning for Jesus's wider audiences as perplexing riddles. If Mark's protagonist understands what his parables do to people, as one might observe, why would he not alter his instructional approach? Put simply, reading Mark 4:12 in the way Hurtado suggests does little more than substitute a pedagogically-inept, scripturally-hamstrung storyteller for an intentionally enigmatic riddler. Rather than address the issues of the "ἵνα→purpose" reading, the "ἵνα→result" approach winds up portraying Jesus as a frustrated rabbi who knowingly speaks over the public's head because Scripture (for some indiscernible reason) requires that he do so.

meaning of his words. The confusion they engender on the public's part thus seems intentional and by design.

Not only does this way of understanding Mark 4:11–12 stand in tension with popular Christian regard for the parables as transparent illustrations of kingdom living, but it also runs afoul of the evidence the Second Gospel affords to the contrary; for in Mark the crowds never really seem to misunderstand the parables and even Jesus's enemies discern his intent whenever he uses the genre to oppose them. Mark refers to Jesus's public use of parabolic speech five times in the Second Gospel: (1) in the Beelzebul Controversy (3:23), (2) before the Sower (4:2), (3) as part of the summary statement concerning Jesus's use of parables (4:33–34), (4) following the saying on defilement (7:17), and (5) for the sake of introducing the Vineyard and the Tenants (12:1). Since three of these contexts refer to Jesus's provision of supplementary private instruction for the disciples (4:14–20, 34; 7:17–23), it is tempting to suppose (especially if one regards Mark 4:12 as a purpose clause) that the public remains just as confused about the precise meaning of Jesus's parabolic speech as the disciples.

Such a judgment would, however, constitute a profound *non sequitor* for nowhere in Mark does the evangelist hint that anyone other than the disciples fails to understand Jesus's figurative mode of address. In 3:23 Jesus deploys parabolic speech to counter a vicious accusation, and the straightforward nature and clarity of his defense seems undeniably convincing. At the conclusion of the Vineyard and the Tenants, moreover, the narrator points out that Jesus's adversaries perceive "that he had told the parable against them" (12:12). Mark 4:33 even goes so far as to affirm the public's "ability to hear" (καθὼς ἠδύναντο ἀκούειν) Jesus's parabolic instruction with understanding. So, despite its popularity among scholars and its supposed prima facie lexico-grammatical probability, understanding Mark 4:12 as a purpose clause remains both unsatisfying for many Christian readers and unsustainable on strictly narrative grounds.[6] As an alternative

---

6. Margaret G. Sim advises against thinking about the meaning of ἵνα clauses in Koine texts in light of the conjunction's predominant lexical gloss. Instead of starting with the English words "in order that" in mind, she suggests readers would do a better job interpreting such clauses if they think of ἵνα as "a procedural marker alerting the reader to expect an indication of the speaker or subject's thought. . . . It is the responsibility of the reader to draw from the text the most relevant logical relation between the clause introduced by ἵνα and the rest of the sentence" (*Marking Thought and Talk*, 20). Sim contends that while the meaning of ἵνα by itself "is undetermined in that it does not have a fixed dictionary meaning," it may introduce a representation of "purpose, result, intention, desire, indirect command or interpretation of the thought of another,

to the "ἵνα→purpose" thesis, I wish to argue it is better to read Mark 4:12 as epexegetic in function; i.e., the verse does not disclose Jesus's rationale for teaching in parables, but instead offers commentary on the unfortunate situation of "those outside" (see ἐκείνοις τοῖς ἔξω in v. 11) God's kingdom. Reading the text in this way allows for an alternative understanding of Mark 4:11–13 that makes good sense both of Jesus's constructive use of parables elsewhere in the Second Gospel and also of Mark's negative characterization of the Twelve: "The mystery about the kingdom of God has been given to you. Yet to those outside everything comes in parables: Those people look closely but still do not understand; they listen intently but still do not comprehend and so might never turn and be forgiven. . . . Now if you do not understand this parable, how will you comprehend the rest?" Put simply, as an epexegetic ἵνα clause, Mark 4:12 presents Jesus's parabolic instruction as a pedagogical concession he makes to imperceptive "outsiders" in an effort to assist them in their attempt to understand the nature of God's rule. For Mark, parables like the Sower are what most Christians have traditionally supposed them to be: readily accessible heuristic devices.[7] Ironically, however, Jesus's close associates in Mark (despite their status as "insiders" and their reception of the kingdom's secret) have somehow failed even to understand such simplified, transparent, and accessible instruction. Defending this thesis will, of course, require a full discussion of ἵνα clause functionality in Mark. Having demonstrated that one of Mark's sixty-four ἵνα clauses is unquestionably epexegetic in function, I will next align the syntactical dynamic at work in Mark 4:11–12 with other New Testament contexts containing epexegetic ἵνα clauses. As a consequence of this demonstration, I hope to show Mark's readers can feel comfortable reading

---

but always a potential rather than actual state of affairs" (42).

7. Whether or not the Historical Jesus's parables were enigmatic is not this paper's concern. It may be that the Jesus of history entertained the public with provocative, polyvalent, open-ended stories that left the task of constructing their meanings up to their audiences. If so, Hedrick would be right to understand Synoptic use of the word παραβολή as referring to *"any saying of Jesus that struck the writer of an early gospel text as an enigma or a banal saying, or any saying whose plain surface meaning does not yield an adequate religious concept"* (*Many Things*, 5, emphasis his). Yet even if one were to agree that the Synoptic writers worked to domesticate the Historical Jesus's brief narrative fictions, I (like Werner Kelber) contend that Mark's act of putting pen to papyrus brought an end to any confusion he may have harbored about the meaning and function of his protagonist's speech; for the Second Gospel's parables shroud no mysteries and point only to what for the Evangelist had become definite, discernable realities even outsiders could apprehend.

Jesus's statement in 4:12 as his elaboration of ἐκείνοις τοῖς ἔξω ("those on the outside") in v. 11, and that doing so provides an understanding of this verse that aligns more easily with the Second Evangelist's broader narrative goals and purposes.[8]

ἽΝΑ IN THE SECOND GOSPEL AS A MARK-ER FOR PURPOSE, RESULT, AND CONTENT CLAUSES

The Second Evangelist displays a rather robust repertoire when it comes to employing ἵνα clauses; for he scatters sixty-four uses of this conjunction across fifty-nine verses to introduce four different types of subordinate clauses. As one might perhaps expect, the majority of Mark's ἵνα clauses serve an adverbial function and so indicate either the purpose or the result of the verbs they modify.[9] Of Mark's thirty "ἵνα→purpose" clauses, thirteen provide the rationale for some sort of command, request, or bit of advice (1:38; 2:10; 3:9b; 5:12, 23b; 6:36; 11:25; 12:2, 13, 15; 14:12, 38; 15:32).[10] In Mark 1:38, for instance, Jesus tells the disciples, "Let us go on to the neighboring towns, so that (ἵνα) I may proclaim the message there also." Here as elsewhere, context clearly indicates the ἵνα clause discloses the purpose behind the main clause's hortatory subjunctive verb form (ἄγωμεν). The remaining seventeen "ἵνα→purpose" clauses have no connection to any sort of imperative and serve one of two functions. Fifteen provide the rationale for a character's action, be it real (3:2, 10, 14; 6:41; 7:9; 8:6; 9:22; 10:13; 14:10; 15:11, 15, 20; 16:1) or merely hypothetical (10:17). The father's description of the demon's treatment of his possessed son in Mark 9:22 provides a good example of this type of "ἵνα→purpose" clause: "It has often cast him into the fire and into the water, so that (ἵνα) it might destroy him; but if you are able to do anything, have pity on us and help us." The two remaining "ἵνα→purpose" clauses aim to define an inanimate

---

8. "The more coherence an interpretation can disclose in a text, the more persuasive it becomes" (Tolbert, *Sowing the Gospel*, 11).

9. Porter notes, "the most common method for forming a purpose clause is with the subjunctive mood form (and occasionally the future form), following either usually ἵνα or occasionally ὅπως" (*Idioms*, 232). "A pure final clause is one whose office is to express the purpose of the action stated in the predicate which it limits" (Burton, *Syntax*, §197).

10. Although Nigel Turner claims "ἵνα in Mk 15:32 καταβάτω ἵνα ἴδωμεν καὶ πιστεύσωμεν is obviously consecutive" (*Syntax*, 102), it seems better to regard this example as naming the purpose behind the chief priests and scribes' mocking request that Jesus come down (καταβάτω) from the cross.

object's *raison d'être*: "He said to them, 'A lamp is not meant to be placed under a bushel basket or under a bed, right? Is it not instead meant to be placed on a lampstand?'" (4:21). The Greek text for this verse carries over into English idiom only with considerable difficulty. It involves two marked rhetorical questions, the first of which expects a negative response (see μήτι in v. 21a), while the second anticipates an affirmative answer (see οὐχ in v. 21b). Also, ὁ λύχνος provides the grammatical subject for ἔρχεται in v. 21a, and v. 21b involves an ellipsis of the words ἔρχεται ὁ λύχνος after οὐχ. For Mark to qualify the lamp's "coming" with a ἵνα clause amounts to little more than broaching the topic of its proper household function.

Two of Mark's ἵνα clauses carry a consecutive meaning and so point to the anticipated result of their main verb's actions.[11] Having described the appropriate use of a lamp in the preceding verse, Jesus declares in Mark 4:22 that "there is nothing hidden, except to be disclosed (ἐὰν μὴ ἵνα ἐφανερωθῇ); nor is anything secret, except to come to light (ἀλλ' ἵνα ἔλθῃ εἰς φανερόν)" Context once again clearly indicates that both must be "ἵνα→result" clauses, since the purpose behind hiding something and/or keeping anything secret by definition aims to prevent both its disclosure and illumination. Put simply, in this verse Jesus describes in good proverbial fashion something he anticipates will come about as a result of the actions of others yet in defiance of their aims, goals, and purposes. A. T. Robertson recognizes as much when he writes, "in Mk. 4:22, ἐὰν μὴ ἵνα φανερωθῇ, we have ἵνα (cf. ἀλλ' ἵνα) used like ὥστε and the inf."[12]

It is important to note that Mark 4:22's ἵνα clauses speak only of anticipated rather than real or actual results, since the scenario Jesus envisions is purely hypothetical, since one would otherwise expect ὥστε to introduce the clauses and for them to use infinitives rather than finite subjunctive verb forms.[13] Indeed, the same holds true for all "ἵνα→result" clauses: "The relation of thought between the fact expressed in the principal clause and

---

11. Maximilian Zerwick articulates the difference between consecutive/result and final/purpose clauses in the following way: "The distinction between consecutive and final clauses lies in the fact that a consecutive clause declares the end which in the nature of things is reached by something, whereas a final clause declares the end which someone intends to reach" (*Biblical Greek* §351). "Consecutive clauses denote the result (intended or actual) of the action indicated by the verb in the main clause.... A ἵνα clause (with the subjunctive) may be substituted for ὥστε and the infinitive of *intended* result" (Funk, *Beginning-Intermediate Grammar*, 519–20, emphasis added). Funk lists 1 John 1:9 as an example of a "ἵνα→result" clause.

12. Robertson, *Grammar*, 999.

13. See Higgins, "NT Result Clauses with Infinitive," 233–41.

that expressed in the clause of *conceived* result introduced by ἵνα is that of cause and effect, but it is recognized by the speaker that this relation is one of theory or inference rather than of observed fact."[14]

Of the Second Gospel's thirty-two remaining ἵνα clauses, thirty are substantival content clauses that function like nouns in their respective contexts.[15] The example at Mark 9:12, for instance, provides a subject for its governing verb: "He said to them, 'Elijah is indeed coming first to restore all things. How then is it written about the Son of Man, that (ἵνα) he is to go through many sufferings and be treated with contempt?'" While Robert A. Guelich seeks to label this an epexegetic clause,[16] it seems better to regard it instead as providing a grammatical subject for the passive verb γέγραπται. Having noted that "a ἵνα clause rarely appears as subject," Funk points to Mark 9:12 as an example.[17]

---

14. Burton, *Syntax*, §219, emphasis added. Just a few pages later Burton claims "there is no certain, scarcely a probable, instance in the New Testament of a clause introduced by ἵνα denoting actual result conceived as such" (ibid., §222). "If actual result is to be denoted an analytical construction with ἵνα cannot, or should not, be substituted . . . .'Ἵνα can be substituted for the infinitive of result (probably also for other kinds, too, in later writers), but hardly for actual result" (BDF, §391). Sim recognizes as much when she notes how the deployment of the subjunctive mood in ἵνα clauses "makes salient the *potential* state of affairs in view" (*Marking Thought and Talk*, 103, emphasis added).

15. "A content clause states the content of some other unit, such as a subject, complement, predicate, and so forth. The conjunctions ὅτι and ἵνα are the most frequent for indicating a content clause" (Porter, *Idioms*, 237, emphasis his). "In classical usage ἵνα with the subjunctive introduced only strictly final clauses, i.e. not object or subject clauses but adverbial ones indicating the end in view. . . . Later it began to be more and more used for the infinitive expressing the object (which in a certain sense is an «end in view») with verbs of asking, commanding or the like. . . . Thus ἵνα is used not only for the object-infinitive with verbs of asking, exhorting, commanding . . . but also for the subject infinitive" (Zerwick, *Biblical Greek*, §§ 406, 408). Robertson describes these as sub final clauses: "There are a considerable number of [ἵνα] clauses which are not pure purpose and yet are not result. They are the bridge, in a sense, between the two extremes. They are found with verbs of striving, beseeching, commanding, fearing. In some instances the clause is hardly more than an object-clause. . . . Thus the ἵνα clause is seen to be either nom. or acc., simply, or in apposition with a substantive" (*Grammar*, 991–92). Robertson's final comment indicates that what this paper refers to as "'ἵνα→epexegetic" clauses he understands instead as a sub-category of "ἵνα→substantive" clauses.

16. In Guelich's estimation, ἵνα in Mark 9:12 "functions epexegetically with reference to the Scriptures" (*Mark 1—8:26*, 211). Guelich's proposed understanding thus seems to require that the ἵνα clause be in apposition to the monolectic subject of γέγραπται, which seems unlikely.

17. Funk, *Beginning-Intermediate Grammar*, 378. See also Burton, *Syntax*, §212. First Corinthians 4:2 and Rev 9:4 contain additional examples of "ἵνα→substantive"

The rest of Mark's "ἵνα→substantive" clauses all provide objects for the main verbs of their governing clauses (3:9a, 12; 5:10, 18, 23a, 43; 6:8, 12, 25, 56; 7:26, 32, 36; 8:22, 30; 9:9, 18, 30; 10:35, 37, 48, 51; 11:16; 12:19; 13:18, 34; 14:35, 49; 15:21). While he would probably agree that most of the examples communicate the content of some desire, command, or advice *via* a statement in indirect discourse,[18] Daniel B. Wallace suggests the initial ἵνα clause of Mark 5:23 provides instead a specimen of an independent imperatival ἵνα clause. For him, this verse and others like it (particularly 10:51; 12:19; 14:49) use ἵνα with the subjunctive in what he takes to be independent clauses in an effort to direct another person's behavior, and so he writes, "It is evident that the ἵνα clause does not logically follow what is previously said and, therefore, is not subordinate to it."[19] Alternatively, one may account for the phenomenon Wallace observes both here and elsewhere in Mark by labeling it an example of anacoluthon involving the ellipsis of the verbal element from the Second Evangelist's default pattern for conveying the content of expressions of desire, request, or command *via* substantival ἵνα clauses.

In Mark 6:25, for instance, Herodias's daughter petitions Herod Antipas in the following way: "I want you to give me at once the head of John the Baptist on a platter." The Greek text for this verse combines its main verb (θέλω/"I want") with a ἵνα clause that discloses the content of Herodias's request *via* indirect speech (ἵνα ἐξαυτῆς δῷς μοι ἐπὶ πίνακι τὴν κεφαλὴν Ἰωάννου τοῦ βαπτιστοῦ/"you to give me at once the head of John the Baptist on a platter"). This same pattern (verb of saying/desiring/requesting/commanding [+ personal object] [+ adverbial πολλά] + substantival ἵνα clause disclosing the content of the statement/desire/request/command *via* indirect discourse) appears regularly elsewhere in Mark.[20] In 10:35, for

---

clauses that provide grammatical subjects for passive voice verbs. The ἵνα clause in John 16:7 functions as the subject for an active voice verb, and the example in 1 Cor 9:13 provides a subject nominative for an elliptical ἐστίν.

18. "*The distinguishing feature for indirect questions and commands is introduction of the indirect speech by means of certain words, in particular the interrogative pronoun for indirect questions and* ἵνα *(among others) for indirect commands*" (Porter, *Idioms*, 274, emphasis his). "An innovation in Hellenistic is ἵνα c. subj. in commands, which takes the place of the classical ὅπως c. fut. indic." (Moulton, *Prolegomena*, 178).

19. Wallace, *Greek Grammar*, 477. See also Turner, *Syntax*, 95, and Robertson who describes ἵνα in Mark 5 23a and 10:51 as "merely an introductory expletive with the volitive subjunctive" (*Grammar*, 933).

20. See 3:9a, 12; 5:10, 18, 43; 6:8, 12, 56; 7:26, 32, 36; 8:22, 30; 9:9, 18, 30; 10:35, 37, 48; 13:18, 34; 14:35; 15:21. The list of verbs Mark deploys in these constructions includes

instance, James and John address Jesus in the following way: "Teacher, we want you to do for us whatever we ask of you." As is the case with Herodias's statement in 6:25, their words combine an expression of longing (θέλομεν) with a "ἵνα→substantive" clause that discloses the exact nature of what they desire from Jesus. If one understands the syntax of the ἵνα clauses in 5:23a, 10:51, 12:19, and 14:49 along similar lines, then in these cases Mark simply omits from the statements of Jairus, Bartimaeus, the Sadducees, and Jesus the verb of desiring that normally appears in such constructions.[21] This way of accounting for the data leaves Mark's readers without cause to regard the ἵνα clauses in 5:23a, 10:51, 12:19, and 14:49 as independent imperatival clauses. Rather, they are all substantival ἵνα clauses for which the main verbs have been elided, and they all disclose the content of an indirect command, request, or desire in a subordinate clause.[22]

Wallace also suggests classifying ἵνα clauses like those one finds in Mark 6:25; 9:30; 10:35; 11:16 as complementary clauses: "The complementary ἵνα *completes* the meaning of a helping verb such as θέλω, δύναμαι, and the like. In Classical Greek this would have been expressed by a complementary infinitive."[23] A simpler explanation that avoids any unnecessary multiplication of pragmatic categories for ἵνα clauses involves regarding these examples instead as substantival in nature; i.e., in Mark 6:25; 9:30; 10:35 the Second Evangelist provides θέλω with an object in the form of a "ἵνα→substantive" clause. The same case is perhaps a bit more difficult to make with the example at Mark 11:16, where the narrator points out that

---

the following: (1) ἀγγαρεύω (Mark 15:21), (2) διαστέλλω (Mark 5:43; 7:36; 9:9), (3) δίδωμι (Mark 10:37), (4) εἶπον (Mark 3:9; 9:18), (5) ἐντέλλω (Mark 13:34), (6) ἐπιτιμάω (Mark 3:12; 8:30; 10:48), (7) ἐρωτάω (Mark 7:26), (8) θέλω (Mark 6:25; 9:30; 10:35), (9) παραγγέλλω (Mark 6:8), (10) παρακαλέω (Mark 5:10, 18; 6:56; 7:32; 8:22), and (11) προσεύχομαι (Mark 13:18; 14:35).

21. One should accordingly supply/infer θέλω for 5:23a; 10:51; 14:49 and θέλει for 12:19.

22. In his section on object clauses after verbs of exhorting, Burton notes "under the head of verbs of *exhorting*, etc., is to be included the verb θέλω when used with reference to a command or request addressed to another. It is frequently followed by an object clause introduced by ἵνα.... In many cases a clause or Infinitive after a verb of *commanding* or *entreating* may be regarded as a command indirectly quoted. It is then a species of indirect discourse" (*Syntax*, §§203-4, emphasis his). For more on indirect commands, see Porter, *Idioms*, 274-75.

23. Wallace, *Greek Grammar*, 476, emphasis his. While Wallace does not include Mark 6:25 and 11:16 in his list of examples, both clearly fit his criteria since the first conjoins θέλω with a ἵνα clause in its predicate, and the second does the same but with a form of ἀφίημι as its main verb.

Jesus "would not allow anyone to carry anything through the temple." While I wish to argue that the ἵνα clause in this verse provides the main verb ἤφιεν with an object, the appearance of ἀφίημι with an infinitival complement at 1:34; 5:37; 7:12, 27; 10:14 perhaps suggests it would be better to regard the ἵνα clause in Mark 11:16 as a verbal complement as well. Before acting on this observation, however, one should note that Mark 5:19, 37; 7:12, 27; 10:14; 11:6; 14:6; 15:37 collectively demonstrate the Second Evangelist's ability to use ἀφίημι in the sense of "permit" along with an accusative object. Mark 15:36 also shares the same structure as Mark 11:16 (a form of ἀφίημι + a subjunctive content clause), albeit without the presence of ἵνα: ἄφετε ἴδωμεν/"permit that we might see." Combining these observations with the parallel use of substantival ἵνα clauses elsewhere in Mark has the effect of making Wallace's suggestion appear otiose.

ἽΝΑ IN THE SECOND GOSPEL AS A MARK-ER FOR EPEXEGETIC CLAUSES

This paper's thesis contends that Mark 4:12 constitutes an epexegetic ἵνα clause. Such clauses involve "the use of ἵνα after a *noun* or *adjective* to explain or clarify that noun or adjective."[24] Sim notes that "ἵνα→epexegesis" clauses "are preceded either by stative clauses, where the subject of the verb 'to be' may be a noun, an adjective or a demonstrative, or by a main clause in which there is a noun or demonstrative which is complemented or expanded by a ἵνα clause."[25] Claiming Mark 4:12 counts as an example of such a clause would prove difficult to maintain were it not for the presence of a clear example in Mark 11:28. In this verse, the chief priests, scribes, and elders query Jesus with the following words: "By what authority are you doing these things? Who gave you this authority to do them?" Their second question contains a ἵνα clause (ἵνα ταῦτα ποιῇς) that essentially defines what the religious leaders mean by "this authority" (τὴν ἐξουσία ταύτην). Here one might be tempted to regard the ἵνα clause as expressing the result of the hypothesized gift of authority, in which case one would render

---

24. Ibid. As such, "ἵνα→epexegesis" clauses offer what amounts to a definition of the noun or pronoun they modify. While Guelich also regards Mark 4:12 as a "ἵνα→epexegesis clause," he suggests it expounds on the preceding verse as a whole. "4:12 qualifies or interprets 4:11b by giving an explication using an OT citation" (*Mark 1—8:26*, 211). While Guelich accurately identifies Mark 4:12's function, he misidentifies its referent. See also Lampe, "Die markinische Deutung," 140–50.

25. Sim, *Marking Thought and Talk*, 99. The ἵνα clause at Mark 4:12 falls into the second of these two categories.

the question as follows: "Who gave you this authority, *such that* you do these things?" The problem with this reading, however, is that the proper provenance of "ἵνα→result" clauses concerns only "anticipated" or "potential" rather than "real" results.²⁶ Since Mark here portrays the chief priests, scribes, and elders as responding to things Jesus has already done, the prospect of Mark 11:28 containing a "ἵνα→result" clause necessarily seems ruled out as a matter of course. The better interpretive option thus sees this ἵνα clause as offering instead an explanation of the words τὴν ἐξουσίαν ταύτην. To the extent that ἵνα ταῦτα ποιῇς describes the reason behind Jesus's reception (ἔδωκεν) of authority, some hint of "purpose" remains present. Yet the combination of τὴν ἐξουσίαν with the near demonstrative pronoun compares well enough with clear examples of "ἵνα→epexegesis" clauses in the rest of the New Testament to confirm this clause's explanatory function. In order to avoid any confusion about the exact meaning of their inquiry, Mark refrains from having the religious leaders ask Jesus a question about "this authority" without clarifying exactly what authority they have in mind. Their curiosity concerns the authority on the grounds of which Jesus "does these things."

The undeniable presence of a "ἵνα→epexegesis" clause in Mark 11:28 thus demonstrates the Second Evangelist's awareness of and facility with using such constructions. Yet before characterizing Mark 4:12 as a second instance of this phenomenon I would like first to examine the use of this type of clause in the Fourth Gospel and the Johannine Epistles in an effort to gain a bit of clarity and perspective about such constructions. While the Johannine literature as a whole contains a higher concentration of "ἵνα→epexegesis" clauses than the rest of the New Testament documents, the epistles in particular exhibit a penchant for using this kind of explanatory clause. Of 1 John's nineteen ἵνα clauses, eight are indisputably epexegetic in function (2:27; 3:1, 8, 11, 23; 4:17, 21; 5:3).²⁷ Two of 2 John's five ἵνα clauses are clearly epexegetic (v. 6), while one of the two ἵνα clauses in

---

26. The use of the subjunctive (i.e., the mood of projection) with ἵνα requires as much.

27. Of the remaining eleven ἵνα clauses, four indicate purpose (1:4; 2:28; 3:5; 5:13), four point to a result (1:9; 2:19; 4:9; 5:20), and three are substantival content clauses (1:3; 2:1; 5:16). It is worth noting that one can make a strong case that the examples at 1:3-4 and 2:1 also serve an epexegetic function provided the demonstrative pronouns of their main clauses are cataphoric rather than anaphoric. Reading these three verses in this way would bring the total percentage of "ἵνα→epexegesis" clauses in 1 John to fifty-eight percent.

3 John functions in this way (v. 4).[28] Hence, at least forty-two percent of the ἵνα clauses in the Johannine Epistles are of the epexegetic variety, compared to a mere three percent in Mark. While "ἵνα→epexegesis" clauses still appear with regularity in the Fourth Gospel, the overall ratio drops to slightly more than ten percent, with fifteen of John's 145 ἵνα clauses carrying an epexegetic meaning.[29]

Many of the epexegetic ἵνα clauses one finds in the Johannine literature exhibit regularly occurring features that help identify or "mark" them as such. While all of them assist readers in unpacking what a writer means by an otherwise ill-defined term in the main clause, the exact role this ambiguous term plays within it can and does vary. Whereas many "ἵνα→epexegesis" clauses help clarify the meaning of a predicate nominative (John 6:29, 39–40, 50; 15:12; 17:3; 1 John 3:11, 23; 4:21; 5:3; 2 John 6), others help define the object of the main clause (John 11:57; 13:15, 34; 15:17; 16:30; John 2:25; 1 John 2:27; 3:1). While some elaborate on the object of an adverbial preposition appearing in the main clause (John 15:8; 18:37; 1 John 3:8; 4:17), others provide more detail about a genitive qualifier (John 15:13; 3 John 4). So while all "ἵνα→epexegesis" clauses involve an appositional relationship with a word in the main clause, that word's precise function within the main clause can vary according to context.[30]

---

28. While a pair of 2 John's three remaining clauses convey purpose (vv. 8, 12), the third example in v. 5 is a substantival content clause. Third John 3b is a purpose clause.

29. See John 2:25; 6:29, 39–40, 50; 11:57; 13:15, 34; 15:8, 12–13, 17; 16:30; 17:3; 18:37. One can make a case that the ἵνα clause in John 13:1 is epexegetic of αὐτοῦ ἡ ὥρα, but it may indicate purpose of the hour's coming instead. As elsewhere in the Johannine literature, the presence of a vague cataphoric pronoun in the main clause usually helps "mark" John's ἵνα clauses as epexegetic in function. Curiously, there are no clearly epexegetic ἵνα clauses in Revelation, even though the author uses the conjunction forty-two times. Indeed, only one of the ἵνα clauses in Revelation deserves consideration as carrying an epexegetic meaning: "And I heard a voice from heaven saying, 'Write this: Blessed are the dead who from now on die in the Lord.' 'Yes,' says the Spirit, 'they will rest from their labors (ἵνα ἀναπήσονται ἐκ τῶν κόπων αὐτῶν), for their deeds follow them'" (13:14). While this ἵνα clause perhaps explicates the predicate adjective μακάριοι by defining the nature of the "blessing," it could just as easily express the blessing's result. Since the proper provenance of "ἵνα→result" clauses concerns "anticipated" or "potential" results rather than "real" results, and given the presence of the deictic indicator ἀπ' ἄρτι, it seems best to classify this as a result clause. See also Rev 16:15, where the ἵνα clause clearly indicates the result of the blessing in a similar construction.

30. The explanatory nature of "ἵνα→epexegesis" clauses accounts nicely for Robertson's description of them as appositional clauses (*Grammar*, 1078). Funk also thinks "ἵνα→epexegesis" clauses fill the slot of an appositive: "Ἵνα may introduce clauses that stand in apposition to some other element in a sentence, usually with a demonstrative

In many instances the structure of the main clause is a simple stative, consisting of three basic elements: (1) a pronominal subject nominative, (2) a form of εἰμί, and (3) an arthrous predicate nominative.[31] More often than not, the main clause's subject will be a fronted, cataphoric demonstrative pronoun.[32] First John 3:23 provides a good illustration: "And this (αὕτη) is (ἐστίν) his commandment (ἡ ἐντολὴ αὐτοῦ), that (ἵνα) we should believe in the name of his Son Jesus Christ and love one another, just as he has commanded us."[33] That the demonstrative αὕτη could have been eliminated and the sentence rewritten in a simpler, more straightforward form (with the ἵνα clause itself filling the slot of the predicate nominative and ἡ ἐντολὴ αὐτοῦ the slot of subject nominative) suggests on the one hand that the writer here seeks to present the "ἵνα→epexegesis" clause as a prominent notion.[34] While it certainly is not the case that the audience knows nothing at all about what interests 1 John's writer (i.e., the Johannine believers must have been aware that Jesus provided them with instructions for communal living),[35] the text's structure intimates they have not yet heard enough

---

pronoun (οὗτος) preceding" (*Beginning-Intermediate Grammar*, 379; see also BDF, §394).

31. Assigning the pronouns in these sentences the role of subject nominative reflects Wallace's advice: "The general principle for distinguishing S from PN is that the S is the *known* entity" (*Greek Grammar*, 42, emphasis his). Hence, even though the predicate nominative is arthrous, the pronoun remains the grammatical subject in the sentence as the "known entity."

32. Steven E. Runge lists cataphoric demonstratives among the ways New Testament writers assign prominence to a target reference. "It is not some special semantic meaning of the part of speech that has the effect of highlighting; it is the fact that it is pointing forward to a yet-to-be-introduced target" (*Discourse Grammar*, 66).

33. Additional examples include 1 John 3:11 and 2 John 6a. The first of these seeks to define the content of the gospel message: "For this (αὕτη) is (ἐστίν) the message (ἡ ἀγγελία) you have heard from the beginning, that (ἵνα) we should love one another." In the second example, "love" receives explication: "And this (αὕτη) is (ἐστίν) love (ἡ ἀγάπη), that (ἵνα) we walk according to his commandments."

34. Such is the case with the ἵνα clause in John 4:34: "Jesus said to them, 'My food (ἐμὸν βρῶμα) is (ἐστίν) to do the will of him who sent me and to complete his work (ἵνα ποιήσω τὸ θέλημα τοῦ πέμψαντός με καὶ τελειώσω αὐτοῦ τὸ ἔργον).'" While this ἵνα clause does indeed explicate ἐμὸν βρῶμα, it accomplishes this task by providing ἐστίν with a predicate nominative. Hence, it is technically a substantival ἵνα clause rather than a "ἵνα→epexegesis" clause. Something similar occurs in John 18:39a: "But it is (ἔστιν) a custom (συνήθεια) of yours that I release someone for you at the Passover (ἵνα ἕνα ἀπολύσω ὑμῖν ἐν τῷ πάσχα)." While the provision of the word "it" in English translation is somewhat misleading, the ἵνα clause here provides ἔστιν with a predicate nominative. The words συνήθεια ὑμῖν fill the slot of subject.

35. Jesus is the antecedent of the pronoun αὐτοῦ, and it constitutes a clear example

about this topic. The writer's method of presentation in 3:23 thus helps his audience recognize believing in Jesus and loving one another as matters of considerable importance that are deserving of parenetic promotion as "his commands."

It also merits mentioning that in many cases a writer's decision to allow the ideological content of a "ἵνα→epexegesis" clause to find representation within the main clause by means of a vague, forward-pointing "stand-in" conveniently addressed two practical needs: (1) it made the writer's complete thought easier for readers to digest by offering its content in two distinct "bites" rather than one (first the main clause, then the epexegetic qualifier), and (2) it made the complete thought less cumbersome for writers to compose by granting them an opportunity to roll the sum total of the idea one finds in the "ἵνα→epexegesis" clause into a subordinate appendage to the main clause. Hence, the more complex or involved the contention of the "ἵνα→epexegesis" clause was, the more indispensable this structure became for efficient communication and composition. This also is easy to see from 1 John 3:23, where "his commandment" finds definition not just in one imperatival clause (ἵνα πιστεύσωμεν τῷ ὀνόματι τοῦ υἱοῦ αὐτοῦ Ἰησοῦ Χριστοῦ) but two (καὶ ἀγαπῶμεν ἀλλήλους), both of which the writer qualifies with a concluding adverbial clause (καθὼς ἔδωκεν ἐντολὴν ἡμῖν). Deciding to withhold a "ἵνα→epexegesis" clause until the end of a sentence *via* the assistance of an intentionally vague term in the main clause (be it a cataphoric demonstrative or some other equally ambiguous part of speech)[36] thus provided Greek language users with a way both to ease the delivery of a complex idea while simultaneously signaling the content of the "ἵνα→epexegesis" clause as prominent for readers.

Following his public performance of the Sower and other parables in Mark 4:1–9, Jesus retreats to a private place in v. 10 where "those around him with the twelve" inquire about the parables' meaning. Having pointed to their prior reception of the kingdom's mystery, Jesus makes the following statement: "Now to those outside (ἐκείνοις δὲ τοῖς ἔξω) everything comes in parables" (v. 11). In this way the Second Evangelist presents his audience with a contrast between those Jesus selects in ch. 3 to "be with him" (see ἵνα ὦσιν μετ' αὐτοῦ in v. 14) and "outsiders." But who exactly are those people on the outside? Tolbert, for one, encourages her readers against

---

of a subjective genitive; i.e., ἡ ἐντολὴ αὐτοῦ alludes to "the commandments Jesus gave."

36. In 1 John 3:1, for instance, the term the "ἵνα→epexegesis" clause explains is ποταπὴν ἀγάπην, "what sort of love," which of course begs for further clarification.

identifying "outsiders" with Jesus's public audience on the grounds that "in the immediately preceding episode 'those outside' denoted Jesus's natural family, while those inside were his new family, people who do the will of God (3:31–35)."[37] Tolbert appears to offer this idea as a means of preserving her earlier suggestion that the parables "were not intended to be confusing, misleading, or obscure."[38] Hence, she suggests "the division between those who are given the mystery, the insiders, and those who hear riddles, the outsiders, is not a simple opposition of disciples versus crowds."[39] While clever, Tolbert's reading ultimately stumbles over her inability to see in the present context what she clearly perceives everywhere else in Mark; namely, the Second Evangelist's scathing critique of the Twelve. This oversight on her part, moreover, comes about as a direct consequence of her having tagged Mark 4:12 as a "ἵνα→purpose" clause.[40]

So the question lingers: Who exactly are those people on the outside? For all my reservations about the particulars of Tolbert's response, she is right to suspect Mark's contrast between "insiders" and "outsiders" in v. 11 involves more than just the latter's physical separation from Jesus. If such were the case, one would have to regard the presence of the demonstrative ἐκείνοις as pleonastic since the substantival adverb τοῖς ἔξω would be enough on its own to draw the contrast between the two groups on either side of the door. So instead of dismissing Mark's inclusion of ἐκείνοις in v. 11 as a wordy flourish, perhaps there is something to gain by allowing the demonstrative to look forward to its target referent rather than backward. For Mark, "those outside" are the type of people Isa 6:9–10 describes: "They look closely but still do not understand; they listen intently but still do not comprehend and so might never turn and be forgiven." It is this sort of audience Jesus apparently tries to benefit by means of his parabolic instruction. His teaching seeks to assure "outsiders" of an opportunity to repent and to find God's forgiveness. Whereas plain statements about the

---

37. Tolbert, *Sowing the Gospel*, 160. Tolbert claims "'Those outside' in 4:11, then, corresponds to that class of people who, for whatever reasons, do not do the will of God" (160).

38. Ibid., 104; see also 87.

39. Ibid., 160.

40. Her reading also fails to realize that both Jesus's family in 3:31–35 and the crowd in 4:11–13 happen to share the same physical location vis-à-vis Jesus; i.e., both groups are "on the outside." Mark 4:11–13, moreover, has nothing to say about "doing God's will," but much about seeing, understanding, hearing, and comprehending. Put simply, there's been a change of topic since 3:31–35 that Tolbert's reading does not acknowledge.

kingdom's mystery may exceed their ability to comprehend, Jesus knows the crowds are at least up to the challenge of understanding his stories.

The narrator's summary statement in 4:33–34 does nothing short of prove him right: "With many such parables he spoke the word to them, since (καθώς) they were able to hear it; he did not speak to them except in parables, but he explained everything in private to his disciples." That καθώς here carries the causal nuance "since" rather than "to the extent that" seems clear in light of its use elsewhere in Mark to speak about the inevitable fulfillment of prophetic utterances (see 1:2; 9:13; 14:16, 21; 16:7).[41] So while BDAG suggests glossing Mark 4:33's use of καθώς with either "as" or "to the extent that" so as to limit the degree to which the contention of the main clause holds true, there seems to be no good reason for doing so provided Mark 4:12 is something other than a purpose clause.[42] Since the Second Gospel's two remaining uses of this comparative adverb both introduce indirect statements rather than exception clauses (see 11:6; 15:8), concluding Mark 4:33 makes an unqualifiedly positive statement about the crowd's comprehension of Jesus's parables seems obligatory. Only in the event Mark 4:12 contains a purpose clause is there any reason to suppose anyone other than the disciples experiences difficulty understanding Jesus's parabolic speech in the Second Gospel.

But what does all of this indicate about the Twelve? Two things suggest it is their failure to understand Jesus's instruction that constitutes the real focus of Mark 4:11–13 rather than the supposedly unfortunate plight of "those outside." Mark's selection of the remote demonstrative ἐκείνοις in v. 11 rather than the near demonstrative τούτοις signals to the reader that while v. 12's description of what it means to be an "outsider" remains significant to the discourse, it is not the most important point the Second Evangelist aims to make in these verses. According to Runge, "when there are other elements in the discourse that potentially compete with the default thematic element, the near and far demonstrative pronouns provide a means for the writer to disambiguate the role that these competing elements play . . . [by providing] an efficient way of marking an entity's thematic importance."[43]

---

41. Cf. Mark's comfortable substitution of ὅτι for καθώς in the citation formula at 14:27.

42. BDAG, "καθώς," 493. In fact, all the examples BDAG provides for this supposed nuance of καθώς can just as easily mean "since," "insofar as," or "in accordance with" (see Acts 2:4; 11:29; 1 Cor 12:11, 18; 15:58; 1 Pet 4:10).

43. Runge, *Discourse Grammar*, 369. Whereas the primary contextual topic is thematic, all other ideas appearing in the same context are athematic.

Whereas writers use the near demonstrative οὗτος to mark thematic ideas, the far demonstrative ἐκεῖνος instead marks athematic concepts. Runge explains, "Use of the far demonstrative as a substitute for a personal pronoun allows the writer the [sic] mark them as athematic, meaning that the center of attention remains focused on some other thematic participant. The athematic participant is only of passing interest."[44] As a consequence, Mark's selection of ἐκείνοις rather than τούτοις in v. 11 suggests that while the situation of "outsiders" remains important for Mark's readers to keep in mind, it does not represent the most significant idea Jesus wishes to communicate in these verses.[45] Appreciating the struggle outsiders experience when trying to understand God's kingdom remains relevant, but only to the extent it helps Mark make another more important point about the disciples' inability to comprehend Jesus's parabolic instruction.

Mark's use of the present tense λέγει in the frame that introduces Jesus's words in v. 13 helps confirm this reading of ἐκείνοις. According to Runge, mid-speech quotative frames of this variety are technically redundant (since they do not facilitate a change of speaker) and generally serve one of two purposes. They either (a) segment a larger speech into smaller units, or else (b) slow the discourse pace just ahead of a significant pronouncement.[46] Mark 4 contains six redundant quotative frames, all of which involve καί and a third-person singular form of λέγω (see vv. 9, 13, 21, 24, 26, 30). Of the six frames, only the one in v. 13 deploys the more heavily marked present tense λέγει rather than the imperfect ἔλεγεν.[47] In Runge's estimation, "if a writer is going to insert an *underspecified* redun-

---

44. Ibid., 370. Matthew 24:42–43 contains an instructive example. The first verse communicates the passage's thematic notion: "Keep awake therefore, for you do not know on what day your Lord is coming." What follows provides an important supplemental example Matthew marks as athematic by means of the far demonstrative pronoun: "But understand this (ἐκεῖνο): if the owner of the house had known in what part of the night the thief was coming, he would have stayed awake and would not have let his house be broken into." Runge quips "Jesus is not focused [in v. 43] on helping people avoid being burglarized; he is simply illustrating his main point" (379). Runge confirms this understanding in "Relative Saliency" by closely examining Stephen H. Levinsohn's treatment of the demonstratives in Mark 4:14–20 (103–25).

45. This constitutes an important difference between the "ἵνα→epexegesis" clause in Mark 4:12 and similar clauses in the Johannine literature, the vast majority of which explicate a cataphoric near demonstrative pronoun.

46. Runge, *Discourse Grammar*, 157.

47. For more information on markedness theory and how it relates to the Greek verbal network, see Porter, *Idioms*, 20–25.

dant frame with the goal of continuing the speech, the imperfect is the most natural choice."[48] Since Mark uses λέγει rather than the default ἔλεγεν in v. 13a, it seems best to infer his adoption of the more heavily marked present tense-form aims to *overspecify* Jesus's announcement in v. 13b thereby designating its idea as the immediately preceding context's thematic element.[49] Unlike the material that follows the five other redundant quotative frames in Mark 4, v. 13b does not begin a new segment of the discourse and the paragraph break that occurs in the NA28 text after Mark 4:12 should instead appear one verse later. Jesus's words in v. 13b thus constitute the climactic capstone of his statements in vv. 11–13. In these verses Jesus seeks to censure the disciples for their failure to understand what even the crowds find readily accessible. Put simply, the presence of λέγει in v. 13a signals to Mark's readers that vv. 11–13 as a whole belong together and have more to do with critiquing the disciples than characterizing the status of outsiders

---

48. Runge, *Discourse Grammar*, 160, emphasis added.

49. While he notes that many grammarians associate the use of what he calls the "historical" present with either discourse boundaries or marked prominence, Levinsohn argues that "the primary motivation for using the historical present (hereafter, HP) is to *highlight* and . . . particularly in Mark and John, what is highlighted by the HP is not so much the speech or act to which it refers but the event(s) that follow" (*Discourse Features*, 200, emphasis his). Levinsohn goes on to write, "It is what follows the event or speech associated with the HP that is highlighted" (ibid., 202). Coming as it does in the middle of Jesus's speech, λέγει in Mark 4:13 highlights not an "event" that follows, but a saying Jesus makes about his disciples. Mark 2:17 provides another illustrative example of λέγει marking one of Jesus's climactic statements: "And when Jesus heard it he said (λέγει) to them, 'The strong have no need for a physician, but those who are ill. I did not come to call the righteous but sinners.'" Other instances where λέγει marks a critical, climactic, or concluding saying of Jesus that remains tied to the preceding context include Mark 1:38, 44; 2:5, 8, 10, 14; 3:4–5, 33–34; 5:19, 36, 39, 41; 6:31, 38, 50; 7:18, 34; 8:12, 17; 9:19, 35; 10:11, 23–24, 27, 42; 11:2, 22, 33; 12:16; 14:13, 27, 30, 32, 34, 37, 41; 15:2. The example in 9:19 is particularly relevant, since the statement λέγει introduces in this verse announces a harsh judgment in the form of a question in much the same way as Mark 4:13: "Answering he said (λέγει) to them, 'You faithless generation, how much longer must I be among you? How much longer must I put up with you? Bring him to me.'" The narrator's change of tense form in Mark 12:16 away from the present λέγει when introducing Jesus's clinching question to the aorist εἶπαν when recording his antagonists' response nicely illustrates the weighted value of their respective input for the dialogue. That Mark could use λέγει at the head of a new paragraph is clear enough from 4:35: "On that day, when evening had come, he said (λέγει) to them, 'Let us go across to the other side.'" Yet even in this instance, the verb still highlights the following statement. Indeed, it is the summary nature of the preceding statement in vv. 33–34 rather than λέγει that facilitates this shift in the discourse. See also Mark 8:1, where the deictic indicator ἐν ἐκείναις ταῖς ἡμέραις rather than λέγει establishes the change of scene.

or establishing a parable theory that characterizes Jesus's stories as riddles. Such is the consequence of understanding Mark 4:12 in a way that allows the public to "see" and "hear" in the parables what the disciples ironically cannot.

Rather than present an obstacle to this paper's thesis, Mark's inclusion of the μήποτε clause at the end of v. 12 actually helps make its point stronger. The New Testament writers deploy μήποτε twenty-four times to mark three different types of clauses: (1) nineteen final/purpose clauses that either (a) provide the negative rationale for an explicit parenetic exhortation (Matt 5:25; 7:6; 13:29; 25:9; 27:64; Mark 14:2; Luke 12:58; 14:8, 12; 21:34; Acts 5:39; 2 Tim 2:25; Heb 2:1; 3:12; 4:1) or (b) name the negative outcome that another non-imperatival clause seeks to preclude as a matter of necessity (Matt 4:6; 15:32; Luke 4:11; 14:29); (2) two interrogative clauses that provide the content of a question in either direct or indirect discourse (Luke 3:15; John 7:26); and (3) three consecutive/result clauses that name the unfortunate consequence of another named circumstance (Matt 13:15; Mark 4:12; Acts 28:27).[50]

Like Mark 4:12, the μήποτε clauses in Matt 13:15 and Acts 28:27 involve citations of Isa 6:10b LXX. As is the case with Mark 4:12a, the first parts of both Matt 13:15 and Acts 28:27 describe a regrettable set of circumstances. While both Matthew and Luke use the μήποτε clause of Isa 6:10b LXX to describe the intended potential result of the claims in Isa 6:10a LXX, Mark instead skips over the content of Isa 6:10a LXX to include the μήποτε clause one finds in Isa 6:10b LXX immediately following his rather free citation of Isa 6:9 LXX. The respective text-forms read as follows:

Mark 4:12	Isa 6:9–10 LXX/Matt 13:14–15/Acts 28:26–27
ἵνα βλέποντες βλέπωσιν καὶ μὴ ἴδωσιν,	ἀκοῇ ἀκούσετε καὶ οὐ μὴ συνῆτε,
καὶ ἀκούοντες ἀκούωσιν καὶ μὴ συνιῶσιν,	καὶ βλέποντες βλέψετε καὶ οὐ μὴ ἴδητε·
μήποτε ἐπιστρέψωσιν καὶ ἀφεθῇ αὐτοῖς.	ἐπαχύνθη γὰρ ἡ καρδία τοῦ λαοῦ τούτου,
	καὶ τοῖς ὠσὶν (αὐτῶν) βαρέως ἤκουσαν
	καὶ τοὺς ὀφθαλμοὺς αὐτῶν ἐκάμμυσαν,
	μήποτε ἴδωσιν τοῖς ὀφθαλμοῖς
	καὶ τοῖς ὠσὶν ἀκούσωσιν
	καὶ τῇ καρδίᾳ συνῶσιν
	καὶ ἐπιστρέψωσιν, καὶ ἰάσομαι αὐτούς.

50. The lone remaining occurrence of μήποτε in the New Testament appears at Heb 9:17. The clause to which it belongs does not merit classification in one of these three ways because μήποτε here serves a purely adverbial function in an explanatory clause marked by ἐπεί.

They look closely but still do not understand, they listen intently but still do not comprehend, and so might never turn and be forgiven.	You hear a report and do not comprehend, and you look closely and do not see. For this people's heart is dull, and they hear with difficulty with their ears, and they shut their eyes; lest they should see with their eyes and should hear with their ears and should understand with their heart, and should turn around and I would heal them.

Even though Mark relocates Isa 6:10b's μήποτε clause to an earlier position in Isaiah's context, its basic function remains essentially unchanged; for both forms of text deploy μήποτε to mark a result clause describing the negative consequences of what precedes. Yet Mark's omission of Isa 6:10a is far from inconsequential. In the shared text of Matt 13:15; Acts 28:27; Isa 6:10 LXX, God's hard-hearted people (see the intransitive and deponent ἐπαχύνθη) hear only with difficulty (βαρέως ἤκουσαν) and shut their eyes (τοὺς ὀφθαλμοὺς αὐτῶν ἐκάμμυσαν). As a direct consequence, they do not (μήποτε) see with their eyes, hear with their ears, understand with their heart, or turn around so that God might heal them. Their failure in this regard, moreover, seems attributable to their own willful activity, and to this extent Isaiah's μήποτε clause carries with it a sense of purpose. The people do not see or hear because they try to avoid doing so.

Mark's text, by way of contrast, credits the crowd with at least attempting to see (βλέποντες βλέπωσιν) and trying to hear (ἀκούοντες ἀκούωσιν), even though their efforts ultimately fail to produce understanding and discernment. By eliminating Isa 6:10a LXX and emending the language of Isa 6:9 LXX, Mark presents public ignorance of the kingdom's mystery as the *unintended* result of their own ineptitude rather than the sort of willful intransigence observable in his source text. Mark's clever editing of Isaiah 6:9–10 LXX thus affords him the opportunity to characterize Jesus's parabolic speech as his protagonist's attempt to help "outsiders" overcome their maladroit intellectual limitations. That it might be otherwise holds true only in the event Mark 4:12 is a purpose clause. If ἵνα does not here point to the reason Jesus uses parabolic speech, any hint of purpose in the following μήποτε clause instantly dissipates and does so as a consequence of Mark's redaction of Isa 6:9–10 LXX.

CONCLUSION

This paper's argument has sought to overcome the problems associated with the standard scholarly interpretation of Mark 4:12 by reading it as a "ἵνα→epexegesis" clause rather than a "ἵνα→purpose" clause. Mark quotes Isa 6:9–10 LXX not to name the rationale behind Jesus's preferred method of communicating with the public, but in order to describe their plight apart from his pedagogical assistance. Both the complex nature of the quotation and the Second Evangelist's desire to mark its content as a prominent idea account nicely for his decision to include it within a "ἵνα→epexegesis" clause. While the preponderance of "ἵνα→purpose" clauses elsewhere in Mark's narrative probably explains the verse's history of interpretation, the presence of an indisputably clear example of a "ἵνα→epexegesis" clause at Mark 11:28 makes my thesis a live possibility. The verse's conformity with the basic structural features of "ἵνα→epexegesis" clauses in the Johannine literature further illustrates its viability. Jesus does not here claim to use figurative stories as a way to obscure truth for outsiders and in an effort to preclude their involvement in the kingdom. Rather, he aims only to contrast their admittedly pitiable condition with that of his disciples. To their credit, the crowds make an effort toward discipleship, and to this extent Rhoads, Dewey, and Michie are right to draw attention to them as the deserving objects of Jesus's compassion.[51] Understanding Mark 4:12 in this way thus allows for the public to discern the meaning of Jesus's parables in the way passages like 4:33–34 and 12:12 seem to require, and is in keeping with Jesus's general disposition toward the public elsewhere in Mark's story.

Someone, however, has to lose, and in this case it is the disciples. Here as elsewhere in the Second Gospel, Mark adds yet another nuance to his unflattering portrait of the twelve by casting them as even less perceptive than the crowds. Despite their "insider" access to the kingdom's mystery, they cannot even understand what "outsiders" find manageable: the message of Jesus's parables. Like an overly-accommodating elementary school teacher, the Markan Jesus compassionately explains the obvious to them time and again (see 4:14–20, 34b; 7:18b–23; 8:19–20; 13:28); yet he does not do so in this context without first venting his frustration over the disciples' lack of

---

51. "In general, the response of the crowds reveals their desire for a leader who will attend to their needs.... As long as Jesus is publicly accessible and the outcome of his activity is undetermined, the crowds follow him, respond to his compassion and power, acclaim him, and are 'glad to hear him'" (Rhoads et al., *Mark as Story*, 134–35). See Mark 6:34; 8:2.

perception in vv. 11–13.[52] So as to avoid inducing confusion on the part of his readers about what constitutes the passage's main idea, Mark has Jesus make cataphoric use of the remote demonstrative pronoun ἐκείνοις in v. 11. The presence of λέγει in the redundant quotative frame at the head of v. 13, moreover, signals not a transition to a new part of the discourse, but the presence of a capstone comment that gives expression to Jesus's exasperation over the dullness of the twelve: "Now if you do not understand this parable, how will you comprehend the rest?"

BIBLIOGRAPHY

Bauer, Walter, et al. A Greek-English Lexicon of the New Testament and Other Early Christian Literature. 3rd ed. Chicago: University of Chicago Press, 2000.

Burton, Ernest DeWitt. Syntax of the Moods and Tenses in New Testament Greek. 3rd ed. Edinburgh: T. & T. Clark, 1898.

Decker, Rodney J. Mark 9–16: A Handbook on the Greek Text. Baylor Handbook on the Greek New Testament. Waco, TX: Baylor University Press, 2014.

Funk, Robert W. A Beginning-Intermediate Grammar of Hellenistic Greek. 3rd ed. Salem, OR: Polebridge, 2013.

Guelich, Robert A. Mark 1–8:26. WBC 34a. Dallas: Word, 1989.

Hedrick, Charles W. Many Things in Parables: Jesus and His Modern Critics. Louisville: Westminster John Knox, 2004.

Higgins, M. J. "NT Result Clauses with Infinitive." CBQ 23 (1961) 233–41.

Hurtado, Larry W. Mark. NIBCNT. Peabody, MA: Hendrickson, 1989.

Lampe, P. "Die markinische Deutung des Gleichnisses vom Sämann, Markus 4, 10–12." ZNW 65 (1974) 140–50.

Levinsohn, Stephen H. Discourse Features of New Testament Greek: A Coursebook on the Information Structure of New Testament Greek. 2nd ed. Dallas: SIL International, 2000.

Moulton, James Hope. A Grammar of New Testament Greek. Vol. 1. Prolegomena. 3rd ed. Edinburgh: T. & T. Clark, 1908.

Porter, Stanley E. Idioms of the Greek New Testament. 2nd ed. BLG 2. Sheffield: Sheffield Academic, 1994.

———. Verbal Aspect in the Greek of the New Testament, with Reference to Tense and Mood. SBG 1. New York: Peter Lang, 1989.

Rhoads, David, et al. Mark as Story: An Introduction to the Narrative of a Gospel. 3rd ed. Minneapolis: Fortress, 2012.

Robertson, A. T. A Grammar of the Greek New Testament in the Light of Historical Research. 4th ed. Nashville: Broadman, 1934.

Runge, Steven E. "Relative Saliency and Information Structure in Mark's Parable of the Sower." BAGL 1 (2012) 103–25.

———. Discourse Grammar of the Greek New Testament: A Practical Introduction for Teaching and Exegesis. Lexham Bible Reference Series. Peabody, MA: Hendrickson, 2010.

---

52. See also 7:18a; 8:17–18; 13:28.

Sim, Margaret G. *Marking Thought and Talk in New Testament Greek: New Light from Linguistics on the Particles* ἵνα *and* ὅτι. Eugene, OR: Pickwick, 2010.

Tolbert, Mary Ann. *Sowing the Gospel: Mark's World in Literary-Historical Perspective*. Minneapolis: Fortress, 1989.

Turner, Nigel. *A Grammar of New Testament Greek*, by James Hope Moulton. Vol. 3. *Syntax*. Edinburgh: T. & T. Clark, 1963.

Wallace, Daniel B. *Greek Grammar Beyond the Basics: An Exegetical Syntax of the New Testament*. Grand Rapids: Zondervan, 1996.

Wrede, William. *The Messianic Secret*. Translated by J. C. G. Greig. London: James Clarke, 1971.

Zerwick, Maximilian. *Biblical Greek: Illustrated by Examples*. Translated by Joseph Smith. Scripta Pontificii Instituti Biblici 114. Rome: Editrice Pontificio Istituto Biblico, 1963.

10

What the Church Should Do to the Sexually Immoral Man

Examining the Ideational Meaning of 1 Corinthians 5

ESTHER G. CEN

INTRODUCTION

IN 1961 JAMES BARR delineated the fallacies regarding the emphasis on word studies in biblical interpretation.[1] Since then, biblical scholars have begun to revisit the traditional grammatical method used in Greek New Testament exegesis. In the 1980s, drawing on modern linguistics, biblical scholars began to develop the notion and methodology of *discourse analysis*.[2] The traditional method has made a lasting contribution to biblical interpretation, but it tends to atomize language into small units and place

---

1. Barr, *Semantics*, 107–257; cf. Carson, *Exegetical Fallacies*, 25–66; Cotterell and Turner, *Linguistics*, 106–87; Silva, *Biblical Words*, 17–34, 101–18.

2. For a review of the discipline of discourse analysis in New Testament studies, see Porter, "Discourse Analysis," 14–35. Cf. Porter, *Linguistic Analysis*, 133–44; Black, *Linguistics*, 170–98; Cotterell and Turner, *Linguistics*, 230–92. Porter writes, "Discourse analysis as a discipline within linguistics has emerged as a synthetic model, one designed to unite into a coherent and unifying framework various areas of linguistic investigation" ("Discourse Analysis," 18). According to Porter, it is not simple to define what discourse analysis (text-linguistics) is because it is not a "thing," it is many "things" such as analyses of discourse boundaries, cohesion, and prominence. In a short definition, discourse analysis emphasizes the function of language in context and looks "above" the clause level at the bigger picture of the discourse. The underlying principle of discourse analysis is the notion that language is not used in discrete and isolated words, phrases, or even sentences, but that larger linguistic units called discourse carry the meaning (*Linguistic Analysis*, 133).

too much weight on the etymology of words. Exegesis, therefore, became a combination of isolated word studies. Modern linguistics, by contrast, is more systematic in understanding and analyzing the language used in the New Testament. It also stresses synchronic over diachronic methods.

Stanley E. Porter has pointed out that an understanding of "Greek language and linguistics [is] essential to understanding the Greek New Testament."[3] In other words, the knowledge of Greek linguistics is worthy of effort for serious biblical students. Departing from the traditional method, I will here draw on the discipline of discourse analysis. In this essay, my research question concerns the *subject matter* of 1 Cor 5, i.e., what is this discourse about?[4] I argue that 1 Cor 5 is about what the church community should *do* to the sexually immoral man. In other words, the primary focus is not the man, but the church as a community, i.e., what the church has failed to do, how the church should view this issue, and what the church should do. To support my argument, first, I will delineate my methodology, including an overview of the linguistic model that I adopt and my method of analysis. Secondly, I will examine and interpret the ideational meaning of 1 Cor 5 using my method. Lastly, I will discuss the limitations of my work and some prospects for future study.

METHODOLOGY

Systemic Functional Linguistics (SFL)

I adopt Michael Halliday's SFL as my linguistic model. This is not the place to discuss the entire SFL theory in detail. I will, however, provide a brief framework here, and will delineate a methodology specifically related to my analytic work in detail in the following sections. SFL is a systemic model that is concerned with usage of language in various social settings. The basic notion of SFL is that language in use has three overarching functions: (1) to describe human experience in the world or inside human minds, (2) to interact with other human beings, and (3) to organize messages in ways

---

3. Porter, *Linguistic Analysis*, 1.

4. It is a standard view that 1 Cor 5 can be treated as a relatively independent discourse unit. See McNamara, "Incestuous Man," 307–26; Mitchell, *Paul*; Moses, "Exclusion," 172–91; Ossom-Batsa, "Community Behavior," 293–310; Rosner, "Temple," 137–45; Smith, *Hand this Man*. Since discourse boundaries of the entire book of 1 Corinthians are not the concern of this essay, I adopt this standard view to analyze 1 Corinthians 5 as a unit.

that make sense.⁵ Based on this notion, SFL proposes three categories—i e., three metafunctions (*ideational, interpersonal*, and *textual*)—as a way to investigate how meanings are created and communicated. On the one hand, each metafunction of the language used in a discourse communicates one particular meaning. On the other hand, each metafunction corresponds to a set of grammatical components.

Although these three metafunctions of language work together to make meaning, each can be analyzed separately for the sake of discussion. First, the *ideational* metafunction concerns the construal of human experience. It creates and communicates ideational meaning, mainly through the content of clauses in terms of the *transitivity* network, i.e., a network of "processes" involving "participants" and certain "circumstances."⁶ The ideational metafunction includes both the *experiential* metafunction realized at the clause level, and the *logical* metafunction realized in logical structures above the clause and between clauses. Second, the interpersonal metafunction concerns the exchange of information and "goods-and-services"⁷ between writers and readers, real or imagined. The interpersonal meaning is expressed in the choices between mood-forms and between clause types, e.g., questions and statements. Simply put, language in use facilitates one of these four exchanges: giving information (statements), demanding information (questions), giving goods-and-services (offers), and demanding goods-and-services (commands). Third, the textual metafunction concerns the organization of the message, i.e., how a speech or a text hangs together by linguistic elements such as conjunctions and deictic indicators so that cohesion and structure (i.e., arrangement of linguistic units) are realized.

Since the objective of this essay is to identify the subject matter of a discourse, I will focus on examining the transitivity system of the experiential metafunction. There is, however, unavoidable overlapping with other metafunctions. For example, the mood-forms will also be examined to distinguish between indicative statements and commands.⁸ In the next two sections, I will lay out my methodology in detail, first of a preliminary

---

5. Thompson, *Introducing Functional Grammar*, 28–44.

6. Thompson, *Introducing Functional Grammar*, 87. Porter, *Linguistic Analysis*, 145–58.

7. Thompson, *Introducing Functional Grammar*, 47.

8. The Greek mood system grammaticalizes attitudinal semantics, which are a component of interpersonal meaning.

lexical-grammatical analysis, and then of an analysis of the experiential metafunction of each clause.

Method of Preliminary Analysis

In the first step of my analysis, I will observe the general lexical and grammatical patterns of the discourse at hand.[9] Although these observations by no means provide a comprehensive picture of what the discourse is about, they often provide helpful information. Halliday and Matthiessen point out that every language dedicates some resources of lexicogrammar to describe human experience.[10] Language names things and classifies them into categories. We, therefore, have names such as *flour, banana,* and *egg* to describe different entities of the category of food. When these words occur in a conversation, they together hint at the subject matter of food. Besides, some words tend to collocate with each other in particular contexts. For instance, when we talk about baking, we use words such as *yeast, flour, oven, preheat,* and *temperature*. Although these words belong to different word classes, their collocation hints at the subject matter of baking. When words are configured into clauses such as *First, I preheated the oven to 350* or *The first step is to preheat the oven to 350*, the syntactical configurations provide even more information about what the writer is doing with these words: narrating a past baking experience or instructing how to bake. The lexical and grammatical patterns provide information that helps identify the ideational meaning. Examining a text is somewhat like detecting a criminal case. Every piece of the puzzle, therefore, is helpful to construct the entire picture, and every irregular pattern requires attention and explanation.

On the one hand, semantic domain theory provides a means to analyze how lexical senses of words form clusters of meanings. Drawing on J. P. Louw and E. A. Nida's lexicon,[11] I examine lexical patterns in terms of

---

9. Porter and O'Donnell, "Semantics," 154–204; Porter, *Letter to the Romans,* 28–30; Porter, "Biblical Discourse," 111.

10. Halliday and Matthiessen, *Introduction to Functional Grammar,* 29.

11. To understand Louw and Nida's methodology of defining domains and classifying words into domains, see the introduction of the Louw-Nida lexicon and Nida's *Componential Analysis*. For the discussions regarding the limitations of Louw and Nida's methodology, see Carson, *Exegetical Fallacies,* 48–54 and Porter, *Linguistic Analysis,* 47–59. Although scholars point out the limitations of the Louw-Nida lexicon, it is the best available lexicon based on semantic domains. The most challenging part of this lexical analysis is that Louw and Nida adopt a polysemic position regarding lexicography; so when a lexeme is classified in different domains, I need to make an interpretive decision about

frequency (f) and *concentration (c)*.[12] During the lexical analysis, I exclude functional words such as those used as discourse markers and referential indicators because my focus here is ideational meaning derived from the experiential metafunction. Therefore, when I analyze the frequency of a lexeme, I only count nouns, verbs, pronouns, adjectives, and adverbs.

On the other hand, Porter's linguistic theory provides a means to analyze verbal aspect and causality.[13] As indicated above, the analysis of ideational meaning entails an examination of the transitivity system at the clause level. Details regarding how to examine the transitivity of clauses will be delineated in the next section. In short, it concerns processes realized in verbal groups, in particular, the relation among aspect (realized in tense-form), causality (realized in voice-form), and agency.[14] Therefore, the preliminary analysis will examine the lexical patterns of words and verbal patterns, in particular, verbal aspect (*perfective, imperfective,* and *stative*)[15] and causality (*direct, indirect,* and *ergative*).[16] Now I will move to delineate the method of examining the transitivity of a clause.

---

which domain and which sense of the lexeme fits best in the context of the discourse at hand. Others might not agree with my decisions.

12. Halliday points out that frequency of a pattern provides information of the prominence of a discourse ("Linguistic Function," 330–68). Regarding statistical significance tests and simple counting, see McEnery and Hardie, *Corpus Linguistics*, 122–66. In this essay, I use a simple counting method. My definition and method of calculating frequency and concentration are as follows: frequency in this essay describes the proportion of the occurrence of a linguistic element compared to the total occurrence of the linguistic category it belongs to. The higher the proportion is, the higher the frequency will be. For instance, if there are x instances of the aorist tense-form, and y instances of verbs counted together, then the frequency of occurrence of aorist tense-form is $(x/y)*(100\%)$. On the other hand, concentration describes the proportion of the occurrence of a linguistic element in a particular part of the discourse compared to all its instances in the entire discourse. For instance, if there are y instances of the aorist tense-form in total, and x of them occur in the first two verses of the discourse, the concentration of the aorist tense-form in these two verses is $(x/y)*(100\%)$. The concept of frequency provides a tool to describe what (both lexical and grammatical choice) are used most frequently. The concept of concentration provides a tool to describe how a linguistic element distributes in the discourse.

13. Porter, *Idioms*, 20–79, 301–4; Porter, *Linguistic Analysis*, 133–43.

14. Porter, *Letter to the Romans*, 29–30.

15. Porter, *Idioms*, 20–49; also see Porter, *Verbal Aspect*.

16. Porter, *Letter to the Romans* 30.

Method of Examining the Transitivity of a Clause

The transitivity system enables the construal of processes involving participants in circumstances—i.e., who does what to whom under what kind of circumstances. According to this definition, therefore, I will examine three elements: processes (usually realized in verbal groups), participants (usually realized in noun groups), and circumstances (realized in various ways).

Halliday, in his functional grammar, proposes a six-category scheme for classifying verbal processes in English, and New Testament scholars such as Reed and Porter apply these categories to study New Testament Greek.[17] Since the definitions of the participants in the ideational metafunction are closely associated with the classifications of processes—i.e., a specific process takes specific participants—I group the processes together with participants in Table 1.

Table 1: Process Types and Participants

Categories of Processes	Sub-Categories	Major Participants
Material Process	Material-action	Actor, Goal
	Material-event	Actor
Mental Process	Perception, Cognition, Emotion, Desideration	Senser, Phenomenon
Relational Process	Attributive	Carrier, Attribute
	Identifying	Token, Value
Verbal Process		Sayer, Receiver
Behavioral Process		Behaver, Behavior
Existential Process		Existence

In regard to circumstances, a variety of forms such as adverbs, prepositional phrases, participles, and infinitives are applied.[18] The two most basic circumstantial categories are *space* and *time*, and our most basic conceptions of them are in terms of point and line. Accordingly, we have four combinations to describe space and time: (a) location-time: "when"; (b) location-space: "where"; (c) extent-time: "how long and how often"; and (d)

---

17. Halliday, *Introduction to Functional Grammar*, 101–57; Thompson, *Introducing Functional Grammar*, 86–140; Reed, *Discourse Analysis*, 62–76; Porter, *Letter to the Romans*, 24–35.

18. Thompson, *Introducing Functional Grammar*, 109–12.

extent-space: "how far in distance." The rest of the circumstantial categories are *manner, cause, accompaniment, role, matter,* and *angle*.

In the next sections, I will present the results and corresponding interpretation of my analysis based on this methodology.

EXAMINING THE IDEATIONAL MEANING OF 1 CORINTHIANS 5

To begin, I will discuss some lexical and grammatical patterns in 1 Cor 5 that lead to a tentative plan of dividing the discourse into three units. Following this, I will describe and interpret the overall pattern of the transitivity system of the discourse and compare the patterns of the three units. Finally, I will describe the subject matter of 1 Cor 5.

Results of the Preliminary Analysis
The Lexical Semantic Patterns

Here I will provide some observations based on the lexical analysis. Among 130 words, excluding the function words, the following are the five most frequent lexemes in 1 Cor 5: σύ ("you," 9x), ἐγώ ("I," 5x), εἰμί ("to be," 4x), κρίνω ("to judge," 4x), and ζύμη ("yeast," 4x).[15] This analysis provides some information concerning the ideational meaning of the discourse: (1) it concerns two major participants (σύ and ἐγώ); ἐγώ refers to Paul, the author of the letter, and σύ refers to the Corinthian church; (2) it consists of relational or existential processes (εἰμί); (3) it also consists of mental-cognition processes (κρίνω); and (4) it mentions ζύμη. The collocation of ζύμη and the other lexemes seems odd and requires explanation in further investigation. This list by no means provides any clear picture of the semantic field of 1 Cor 5, but the analysis below indicates that the discourse is about what Paul ("I") expected the Corinthians ("you") to do—i.e., to perform their responsibility as a congregation by "judging" insiders and taking action in church

---

19. Among the 130 words, there are 85 different lexemes. Of the 85 lexemes, 61 occur one time, 14 two times, 5 three times, 3 four times, 1 five times, and 1 nine times. It is obvious that those lexemes that occur one or two times (75 out of 85) are not worthy of consideration in terms of finding lexical patterns. However, the individual exegete must decide between looking at either the ten or five most frequent lexemes in this case. On the one hand, the consideration of more lexemes carries more information in relation to the subject matter. But, on the other hand, considering more lexemes can also confuse the subject matter. A more objective method regarding this issue will be developed in my future work.

discipline. To justify his exhortation, Paul used a metaphorical illustration related to "yeast." Therefore, this list corresponds to the subject matter.

Excluding the function words as well as the pronouns,[20] which amount to 98 instances, the following are the three semantic domains that predominate in the discourse: Domain 88 (Moral and Ethical Qualities and Related Behavior, f: 11% of 98 instances), Domain 33 (Communication, f: 7%), and Domain 5 (Food and Condiments, f: 7%).[21] Domain 88 spreads throughout the entire discourse. This indicates that the discourse might be about moral and ethical qualities and related behavior in general. On the other hand, the distribution of Domain 33 (c: 54% of 7 instances) centers in vv. 9–13,[22] and Domain 5 (c: 100% of 7 instances) is concentrated in vv. 6–8. Since 1 Cor 5 is not about making bread when the concrete meaning of yeast is most likely communicated, the occurrence of Domain 5 is regarded as a metaphorical illustration.

Since all the occurrences of Domain 5 are found in vv. 6–8, and these verses together consist of a metaphorical illustration, they could be regarded as a unit of their own compared with the co-text (i.e., the text around it). Before a tentative plan to divide the discourse is made, I will discuss more observations about the grammatical patterns, in particular, the causality and aspectuality of the verbal groups.

The Grammatical Semantic Patterns

I examined the 34 verbs in 1 Cor 5, including finite (i.e., indicative, imperative, and subjunctive) and non-finite (i.e., infinitive and participle). The analysis indicates that direct causality (f: 65% of 34 verbs) is overwhelmingly predominant in the entire discourse, while indirect causality (f: 16% of 34) and ergative causality (f: 19% of 34) are used less frequently. This usage of direct causality in relation to indirect and ergative causality follows

---

20. Many pronouns such as relative and demonstrative pronouns are used to hang the text together. Their occurrences are usually frequent but do not contribute much to the ideational meaning. However, in my lexical analysis, I want to include the personal pronouns, which encode information about participants.

21. Here, I apply the same method discussed in note 11 to determine "predominance," i.e., high frequency. There are 98 instances from 39 different domains in 1 Cor 5. These three domains, Domains 88, 33, and 5, account for 25% of the instances. I regard it reasonable to say these three domains predominate in the discourse.

22. It is not surprising to have a high frequency of Domain 33 (Communication) in a letter if we take genre or register into consideration. In 1 Cor 5, words such as ἀκούεται (hear) and ἔγραψα (write) account for the high frequency of Domain 33.

the normal pattern of causality in the body and parenesis of Pauline letters.[23] Using the language of slot and filler, this general pattern of causality indicates that in most of the processes, the direct agents fill the slot of subject (*f*: 84%).

On the other hand, the analysis of aspectuality indicates that the imperfective (present, *f*: 51% cf 34; imperfect, *f*: 3% of 34) significantly predominates the discourse, and the frequency of the perfective (aorist, *f*: 37% of 34) comes second. Since 1 Corinthians is generally accepted as a letter, where exposition material predominates, it is not unusual for the present tense-form to predominate. First Corinthians 5 includes three instances of the stative aspect (perfect, *f*: 9% of 34), πεφυσιωμένοι ("to cause someone to be arrogant," v. 2), κέκρινα ("to judge," v. 3), and οἴδατε ("to know," v. 6). According to Porter, these three uses of the stative aspect imply emphasis worthy of further examination in the next step of exegesis.[24]

Besides the pattern of frequency, it is also worth observing the pattern of the distribution of aspectuality. While the distribution of the present tense-form spreads throughout the entire discourse, the distribution of the aorist tense-form is relatively concentrated in vv. 1–5 (*c*: 54% of 13 instances of the aorist). This indicates that vv. 1–5 might have more narrative material, the so-called background material in a discourse of exposition.[25] The examination below affirms this speculation. In vv. 1–5, the matter in question is first introduced: what the man did and what the church failed to do. The preliminary analysis provides information that leads to a tentative plan of dividing the chapter into three groups of ideational meaning, A (vv. 1–5), B (vv. 6–8), and C (vv. 9–13). Now I will move on to more detailed analysis.

The Ideational Patterns of 1 Corinthians 5

In this section, I will identify and interpret some ideational patterns of the discourse.[26] First, I will discuss the overall patterns of process types and participants of the entire discourse, then I will compare the ideational patterns of Units A, B, and C. Table 2 indicates that the clauses of the entire

---

23. Porter, *Letter to the Romans*, 30.
24. Porter, *Idioms*, 23, 302–4.
25. Ibid., 23.
26. Thompson, *Introducing Functional Grammar*, 126–35; Halliday, "Linguistic Function," 330–68.

discourse mainly involve action processes (*f*: 50% of 38 processes), mental processes (*f*: 25%), and attributive processes (*f*: 21%).

As regards the overall patterning of the action clauses, most of the action clauses are transitive (*f*: 74% of 19 action processes). Actors and goals are the major participants, and most of the actors (*f*: 92% of 13 actors) and the goals (*f*: 71% of 14 goals) are human. Most of the actors fill the subject slots (*f*: 79% of 13 actors). There are not many circumstances in this discourse, and most of them are located in Unit A (*f*: 74% of 15 circumstances).[27] All of this indicates that 1 Cor 5 is mainly about people acting on people, and it is expressed without much adverbial modification. More specifically, half of these transitive action clauses (*f*: 50%) are related to verbs denoting the meaning of "to remove" or its equivalents in this particular context, e.g., "not to associate with" and "not to eat with." Within these processes, "you" is always the actor, and "the man" is often its corresponding goal. The only exception is found in v. 7, where "yeast" is the goal. The entire discourse has three commands, παραδοῦναι ("hand over," v. 5), ἐκκαθάρατε ("clean out," v. 7), and ἐξάρατε ("remove," v. 13). All three are action processes and related to what the church should do to the man. Two of them (ἐκκαθάρατε, v. 7; ἐξάρατε, v. 13) clearly denote the meaning of "to remove." All these point to the "syntactic imagery" of an expectation to remove the man.[28]

As regards mental clauses, most of the mental clauses involve mental-cognition processes (*f*: 67% of 9 mental clauses), which are mainly (*f*: 67% of 6 mental-cognition clauses) related to one of the five most frequent lexemes, κρίνω ("to judge"). Its first occurrence is in the stative aspect in v. 3: ἤδη κέκρικα ὡς παρὼν τὸν οὕτως τοῦτο κατεργασάμενον ("I have already judged the one who did this as I am present"). This indicates that Paul wished to see his judgment of the man as a given state of affairs. The language gives an impression that there was no need to discuss whether the man should be judged or not. It was a done deal. Therefore, although it was the cause of the discussion, it was no longer the focus. The rest of the mental-cognition processes related to κρίνω are located in Unit C (most of them in vv. 12–13), where Paul and the Corinthians are the sensers in

---

27. Manner-quality (36% of 14 instances of circumstance types), location-time (14%), location-space (14%), accompaniment-comitative (14%), manner-comparison (7%), manner-means (7%), cause-purpose (7%).

28. Halliday points out, "The foregrounding of certain patterns in syntax as the expression of an underlying theme is what we understand by 'syntactic imagery'" ("Linguistic Function," 437).

the judge-insiders collocation, and God is the senser in the judge-outsiders collocation. The pattern of the "judge" clauses parallels the pattern of the "remove" clauses. The former clauses stress perception, and the latter stress action. This parallel indicates that Paul did not only deal with the "doing" of the church, but also with the "knowing" that motivated their "doing."

Regarding attributive clauses, the majority of the carriers of the attributive clauses are related to the Corinthians (f: 57% of 6 attributive clauses, indicated in "you" and "your boasting"). One of them is linked to the perfect participle πεφυσιωμένο ("to cause someone to be arrogant," v. 2), one of the three instances of stative aspect. As discussed above, the language of v. 3 indicates that the judgment on the man was already made. It is possible that the Corinthians had already known Paul's point of view on the man. However, what they probably did not know was Paul's judgment on them. The attributive clause with the perfect participle is Paul's first judgment on them—i.e., ὑμεῖς πεφυσιωμένοι ἐστέ ("you are arrogant"). According to Louw and Nida, φυσιόομαι is "a figurative extension of meaning of φυσιόω 'to puff up, to inflate,' not occurring in the NT."[29] The use of ergativity here indicates that the Corinthians were viewed as both the agent and the receiver of the action of puffing up. The use of the structure of "εἰμί + perfect participle" indicates "double markedness."[30] In conclusion, in Unit A, Paul makes two judgments, one related to the man and the other related to the Corinthians. Regarding his judgment on the man, Paul stresses the state of the action of judging. On the other hand, regarding his judgment on the church, he stresses the content of his judgment, stating it explicitly and emphatically. The prominence of the latter suggests that Paul is more concerned with the church than the man. It was their prideful attitude that led to the failure of correctly viewing and handling the issue related to the man. Again, although the subject matter in question began with the man, Paul's major concern seems to be the church as a whole community. Using action clauses, cognition clauses, and attributive clauses, Paul deals with the "doing," "knowing," and "being" of the church related to the man.

Now I will move to compare the ideational patterns of Units A, B, and C in order to identify the flow of the ideational meanings and to finalize the grouping of them. I have already mentioned some of them above. Unit A consists of half of the action clauses (c: 53% of 19 action processes). In those clauses, the major actor is the man. Its corresponding goal is mainly

---

29. Louw and Nida, *Greek-English Lexicon*, 1:765.
30. Porter, *Verbal Aspect*, 466.

"the deed." As indicated above, most of the circumstances are found in Unit A. In v. 3, Paul uses the manner-quality types to explain in what manner he made the judgment on the man: despite Paul's absence, his spirit was present with the Corinthians. In v. 4, a location-time is used to describe when the church should "hand over the man to Satan"—it is when they gather together, which stresses the fact that it should be a decision and an action done by the whole community. In Unit A, therefore, Paul introduces the matter in question, but quickly moves on to describe what the church did or failed to do in response to that matter. Besides, Paul also points out that the church has failed to respond correctly because they have failed to have the right point of view regarding the matter.

Unit B begins with an attributive clause, οὐ καλὸν τὸ καύχημα ὑμῶν ("your boasting is not good"). It echoes Paul's judgment about the church and also introduces the metaphor of yeast and dough. This metaphor illustrates the relationship of the church and the man. In Unit B, we encounter the only instance of the "remove" process that collocates with "yeast" instead of "the man." According to Louw and Nida, ἐκκαθάρατε denotes "to make clean by removing that which is unclean."[31] Since the remaining instances of the "remove" group take "the man" as their goal, it is reasonable to regard the man as compared to "yeast" and the church to "dough." The language points to the issue of cleanness and uncleanness involved in the feast of Passover. Here other methods such as intertextuality might be helpful for a more thorough investigation of the metaphor,[32] but it is beyond the scope of this project. Regardless of how the metaphor should be interpreted, Paul uses the metaphor to illustrate the seriousness of neglecting the immoral case. Unit B provides a theological foundation for the exhortation in Unit C.

Unit C contains most of the "remove" clauses and most of the "judge" clauses. In both the action and cognition processes, the church ("you") is the prominent agent (*f*: 100% of 5 agents of the action processes; 50% of 4 agents of the cognition processes). In Unit A, Paul ("I"), the church ("you"), and the man have approximately equal occurrence as agents (i.e., actor or sensor). In Unit C, however, the church becomes the dominant agent, while the man moves completely to the position of object (i.e., goal or phenomenon). This shift indicates that as the discourse is developed, Paul's concern is moved to what the church should do to the man.

31. Louw and Nida, *Greek-English Lexicon*, 1:700.
32. An example will be Ciampa and Rosner, "I Corinthians," 708.

CEN—*What the Church Should Do to the Sexually Immoral Man*

To conclude my analysis, I will present an outline of 1 Cor 5 by grouping and summarizing the ideational meanings based on the discussion above. The discourse can be divided into three units Unit A, as the opening of the discourse, introduces the matter in question and Paul's view on this matter. Paul first points out the wrong attitude of the church and then moves to state his expectation. Unit B, as the transition and theological reflection, illustrates the justification of Paul's exhortation. Paul uses the metaphor of yeast and dough to illustrate his point. Lastly, Unit C returns to what Paul expected them to do. In this section, another justification of Paul's exhortation is provided, i.e., it is the church's responsibility to make a decision to discipline *insiders*. Grouping the ideational meanings, 1 Cor 5 can be summarized according to the following structure:

A. 1 Cor 5:1–5 The matter: what the sexually immoral man did and what the church failed to do.
   1. 1 Cor 5:1 Introduction of the matter.
   2. 1 Cor 5:2 Paul's *judgment* on the Corinthians' attitude regarding the matter.
   3. 1 Cor 5:3 Paul's judgment on the matter.
   4. 1 Cor 5:4–5 Paul's *exhortation* for the Corinthians regarding the matter.

B. 1 Cor 5:6–8 Paul's specification of his *judgment* and justification.
   1. 1 Cor 5:6a Paul's *judgment* on the Corinthians' attitude regarding the subject
   2. 1 Cor 5:6b–8 Paul's justification: the metaphor of yeast and dough.

C. 1 Cor 5:9–13 Paul's specification of his *exhortation* and justification.
   1. 1 Cor 5:9–11 Paul's *exhortation* for the Corinthians regarding the matter.
   2. 1 Cor 5:11–13 Paul's justification: the responsibility of judging insiders.

The Subject Matter of 1 Corinthians 5

At first glance, the discourse seems to be about the sexually immoral man. Both the frequent occurrence of lexemes related to moral quality and behavior (Domain 88) and Paul's attitude toward the man point in that direction. However, when the church is moved to the position of agent realized in direct causality in the discourse, and the man is moved to the position of object on which the church should judge and act, the focus is shifted to what the church should do to the man. Though the man is the initiated subject in question, the church, as a whole community, is Paul's major concern here.

The subject matter of this discourse, therefore, is what the Corinthians, as a whole, should do to the man, who is an insider, i.e., a believer and a member within the church. Paul repeats what he expects the Corinthians to do in a variety of ways: ἀρθῇ ("might be removed," [v. 2]), παραδοῦναι τὸν τοιοῦτον τῷ σατανᾷ ("hand over the man to Satan," [v. 4]), ἐκκαθάρατε τὴν παλαιὰν ζύμην ("remove the old yeast," [v. 7]), μὴ συναναμίγνυσθαι πόρνοις ("not to associate with sexually immoral men," [vv. 9, 11]), τῷ τοιούτῳ μηδὲ συνεσθίειν ("do not eat with such one," [v. 12]), and ἐξάρατε τὸν πονηρὸν ἐξ ὑμῶν αὐτῶν ("remove the sexually immoral man out of you," [v. 13]). All these are action processes, so this removal that Paul expects the Corinthians to enact is a physical one. The more specific details given in the third section indicate that this removal includes a cessation of fellowship, including table fellowship, with the man.

The repetition of the "judge" and "remove" is significant. Paul's emphasis on his expectation for the Corinthians sounds resolute. The reason for such an emphasis is indicated in vv. 2–3, 6a—i.e., the Corinthians are arrogant. It is not easy to determine what Paul means based on this analysis; either the Corinthians were generally arrogant (indicated in other places in the letter), or the Corinthians were specifically arrogant about this matter. The close relationship between v. 6a and v. 6b seems to imply the latter. However, it is even more difficult to explain why the Corinthians could have boasted about such a matter, which was not even common for the pagan world outside the church. If we look beyond the discourse and consider it in its co-text, 1 Cor 6:12–17 might provide a hint as to how the Corinthians' boasting might have been possible. They might have boasted about their freedom and tolerance of sexual immorality in general.

Despite the difficulty determining what caused the Corinthians' arrogant attitude toward this matter, one thing in 1 Cor 5 is clear: they have failed to do what they should as a Christian community. Because of this, Paul repeats his expectation in different ways with one focus: the Corinthians should remove the man from among them. An analogy of parenting can illustrate Paul's concern. Parents should be responsible to train their children to behave well. If the children misbehave and the parents fail to discipline, the parents should take more blame. In the same way, when the church fails to attend to and take action to discipline the man, the church takes more responsibility. In conclusion, the subject matter of the discourse is what the church should do as a whole community, in particular, to the sexually immoral man—i.e., to remove him from the community.

LIMITATIONS AND FUTURE WORK

I have delineated a linguistic methodology, presented an analysis of 1 Cor 5, and addressed the issue of subject matter. I have not tackled some of the most challenging exegetical questions related to 1 Cor 5, such as what Paul means in 1 Cor 5:5.[33] Neither have I dealt with some of the most pressing practical questions, such as how might 1 Cor 5 guide contemporary churches in North America in the handling of sexual immorality among Christians? I regard these questions as important. However, exegetical questions regarding particular details in a biblical discourse ought to be, and indeed can be, better interpreted in light of a more complete picture, namely, what the discourse is about. What I attempt to present here, therefore, is an alternative or hopefully more robust method to answer some basic questions such as subject matter, which are often neglected or presumed.

I admit that my methodology is limited. Some of these limitations relate to the manner in which I have performed my analysis. For instance, my quantitative method is limited to a small pool of data. Also, I have used Microsoft Excel to do all of my calculations, which requires manual data entry. Any mishandling of the data will influence the mathematical results, which will in turn affect the interpretation. My method to observe the lexical and grammatical patterns will meet challenges when it is applied to a larger pool of data. If I analyze the entire book of 1 Corinthians, how can the data be handled in a more efficient way that guarantees high accuracy? How can the data be handled in such a way that useful information will not be lost in "data mining"? Besides, the criteria of determining prominence need to be further investigated, i.e., what is the relationship between frequency and prominence? Can it even be quantified?

Other limitations pertain to the scope of my method and my analysis. The linguistic method in my work makes an explicit attempt to answer

---

33. See Campbell, "Flesh and Spirit," 331–42; Kistemaker, "Satan," 33–46; Liu, *Temple*; Moses, "Exclusion," 172–91; Obenhaus, "Sanctified Entirely," 1–12; Ossom-Batsa, "Community Behavior," 293–310; Smith, *Hand this Man*; Rosner, "Temple," 137–45.

questions related to basic issues such as subject matter, discourse boundaries, and textual integrity. On the one hand, this transforms normally intuitive judgments into explicitly methodological tasks. When we encounter phenomena such as Paul's metaphor of yeast and dough, however, different approaches become relevant. For instance, in order to determine what the metaphor means and how it functions, we need to integrate other methodologies such as historical investigation, social-scientific method, and literary techniques. In conclusion, research questions influence the choice of methodology, or vice versa, and together they shape our understanding and interpretation.

Table 2: Analysis of Process Types and Participants in 1 Corinthians 5

		Material-Action (f=50%)			Mental (f=25%)		Attribution (f=21%)	Verbal (f=4%)	Total
		Trans. (74%)		Intrans. (26%)					
		other	"remove"	other	other	"judge"			
A (vv.1–5)	I			3		1			4
	You		1		2		1		4
	The Man	3^A							3
	God/Jesus								
	We								
	Others (The case)						1		1
		3	1	3	2	1	2		12
B (vv.6–8)	I								
	You		1		1			2	4
	The Man								
	God/Jesus								
	We			1					1
	Others	1					1		2
		1	1	1	1		3		7

C (vv.9-13)							Total
I				1	2		3
You	4	1	1	1			7
The Man							
God/Jesus				1			1
We							
Others						3	3
	4	1	1	3	3	2	14

A. Only the processes in direct causality are shown here. Therefore, the number might not reflect the complete information of a particular process. E.g., "3" here should be interpreted as Unit A consists of three transitive processes apart from the "remove" process, where "the man" is the actor and also occupies the slot of subject.

BIBLIOGRAPHY

Barr, James. *The Semantics of Biblical Language*. London: Oxford University Press, 1961.

Black, David Alan. *Linguistics for Students of New Testament Greek: A Survey of Basic Concepts and Applications*. 2nd ed. Grand Rapids: Baker Academic, 1995.

Campbell, Barth Lynn. "Flesh and Spirit in 1 Cor 5:5: An Exercise in Rhetorical Criticism of the NT." *JETS* 36 (1993) 331–42.

Carson, D. A. *Exegetical Fallacies*. Grand Rapids: Baker Academic, 1984.

Ciampa, Roy E., and Brian S. Rosner. "1 Corinthians." In *Commentary on the New Testament Use of the Old Testament*, edited by G. K. Beale and D. A. Carson, 695–752. Grand Rapids: Baker Academic, 2007.

Cotterell, Peter, and Max Turner. *Linguistics and Biblical Interpretation*. Downers Grove, IL: InterVarsity, 1989.

Halliday, M. A. K. *An Introduction to Functional Grammar*. London: Arnold, 1985.

———. *An Introduction to Functional Grammar*. Revised by Christian M. I. M. Matthiessen. 3rd ed. London: Hodder Education, 2004.

———. "Linguistic Function and Literary Style: An Inquiry into the Language of William Golding's *The Inheritors*." In *Literary Style: A Symposium*, edited by Seymour Benjamin Chatman, 330–68. London: Oxford University Press, 1971.

Kistemaker, Simon. "'Deliver This Man to Satan' (1 Cor 5:5): A Case Study in Church Discipline." *MSJ* 3 (1992) 33–46.

Liu, Yulin. *Temple Purity in 1-2 Corinthians*. WUNT 2.343. Tübingen: Mohr Siebeck, 2013.

Louw, Johannes P., and Eugene A. Nida. *Greek-English Lexicon of the New Testament Based on Semantic Domains*. 2 vols. 2nd ed. New York: United Bible Societies, 1989.

McEnery, Tony, and Andrew Hardie. *Corpus Linguistics: Method, Theory and Practice*. CTL. Cambridge: Cambridge University Press, 2012.

McNamara, Derek Michael. "Shame the Incestuous Man: 1 Corinthians 5." *Neot* 44 (2010) 307–26.

Mitchell, Margaret Mary. *Paul and the Rhetoric of Reconciliation: An Exegetical Investigation of the Language and Composition of 1 Corinthians*. Louisville, KY: Westminster, 1993.

Moses, Robert E. "Physical and/or Spiritual Exclusion? Ecclesial Discipline in 1 Corinthians 5." *NTS* 59 (2013) 172–91.

Obenhaus, Stacy R. "Sanctified Entirely: The Theological Focus of Paul's Instructions for Church Discipline." *ResQ* 43 (2001) 1–12.

Ossom-Batsa, George. "Responsible Community Behavior or Exclusion: Interpreting 1 Cor 5:1–13 from a Communicative Perspective." *Neot* 45 (2011) 293–310.

Porter, Stanley E. "Discourse Analysis and New Testament Studies: An Introductory Survey." In *Discourse Analysis and Other Topics in Biblical Greek*, edited by Stanley E. Porter and D. A. Carson, 14–35. JSNTSup 113. Sheffield: Sheffield Academic, 1995.

———. "How Can Biblical Discourse Be Analyzed?" In *Discourse Analysis and Other Topics in Biblical Greek*, edited by Stanley E. Porter and D. A. Carson, 107–17. JSNTSup 113. Sheffield: Sheffield Academic, 1995.

———. *Idioms of the Greek New Testament*. 2nd ed. BLG 2. Sheffield: Sheffield Academic, 1994.

———. *The Letter to the Romans: A Linguistic and Literary Commentary*. NTM 37. Sheffield: Sheffield Phoenix, 2015.

———. *Linguistic Analysis of the Greek New Testament: Studies in Tools, Methods, and Practice*. Grand Rapids: Baker Academic, 2015.

———. *Verbal Aspect in the Greek of the New Testament: With Reference to Tense and Mood*. SBG 1. New York: Peter Lang, 1989.

Porter, Stanley E., and Matthew Brook O'Donnell. "Semantics and Patterns of Argumentation in the Book of Romans: Definitions, Proposals, Methods and Experiments." In *Diglossia and Other Topics in New Testament Linguistics*, edited by Stanley E. Porter, 154–204. Sheffield: Sheffield Academic, 2000.

Reed, Jeffrey T. *A Discourse Analysis of Philippians: Method and Rhetoric in the Debate over Literary Integrity*. JSNTSup 136. Sheffield: Sheffield Academic, 1997.

Rosner, Brian S. "Temple and Holiness in 1 Corinthians 5." *TynBul* 42 (1991) 137–45.

Silva, Moisés. *Biblical Words and Their Meaning: An Introduction to Lexical Semantics*. Grand Rapids: Zondervan, 1983.

Smith, David Raymond. *"Hand This Man Over to Satan": Curse, Exclusion and Salvation in 1 Corinthians 5*. LNTS 386. London: T. & T. Clark, 2009.

Thompson, Geoff. *Introducing Functional Grammar*. 2nd ed. London: Arnold, 2004.

Index of Modern Authors

Abeillé, Anne, 40
Acosta, Olga, 107
Adams, Sean A., 43, 52
Ahlsén, Elizabeth, 12
Andrews, E., 66
Andrić, Ico, 154
Anttila, Raimo, 127
Aronoff, Mark, 10
Aubrey, Michael, 53

Baltazar Hernández, Felix, 159, 162
Bamman, David, 89
Bański, Piotr, 40
Barker, Kenneth L., 158
Barnwell, Katharine, 146
Barr, James, 15, 90, 121, 175, 188, 189, 194, 233
Bartholomew, Craig G., 126
Battistella, Edwin L., 66
Bauer, Laurie, 13
Baugh, Albert C., 150
Bell, Allan, 118, 119, 121, 124, 125
Bernstein, Basil, 137, 138
Berthaiume, Scott Charles, 156
Black, David Alan, 90, 105, 233
Blass, Fredrich, 187, 189, 190, 197
Blomberg, Craig L., 170, 193, 194, 211
Bock, Darrell L., 167
Boring, M. Eugene, 211
Boucher, Madeleine, 211
Brannan, Rick, 36, 41, 56
Brown, Gillian, 66
Brugmann, Karl, 197
Bultmann, Rudolf, 64, 115, 131
Burdick, Donald W., 153

Burggraff, Philip D., 52
Burton, Ernest deWitt, 214, 216
Burton, Strang, 19
Busa, Roberto, 38
Bussmann, Hadumod, 10, 11

Caird, George B., 189
Callow, Kathleen, 65
Campbell, Barth Lynn, 247
Caragounis, Chrys C., 30, 171
Carson, D. A., 233, 236
Casey, Maurice, 167, 168, 169
Chau, Simon S. C., 128
Chemin Bässler, Heidi, 156, 159
Chesterman, A., 182
Chilton, Paul, 118
Chomsky, Noam, 11, 13, 198
Church, Kenneth Ward, 103
Ciampa, Roy E., 244
Cirafesi, Wally V., 15
Clark, Billy, 101
Clément, Lionel, 40
Collins, Ellen, 24
Conzelmann, Hans, 64, 188
Cotterell, Peter, 90, 105, 117, 121, 233
Coupland, Nikolas, 118
Cowie, Moira, 147
Crane, Gregory, 89
Cranfield, C. E. B., 211
Croft, William, 88, 96
Crossan, John Dominic, 211
Cruse, D. Alan, 88, 96
Crystal, David, 135
Culpepper, R. Alan, 211
Čutura, Ilijana, 151–55

251

Index of Modern Authors

Debrunner, Albert, 187, 189, 190, 197
Declerck, T., 40
Delbrück, Berthold, 197
Deleuze, Gilles, 137
Dodd, C. H., 211
Donahue, John R., 211
Dooley, Robert A., 201–4
Dow, Lois K. Fuller, 28
Dry, Helen A., 65
Dvorak, James D., 42

Ehro, Ted M., 172
Erickson, Richard J., 192, 193
Evans, Vyvyan, 204, 205
Eve, Martin Paul, 21, 23

Fairclough, Norman, 118
Fawcett, Robin P., 95
Fee, Gordon D., 64, 81, 189, 190
Fewster, Gregory P., 101
Fleischman, S., 66
Frede, Michael, 10
Freud, Sigmund, 135–37
Funk, Robert W., 187, 189, 216, 221, 222

Gadamer, Hans-Georg, 112–14, 121, 123, 126, 127, 129, 130, 138
Gee, James Paul, 18, 24
Geeraerts, Dirk, 88–90, 96, 100, 101, 103, 126
Gibson, Arthur, 189
Givón, Talmy, 201, 202
Golding, William, 65
Gorman, Michael J., 191, 192
Granger, Sylviane, 15
Greaves, Chris, 15
Green, Melanie, 204, 205
Grudem, Wayne A., 174
Guattari, Felix, 137
Guelich, Robert A., 216, 219
Gundry, Robert H., 211
Gutiérrez, Gustavo, 64

Hale, Ken, 65, 66
Halliday, M. A. K., 65–69, 80, 101, 103, 116, 135, 137, 138, 166, 202, 234, 236–38, 241, 242

Hanks, Patrick, 88, 103
Hansen, G. Walter, 81
Hardie, Andrew, 237
Harris, Tony, 11
Harris, Zellig S., 101, 118
Hasan, Ruqaiya, 14, 138, 166
Hasselgård, Hilde, 14
Hayes, John H., 188, 189
Hedrick, Charles W., 211, 213
Hegel, G. W. F., 113, 114, 129
Heidegger, Martin, 126, 127, 131–35, 138
Herbst, Thomas, 15
Higgins, M. J., 215
Holladay, Carl R., 188, 189
Hooker, Morna Dorothy, 79
Hopper, Paul J., 69
Howard, W. F., 188, 190
Hultgren, Arland J., 211
Hurtado, Larry W., 211

Ide, Nancy, 40
Israel, Hephzibah, 148, 149

Jaworski, Adam, 118
Jeremias, Joachim, 211
Johnson-Laird, Philip N., 202
Jones, Steven, 107

Kaiser, Otto, 187
Kaiser, Walter C., 121
Kant, Emmanuel, 112
Kapor, Mamo, 152
Kelber, Werner, 213
King, Magda, 132
Kintsch, Walter, 105, 108
Kistemaker, Simon, 247
Koester, Almut, 16
Kroneman, Dick, 149
Kümmel, Werner G., 187, 188

Lakoff, George, 204
Lakoff, Robin, 10
Lambrecht, Knud, 202
Lampe, P., 219
Land, Christopher D., 16
Landauer, Thomas K., 104, 108
Larkin, William J., 185

Index of Modern Authors

Lee, Jae Hyun, 42
Lee, John A. L., 92, 96, 97
Levinsohn, Stephen H., 201–5, 227
Libby, James A., 42, 43
Lindemann, Andreas, 64, 188
Liu, Yulin, 247
Longacre, Robert E., 80
Louw, J. P., 44, 91, 92, 106, 121, 122, 180, 189, 236, 243, 244
Luhmann, Niklas, 120
Lyons, John, 88, 91, 195

Mangalath, Praful, 105, 108
Marcus, Joel, 211
Marcus, Mitch, 40
Markley, Jennifer Foutz, 193, 194
Marshall, Donald G., 114
Martin, J. R., 137, 138
Martin, Ralph P., 79, 81
Martín-Asensio, Gustavo, 64–66, 68, 69, 83, 138
Marx, Karl, 136
Matthews, P., 198
Matthiessen, Christian M. I. M., 101, 103, 116, 236
McCarthy, Michael, 12
McEnery, Tony, 99, 237
McLean, Bradley H., 131, 134, 135, 137
McNamara, Derek Michael, 234
Meunier, Fanny, 15
Meyer, Michael, 118
Mitchell, Margaret Mary, 234
Moses, Robert E., 247
Moule, C. F. D., 187–89
Moulton, James Hope, 188, 190, 197, 217
Munro, Pamela, 12
Murphy, M. Lynne, 88

Nida, Eugene A., 44, 88, 91, 92, 105, 106, 180, 189, 236, 243, 244
Nietzsche, Frederick, 135
Nord, Christiane, 181
Norden, Eduard, 188

O'Brien, Peter T., 81
O'Donnell, Matthew Brook, 16, 28–34, 37, 42, 43, 45, 52, 56, 69, 101, 236

O'Keeffe, Anne, 12
Obenhaus, Stacy R., 247
Ogden, C. K., 188
Ong, Hughson T., 166, 168, 169
Ossom-Batsa, George, 234, 247

Palmer, Micheal, 11
Palmer, Richard E., 114
Pang, Francis G. H., 16, 33
Pearson, Brook W. R., 30
Peek, Robin, 20, 21
Pellauer, David, 124
Peters, Ronald D., 42
Peterson, John Michael, 166
Picirilli, Robert, 35
Pitts, Andrew W., 15, 42, 43, 52, 70, 72, 116
Pomerantz, Jeffrey, 20, 21
Porter, Stanley E., 9, 11, 12, 14–16, 28–33, 42, 63, 66, 74, 92, 97, 98, 109, 115–17, 127, 134, 168, 169, 185, 195, 197, 202, 206, 210, 214, 216, 218, 226, 233, 234, 236–38, 241, 243
Poynton, Cate, 129, 130
Poythress, Vern S., 174
Pratt, Mary Louis, 125
Proctor, Mark, 43
Prokopidis, Prokopis, 102
Pym, Anthony, 146, 170, 176, 179

Radermacher, Ludwig, 187, 188
Rajagopalan, Kanavillil, 11
Rasmussen, Jens, 120
Rastier, François, 122
Ravin, Yael, 99
Reed, Jeffrey T., 15, 28–32, 66, 80, 116, 117, 206, 238
Rees-Miller, Janie, 10
Rehkopf, Friedrich, 187
Reynaert, Martin, 40
Rhoads, David, 210, 230
Richards, I. A., 188
Ricoeur, Paul, 118, 119, 123–26, 135–38
Riemer, Nick, 93, 94, 107
Robertson, A. T., 189, 190, 197, 215–17, 221

253

Index of Modern Authors

Robie, Jonathan, 16, 42
Robinson, Ian, 198
Robinson, Jason, 117, 134
Romary, Laurent, 40
Rosner, Brian S., 234, 244, 247
Ruhl, Charles, 88, 94, 106
Runge, Steven E., 201–6, 222, 225–27

Saeed, John I., 88
Sandborg-Petersen, Ulrik, 55
Santos, Diego, 32
Saussure, Ferdinand, 195
Savić, Vera, 151–55
Sawyer, John F. A., 122
Schendl, Herbert, 151
Schenk, Wolfgang, 116
Schiffrin, Deborah, 14, 118
Schliermacher, Freidrich, 113, 114
Schnelle, Udo, 187
Schreibman, Susan, 38
Schüssler Fiorenza, Elizabeth, 64
Schweitzer, Albert, 64, 81
Scott-Baumann, Alison, 125
Shuttleworth, Mark, 147
Silva, Moisés, 89, 90, 94, 105, 233
Sim, Margaret G., 212, 219
Simpson, James, 10, 14
Sinclair, John M., 15, 101
Skaffari, Janne, 150, 151, 156
Smith, Catherine J., 32, 34, 37, 42, 43, 57
Smith, David Raymond, 234, 247
Smith, James K. A., 126
Snodgrass, Klyne, 211
Soustelle, Jacques, 156, 159
Sperber, Dan, 149, 150
Stenger, Werner, 190, 191
Stevens, Chris S., 79
Storjohann, Petra, 88, 96
Strimple, Robert B., 81
Stubbs, Michael, 12
Stührenberg, Maik, 40
Suber, Peter, 20–22
Swan, Alma, 13, 20

Taber, Charles, 180, 189
Tan, Randall K., 34, 35, 52
Tauber, James, 55
Taylor, Vincent, 211
Teubert, Wolfgang, 122
Thiselton, Anthony C., 122, 123, 132, 135
Thompson, Geoff, 67, 234, 238, 241
Thompson, Sandra A., 69
Tippett, A. R., 147
Toffelmire, Colin M., 138
Tolbert, Mary Ann, 210, 214, 224
Turner, Max, 90, 105, 117, 233
Turner, Nigel, 190, 214, 217

van Dijk, Teun A., 118, 120
Van Gompel, Maarten, 40
Van Hecke, Pierre, 123, 124
Venuti, Lawrence, 152, 153
Vermeer, Hans, 181
Villemonte de la Clergerie, Éric, 40

Wallace, Daniel B., 189, 192, 197–99, 217–19, 222
Walton, Ryder Dale, 42
Warren, Martin, 15
Westfall, Cynthia Long, 65, 80, 166
Westphal, Merold, 127
Wierzbicka, Anna, 88
Wilson, Andrew, 99
Wilson, Deirdre, 149, 150
Winther-Nielson, Nicolai, 18
Wodak, Ruth, 118, 120
Wrede, William, 169, 210, 211
Wright, Laura, 151

Xue, Xiaxia E., 42

Yarbro Collins, Adela, 211
Young, Robert, 157
Yule, George, 66

Zegarac, Vladimir, 202
Zerwick, Maxmilian, 215, 216
Zhou, Jiayu, 106, 107

Index of Ancient Sources

OLD TESTAMENT

Genesis

11:1–9	118, 125
21:10	172

Numbers

23:19	171

Job

12–14	124

Psalms

8:4–6	167
8:4	169, 171
144:3	171

Isaiah

6:9–10	224, 228
6:9	228
6:10	229
6:10a	228, 229
6:10b	228, 229

Daniel

2:4—7:28	167
7	167–69, 175
7:13	167, 171, 183
8:17	171

PSEUDEPIGRAPHA

1 Enoch

37–71	171
46:1–4	171
48:2–11	171

NEW TESTAMENT

Matthew

4:6	228
5:9	173
5:25	228
7:6	228
9:6	167
9:8	167
12:22–37	187
13:14–15	228
13:15	228, 229
13:29	228
14:16	49, 51
15:32	228
16:13–14	168
16:15–16	168
24:1–51	168
24:42–43	226
25:9	228
26:63–64	168
27:64	228

Mark

1—8:26	219

Mark (continued)

Reference	Pages
1:2	225
1:34	219
1:38	214, 227
1:44	227
2:5	227
2:8	227
2:10	214, 227
2:14	227
2:17	227
2:33–34	227
3:2	214
3:4–5	227
3:9	218
3:9a	217
3:9b	214
3:10	214
3:12	217, 218
3:14	214, 223
3:17	172
3:23	212
3:31–35	224
4:1–9	223
4:2	212
4:9	226
4:10–12	210
4:11–13	213, 224, 225, 227, 231
4:11–12	211–13
4:11	214, 223, 224, 226, 231
4:12	4, 210, 211–14, 219, 220, 224, 225, 227–30
4:12a	228
4:13	226, 227, 231
4:13a	227
4:13b	227
4:14–20	212, 226, 230
4:21	215, 226
4:21a	215
4:21b	215
4:22	215
4:24	226
4:26	226
4:30	226
4:33–34	212, 225, 227, 230
4:33	211, 212, 225
4:34	212
4:34b	230
4:35	227
5:3	217
5:10	217, 218
5:12	214
5:18	217, 218
5:19	219, 227
5:23a	217, 218
5:23b	214
5:36	227
5:37	219
5:39	227
5:41	227
5:43	217, 218
6:8	217, 218
6:12	217
6:25	217, 218
6:31	227
6:34	230
6:36	214
6:38	227
6:41	214
6:50	227
6:56	217, 218
7:9	214
7:12	219
7:17–23	212
7:17	212
7:18	227
7:18a	231
7:18b–23	230
7:26	217, 218
7:27	219
7:32	217, 218
7:34	227
7:36	217, 218
8:1	227
8:2	230
8:6	214
8:12	227
8:17–18	231
8:17	227
8:19–20	230
8:22	217, 218
8:27–29	168
8:30	217, 218
9:2	216
9:9	217, 218
9:12	216

Index of Ancient Sources

9:13	225	14:38	214
9:18	217, 218	14:41	227
9:19	227	14:49	217, 218
9:22	214	14:62	168
9:30	217, 218	15:2	227
9:35	227	15:8	225
10:11	227	15:11	214
10:13	214	15:15	214
10:14	219	15:20	214
10:17	214	15:21	217, 218
10:23–24	227	15:32	214
10:27	227	15:36	219
10:35	217, 218	15:37	219
10:37	217, 218	16:1	214
10:42	227	16:7	225
10:48	217, 218		
10:51	217, 218		
11:2	227	**Luke**	
11:6	219, 225	3:15	228
11:16	217–19	4:11	228
11:22	227	6:6	174
11:25	214	9:18–20	168
11:28	219, 220, 230	10:5–6	173
11:33	227	10:6	173
12:1	212	12	228
12:2	214	12:58	228
12:12	212	14:8	228
12:13	214	14:29	228
12:15	214	20:34	173
12:16	227	21:5–36	168
12:19	217, 218	21:34	228
13:1–37	168	22:69	169
13:18	217, 218		
13:28	230, 231	**John**	
13:34	217, 218		
14:2	228	1:29	180
14:6	219	2:25	221
14:10	214	4:34	222
14:12	214	6:29	221
14:13	227	6:39–40	221
14:16	225	6:50	221
14:21	225	7:26	228
14:27	227	11:57	221
14:30	227	12:34	167, 168
14:32	227	13:15	221
14:34	227	13:34	221
14:35	217, 218	15:8	221
14:37	227	15:12–13	221

257

Index of Ancient Sources

John *(continued)*

15:12	221
15:13	221
15:17	221
16:7	217
16:30	221
17:3	221
18:37	221
18:39a	222

Acts

2:4	225
5:39	228
7:56	167
11:29	225
28:26–27	228
28:27	228, 229

Romans

1:4	172
5:1–11	187
8:4	172
8:14	173
8:19	172
9:26	172
9:27	172

1 Corinthians

5	4, 234, 239, 240, 245–47
5:1	245
5:1–5	241, 245
5:2–3	246
5:2	243, 245, 246
5:3	242, 243, 245
5:4–5	245
5:4	246
5:5	247
5:6–8	240, 241, 245
5:6a	245, 246
5:6b–8	245
5:6b	246
5:7	242, 246
5:9–13	241, 245
5:9–11	245
5:11–13	245
5:11	246
5:12–13	242
5:12	246
5:13	242, 246
6:12–17	246
9:18	217
12:11	225
12:18	225
15:38	225

2 Corinthians

1:19	172
3:7	172
3:13	172

Galatians

2:9	47
2:20	172
3:7	172
3:26	172
4:30	172

Ephesians

2:2	172
3:5	167
4:13	172
5:5	172
5:6	172

Philippians

1:1	66, 70, 71, 73, 79
1:2	70, 71, 73, 79
1:3	66, 73, 78
1:6	73, 78
1:7	73, 79
1:8	66, 73, 74, 78, 84
1:9–10	73
1:9	73, 74, 78
1:10	78, 79, 84
1:12	73, 78
1:13	71, 73
1:14	78, 79
1:15	73, 78

Index of Ancient Sources

1:16	73, 78	2:23	74, 78
1:17	73, 75, 79	2:24	73, 78, 79, 84
1:18	73, 78	2:25	74
1:19–20	73, 75	2:26	73, 74, 78
1:19	73, 78, 79	2:27	73, 74, 78, 79
1:20	73, 78	2:28	70, 73, 74, 78, 79
1:21	73, 74, 79	2:29	73, 74, 78
1:22	73, 74, 78, 79	2:29a	68
1:23	73, 74, 78	2:30	73, 74, 78
1:25	73, 78	3:1	73, 74, 78, 79
1:26	73, 78	3:2	73, 74, 78
1:27–28	78	3:3	73, 79
1:27	70, 73, 74, 78	3:4	73, 78, 79
1:28	73, 74, 78, 79	3:5–6	78
1:29	79	3:5	74
1:30	74, 78	3:7	73, 74, 79
2	3, 64, 74, 78–80, 81	3:8	73, 74, 78
2:1–2	67	3:9–10	78
2:1	73, 78, 79	3:9	73
2:2–5	80	3:11	78
2:2	73, 74, 78	3:12	73, 78
2:3	74, 78	3:13–14	78
2:4–11	74, 79–81	3:13	73, 78
2:4–5	73–75, 79, 80	3:15	73, 74, 78, 79
2:4	73, 74, 78, 79, 81, 82	3:16	73, 74, 78
2:5–11	81	3:17	73, 74, 78
2:5	73, 74, 78	3:18	73, 74, 78
2:6–11	79, 81	3:19	73, 74, 78, 79
2:6	73, 74	3:20	73, 74, 78
2:7–8	78	3:21	73, 74, 79
2:7	74, 78	4:1	78
2:8	78	4:2	73, 74, 78
2:9	73, 74, 78, 79	4:3	70, 73, 74, 78, 79, 83
2:10	78	4:4	73, 78
2:11	73, 74, 78	4:5	73, 74, 79
2:12	73, 78	4:6	73, 78
2:13	73, 74, 79	4:7	73, 79
2:14	78	4:8	73, 74, 78, 79
2:15–16	78	4:9	73, 74, 78
2:15	73, 74, 78	4:10	73, 78
2:16	73, 78	4:11	73, 78, 79
2:17–18	68	4:12	73, 78
2:17	73, 78, 84	4:13	74, 78
2:18	73, 74, 78, 79	4:14	78
2:19	73, 74, 78	4:15	73, 74, 78, 84
2:20	73, 74, 78, 79	4:16	73, 78
2:21	73, 74, 78	4:17	70, 73, 74, 78
2:22	73, 74, 78	4:18	73, 74, 78, 84

Philippians *(continued)*

4:19	73, 79
4:20	74, 78
4:21	73, 78, 79
4:22	73, 79
4:23	73, 78

Colossians

3:6	172

2 Thessalonians

2:3	172

1 Timothy

2:5	174

2 Timothy

2:25	228
3:16	157

1 Peter

4:10	225

Hebrews

2:1	228
2:6–8	167
2:6–8a	170
2:6	169, 170
2:8b–9	170
2:10–18	170
3:12	228
4:1	228
9:17	228
10	49
10:1	49, 50

1 John

1:3–4	220
1:3	220
1:9	215, 220
2:1	220
2:19	220
2:27	220, 221
3:1	220, 221, 223
3:8	220, 221
3:11	220–22
3:23	220–23
4:9	220
4:17	220, 221
4:21	220, 221
5:3	220, 221
5:16	220
5:20	220

2 John

5	221
6	220, 221
6a	222
8	221
12	221

3 John

4	221
8b	221

Revelation

1:13	167
13:14	221
14:14	167

www.ingramcontent.com/pod-product-compliance
Lightning Source LLC
Chambersburg PA
CBHW051517230426
43668CB00012B/1643